CAMBRIDGE CLASSICAL STUDIES

General editors: M.I.Finley, E.J.Kenney, G.E.L.Owen

STUDIES IN ROMAN PROPERTY

STUDIES IN ROMAN PROPERTY

BY THE CAMBRIDGE UNIVERSITY RESEARCH SEMINAR
IN ANCIENT HISTORY

Edited by
M.I.FINLEY
Professor of Ancient History in the
University of Cambridge

CAMBRIDGE UNIVERSITY PRESS
Cambridge
London : New York : Melbourne

Published by the Syndics of the Cambridge University Press

The Pitt Building, Trumpington Street, Cambridge CB2 1RP

Bentley House, 200 Euston Road, London NW1 2DB

32 East 57th Street, New York, NY 10022, USA

296 Beaconsfield Parade, Middle Park, Melbourne 3206, Australia

ISBN 0 521 21115 8 hard covers

First published 1976

Printed in Great Britain
at the University Printing House, Cambridge
(Euan Phillips, University Printer)

CONTENTS

PREFACE

For two years our research seminar examined various aspects of
Roman property. Some twenty people participated regularly and
another ten or twelve attended when they could, not all from
Cambridge. Several of the topics discussed are not properly, or
not at all, represented in this volume: the more obvious absentees
are land-values and methods of valuation (including sale by auction
and the relationship between rents and prices) and the link between
land and debt, generally as well as in the publicized crises of 49
B.C. and A.D. 33. The decision to publish or not was an individual
one, depending solely on the author's personal judgement, whether
because the investigation of a particular topic had been completed
or because a survey of the current state of our information was a
clear desideratum or because a neglected aspect of Roman property
needed to be brought to the fore for further research.

Not only was every chapter discussed in the seminar but subsequent drafts were read and criticized by individual participants.
This volume therefore represents common work (hence no thanks are
expressed in the notes to members of the seminar) but not collective
work. That is, no doctrines or agreed conclusions were imposed, or
even sought, though there was fairly general agreement about the
questions to be asked. As a result, though some disagreements were
resolved, either in the seminar or in private discussion, others
remain. Editorial intervention was restricted to the elimination
of excessive duplication and overlapping. To that extent, the
volume can be read as a coherent unit.

My colleagues will not, I think, consider it invidious if I
take the opportunity to thank C.R.Whittaker, without whose help on
the editorial side the volume would have been long delayed.

August 1975   M.I.F.

1: INTRODUCTION

M.I.Finley (Jesus College)

The dominant place of the land in the economy and society of
classical antiquity is a commonplace. Yet no synoptic view of the
subject has been attempted in the past half-century, none on Rome
alone for more than eighty years.[1] This book does not pretend to
fill that gap. To begin with, a narrow focus was selected for the
inquiry, which may be defined crudely as Roman investment in property. That ruled out some of the best known aspects of the larger
theme, such as land tenure or the history of the *ager publicus*
during the Republic -- not because these are less important aspects
but because, for intensive cooperative study, it was necessary to
restrict the field to something which would be manageable (given
our limited resources) and yet permit us to look at the same
questions from several viewpoints. That is also why slavery was
taken for granted, so to speak, and not investigated except as it
had to be set against tenancy, for example.[2]

Just what the notion of 'investment' meant in Roman society is
one of the subjects of the inquiry: no presuppositions about maxi-
mization of income and the like were implicit in the choice of the
word. Nor, in so far as that was possible, did we start from, or
even give much attention to, the familiar and explicit Roman value
judgements on the subject of land, whether in Cato or in Cicero or
in anyone else. What Romans did receives priority over what they
said, or, more precisely, over what they said they ought to do.
How much land did individual Romans possess? Emperors and members
of the imperial family? How concentrated or how scattered? How
did they organize the labour on their estates? Were there differences between investment in rural and in urban property, either in
profitability or in operationally revealed (not just verbally
expressed) preferences? When, to what extent, and for how long a
time did marginal lands come into, or go out of, cultivation?[3]

These are painfully obvious questions, but anyone familiar
with the available modern publications on the Roman economy or on

Roman history more generally will know how little they have been
investigated. It is also obvious that they are questions about the
richer members of the Roman world. Investment is not a concept
relevant to peasants, slaves or landless labourers, who are nevertheless implicit, and sometimes explicit, throughout this book as
the labour force, actual or potential, or the rent-payers without
whom investments would have ceased to be useful or profitable.

Although the ancient sources overwhelmingly reflect, and
normally emanate from, the same upper strata of the population,
their indifference to the matters this book is concerned with is
shattering. Even when an ancient writer makes a relevant comment,
it is more often than not incidental to some other concern, most
clearly and most frustratingly in the large corpus of Roman juristic writing. If some Roman writer had collated a few data on the
size and range of landholdings in early imperial Italy (or anywhere
else in the empire), we should still welcome the control and the
amplification provided by epigraphical and archaeological finds,
but we would not be driven, as we are, to squeeze something from
half a dozen chance finds scattered widely in time and place,
without contemporary guide-lines. Moralizing statements - 'the
latifundia are destroying Italy' (Pliny, *N.H.* 18.35) - are, as I
have already said, not helpful for this purpose, not even when they
imply factual statements, no matter how often they are quoted in
modern accounts.

It is therefore not surprising that much of this volume has
the appearance of a battle with, rather than a deployment of, the
ancient sources. More correctly, perhaps, there is a constant
struggle against what has been called, rather crudely, the anecdotal method, founding an analysis on individual passages or
occurrences, as if every statement in one of the 'better' ancient
authors is both factually accurate and universally valid unless
the contrary can be proved, which is rarely the case. No historian
admits to so crude a procedure, of course, but how many times do
we read that X is Y, backed by a footnote, 'Pliny (or whoever)
says...', which is supposed to remove all doubts? Above all, there
is a tendency to overlook the vast amount of ignorance that pre-
vailed about many subjects in antiquity, even among the best
authors. I have already mentioned the absence in our sources of

any data or statements about the size and range of landholdings, which I used to exemplify their indifference to such questions. I now ask, Did anyone in fact know? Pliny presumably had some idea about the region of Lake Como; someone in one of the imperial departments had an even more precise idea about Veleia in the reign of Trajan. But did anyone know about Italy as a whole, let alone other regions of the empire?

My answer to that question is an unqualified negative: no one had even an impression worthy of credence, and certainly nothing resembling a quantitative notion. Numbers in ancient authors exercise a remarkable magnetism. Because Columella, in a hypothetical calculation that crumbles on scrutiny, began with the assumption that seven *iugera* of land suitable for vineyards were purchased for HS7,000 (3.3.8), the figure of HS1,000 per *iugerum* has become 'the price' or 'the average price' or 'the standard price' of good land in Italy in the first century A.D., the foundation for calculations of land values, annual income from land, rents, and, finally, rates of profit on investment. There could be no better illustration of the anecdotal method. Of course Columella knew what he paid for any piece of land he bought, what friends paid, when prices rose or dropped noticeably for one reason or another, what he may have read in the Sasernas or elsewhere about other individual transactions -- but he had neither any idea nor the techniques of getting an idea of the averages, the fluctuations, the ratios over any expanse of territory or range of time.

Proper quantitative analysis of economic and social phenomena is difficult: it is not merely a matter of adding, subtracting, multiplying and dividing the available figures. Among the most difficult are questions pertaining to land economy. The opportunities for such analysis of the ancient economy are rare. Paradoxically, they exist only where there is 'accidental' evidence, lists and catalogues which were compiled (and survived) for reasons unrelated to the interests of the modern investigator, not where the evidence appears to be directly relevant, such as Columella's vineyard calculations or the scattered land prices and yield figures that have been recorded.

It follows that the few meaningful quantitative statements we are able to present with some assurance are isolated deductions or

conclusions. In general, few trends or even comparisons (between
the eastern and western halves of the empire, for example) occupy
much attention in this volume -- not because we believe that what
cannot be quantified (in the correct sense) cannot be organized
serially, and certainly not because we believe the historian's
function to be restricted to the recording of data, but because,
in the present state of knowledge, we are unable to compensate for
the 'bunching' of the evidence. We are agreed, I think, in reject-
ing one familiar method: we avoid inferences from the fact that,
of the three surviving agricultural writers, Cato, Varro and
Columella, spaced at roughly century intervals, one mentions or
stresses a particular practice or institution which is absent or
underplayed in either or both of the others; or from the fact that
more attention is devoted to an institution or problem in the
Digest excerpts from Severan jurists than from late Republican or
early Imperial jurists. These differences *may* reflect institutional
changes, but the presumption is too strong that nothing more than
'literary history' lies behind them. Any substantive implications
have to be demonstrated, not merely assumed.

This negative methodological principle is not a counsel of
despair. There are possibilities, which have not been sufficiently
exploited, of forcing answers from the badly located and often
inadequately presented evidence. For example, a note of unease, of
indecision and lack of agreement will be detected in this volume
about the extent and nature of a real-property market in the Roman
world. I have elsewhere expressed the view that there was no
'recognizable real-property market', that 'the normal purchase of
land...was windfall purchase'.[4] Not all my colleagues agree, at
least not with my sharp formulation. It is now more evident than
perhaps it had been previously that the age of Cicero was marked
by relatively frequent transfers of land and houses. Related is
the phenomenon of family continuity on the land. This is not only,
and often not primarily, a matter of economic consideration; senti-
ment, values, social and political status all impinge, at least
within the social and political élite we are discussing, and the
nuances are not easy to capture. If, as appears to be the case,
the circles in which Cicero moved were less concerned with continuity, less attached to the family estate, than similar strata in

some other societies, the question arises whether or not these were
time-bound phenomena brought about by the 'Roman revolution' and
the civil wars. Nor can the practical consequences of the Roman rules of
inheritance be overlooked. The law on the subject has been studied
and re-studied, but I am unaware of any attempt to examine the
practice: how often was an inherited estate sold, by auction or
otherwise, and the cash proceeds divided among the heirs, how often
was the estate itself divided by agreement, how often was it retained and exploited by multiple heirs as a single unit? 'How
often' invites quantitative answers and it would be idle to pretend
that the evidence lends itself to quantitative analysis, but the
mere posing of the questions at least takes us one step further
than the usual references to the Digest about inheritance and
auctions. Two well known documents, Cicero's *pro Caecina* and the
Veleian tablet, are sufficient to demonstrate that practice was
more flexible and more varied (apart from the chicanery alleged by
Cicero) than the law books reveal. It was of no interest to
jurists that by tacit agreement a widow was allowed to buy an
estate at auction without competitive bidding, as happened in the
Caecina story (sect. 16).

One other theme recurrent in this volume requires extensive
research: the impact of the state on private investment in land.
Again we are concerned with familiar actions but insufficiently
examined consequences. Taxation is the most obvious, together with
two related matters, the provision of corn for the inhabitants of
Rome and the evolving *annona* programme of the emperors. But there
are also the efforts to compel senators to hold land in Italy and
the spasmodic imperial attempts to bring marginal land into cultivation, not to mention the whole compulsory system of the later
Empire. Perhaps the impact of imperial domains should be added to
the list: it is not clear to me, at least, what the effect was,
or whether there was one, apart from the losses to individuals
whenever land was confiscated.

The balance-sheet of our two years of work, in sum, reveals
many unanswered questions, topics for further research, as well as
positive results.[5] But we have been asking some of the right
questions, rigorously, and that has led to revisions of received

views and to new, or at least sharper, conceptions of certain central institutions and developments in Roman society.

2: SOME CONFIGURATIONS OF LANDHOLDING IN THE ROMAN EMPIRE

R.P.Duncan-Jones (Gonville and Caius College)

If a map survived of part of the Roman world, say Italy in A.D. 100, showing the ownership and juridical status of land, it would reveal a number of different types. We should see for example some state land, some imperial land, and some city land, as well as a host of privately owned properties of varying size. This essay will attempt to assess the relative importance of the various types very briefly, before considering differences of size among private estates. The surviving evidence for private landownership is so distributed as to give a strong Egyptian bias to any exhaustive treatment of the empire as a whole. A selective discussion like the present one can at least attempt to avoid this imbalance.[1]

Land generally fell into one of six categories (if both the nuances of legal title and the more complex situation in Egypt are ignored).[2] There is no obvious hierarchy among these categories, but private land has deliberately been left until last here, because evidence for it is abundant enough to justify fuller consideration.

I AGER PUBLICUS

The first type is *ager publicus*, land belonging to the *populus Romanus*, the Roman state. Such land, if cultivated, was generally in the hands of private tenants of the state. The extent of *ager publicus* was originally immense, since Rome's practice was to expropriate the land of conquered peoples, at any rate in name.[3] But the extent of *ager publicus* diminished as cultivable land was gradually assigned to veterans, civilian colonists, or purchasers. As late as the time of Trajan, *ager publicus* made up almost a quarter (22%) of peripheral holdings in a list of lands owned by private individuals and cities at Veleia in the north of Italy. Not all of this land was necessarily cultivated, since Veleia stood in a mountainous and infertile region; some may have been pasture.[4] In a similar list from Ligures Baebiani in southern Italy of the same period, *ager publicus* forms 10% of the peripheral holdings.[5]

II IMPERIAL LAND

A second category was land owned by the emperor.[6] Though some
regional figures are available, to look for any one index of its
extent would be mistaken. The modes by which the emperor acquired
land were so various and so haphazard that the scale of his estates
is bound to have varied greatly from one region to another.

The Baebian and Veleian land-registers, which belong to a
relatively early phase in the history of imperial accumulation of
property, show the emperor as owning respectively 12% and less than
1% of peripheral holdings.[7] Two centuries later, Constantine was
able to give the churches of Rome landed property in Italy and
Sicily with rents worth nearly 15,000 *solidi*; their total area was
probably of the order of 100 km^2.[8] Figures are available from the
fifth century which show that the emperor owned substantial parts
of the provinces. In North Africa he held about 18% of the total
area of Zeugitana and 15% of Byzacena. At one Syrian town,
Cyrrhus, he owned 16% of the territory.[9]

III CITY LAND

New city foundations were commonly provided with a dowry of directly
owned territory, from whose revenues the needs of local administration and local government could be met, at least in part. Some
notion of the overall magnitude of city lands at the end of the
Republic is given by the enormous compensation payments that Augustus made to cities for land which he gave to veterans. Augustus
paid out HS600 million in Italy and HS260 million in the provinces
(Augustus, *Res Gestae* 16.1).[10] The veteran settlement of Arausio
in Gallia Narbonensis colonized by Augustus owned 7,330 *iugera*
(18.4 km^2), more than one seventh of the area shown in fragmentary
registers of the time of Vespasian and his successors. Since over
one third of the remaining territory was apparently uncultivated,
the town's share of cultivated territory was evidently as high as
one fifth.[11] The towns of Veleia and Ligures Baebiani (neither a
veteran colony) appear to have owned rather less. 5% of peripheral
holdings at Veleia and 3% at Ligures Baebiani were owned by the
city. In addition, 2% of land actually declared at Ligures
Baebiani belonged to the city; while 12% of the land declared at
Veleia was the property of another city, Luca.[12]

City land at Arausio was leased to private individuals on what were evidently perpetual leases, in return for payment of a low rent or *vectigal*.[13] The *vectigalia* which bore on some of the private ate estates at Veleia suggest that these estates included city land; this would of course increase the apparent total of such land at Veleia.[14]

In the stringent conditions of the fourth century the state began to absorb the assets of other collectivities. Civic lands as such were confiscated by Constantius II. Though temporarily restored by Julian, they were once more confiscated by Valentinian and Valens. Valens however returned one third of the revenue to the cities from A.D. 374 onwards.[15]

IV TEMPLE LAND

Though ownership of land by temples was widespread in the Greek world, it is hardly ever found on a significant scale in the evidence from non-Hellenized areas of the Roman empire.[16] We happen to know, for instance, that in the Hellenistic period large parts of the islands of Delos and Rhamnos in the Aegean were owned by the temple of Apollo.[17] But few direct indices of scale are available for any region in the Roman period. Strabo mentions impressive totals for temple slaves in parts of Asia: 6,000 slaves of the temple of Ma at Pontic Comana (Strabo 12.3.34), and nearly 3,000 at the temple of Zeus at Morimene in Venasa (12.2.6). According to Diodorus, the temple of the Mothers at Engyum in Sicily owned 3,000 head of cattle and much arable land in the first century B.C. (Diodorus 4.80.5).

The only figures from Italy are effectively pre-Roman. The inscription from Heraclea to which they belong is variously dated between the fourth and second centuries B.C. The lands of the temple of Dionysos were measured as 3,320 square *schoeni*; those shown as belonging to the temple of Athena covered approximately 930 *schoeni*, but the list breaks off before the total has been reached. The size of the local *schoenus* is not certain, but the total area of these lands is evidently between 4 and 7 km^2.[18] This implies that a sizeable part of the territory of Heraclea was owned by temples.

The Romans showed some tendency to expropriate the property of

temples in the provinces from an early date. Sulla and Pompey for
example seized temple treasure in Asia and Greece; and Augustus
took over temple land in Egypt.[19] But there was still some temple
land at a much later date. Constantine appears to have confiscated
the lands which existed in his day. They were soon restored by the
pagan emperor Julian, but were again confiscated (finally, it appears) by Jovian in the late fourth century.[20] Meanwhile, the
Christian church received massive endowments of property both from
the emperor Constantine and from private sources.[21]

V LAND ASSIGNED BY THE STATE (AGER ASSIGNATUS)

As mentioned above, much of the *ager publicus* that Rome acquired by
conquest was re-distributed in the form of land grants to individuals.[22] To a certain extent this created stereotyped allotment
patterns. The size of allotments varied however from one distribution to another. On occasion the module of assignment could be
arrived at by dividing the number of colonists into the amount of
land that proved to be available on the site concerned (cf. Livy
35.9). Other sources of variation were compensation for differences
in the fertility of land, and the assignment of larger land-units
to recipients of higher standing.[23] Very wide variations are sometimes found between distributions that took place within a few
years of each other. For example, infantry veterans settled at
Aquileia in 181 B.C. received lots of 50 *iugera* (12.6 hectares),
while Latins (politically inferior by definition) who were given
viritim grants of land on the territory of the Boii in 173 received
only 3 *iugera* (0.75 hectares) each (Livy 40.34; 42.4).

Though land grants continued under the late Republic and
Empire, their size is not well documented. The last explicit figures refer to allotments by Caesar to civilians with 3-4 children
in the Ager Campanus and Ager Stellas. The units planned here were
respectively 10 and 12 *iugera* (2.5-3 hectares) (Cicero, *ad Att.*
1.16.1; *de leg. agr.* 2.85). The most massive land allotments of
all, those carried out by Augustus at the end of the Civil Wars
when the scale of armed forces was drastically reduced, are not
documented in detail. Brunt's reconstruction suggests that the
land allotments to veterans in 30 and 14 B.C., on which Augustus
states that he spent HS860 million (600 million in Italy, the rest

in the provinces), went to 155,000 men (Augustus, *Res Gestae*
16.1).[24] This implies an average of HS5,500 per head, and interpreted (with Brunt) in the light of Columella's land-price of
HS1,000 per *iugerum*, it leads to an average holding as low as 5½
iugera. But Columella's price for ordinary land appears exaggerated,
perhaps by twofold for Italy and probably by a larger factor for the
provinces.[25] Average allotments of the order of 10 *iugera* (comparable to Caesar's land allotments to civilians) thus seem possible.
The land equivalent of the cash retirement bonus of HS12,000
which was substituted for land in 13 B.C. (Dio 55.23.1) would be of
the order of 20-25 *iugera* on the same arithmetic. But not all the
sum need have been intended as a direct *quid pro quo* for land; the
cash bonus probably represented an advance in generosity over previous practice. This was not the end of direct allocation of land
to veterans, since veteran colonies (whose genesis implies specific
land grants) continued to be founded.[26] Later Egyptian figures
(accessible only in résumé) reveal the size of some actual veteran
landholdings. 18 veterans held an average of 13.75 *arourae* (15
iugera or 3.8 hectares) at Philadelphia in the Fayum in A.D. 216;
the same list shows 10 soldiers as holding on average 13.66 *arourae*
(14.9 *iugera*).[27] Though the figures apparently vary from one man
to the next, they may still be consistent with a situation in which
each veteran acquired his land for the same amount of cash. Even
at this date 15 *iugera* of Egyptian land would not necessarily have
cost more than the amount of the Augustan retirement bonus of
HS12,000.[28]

Figures from the late Empire (CTh.7.20.3) suggest land allotments of more generous size than those of the Principate, though
they were apparently made from deserted land, whose profitability
may often have been marginal. Under Constantine veterans received
a yoke of oxen, 100 *modii* of seed corn, and 25 *folles* for expenses,
in addition to an unspecified quantity of land. The implications
of these amounts are not consistent. But since the veteran who was
given oxen at all could hardly receive a fraction of a yoke or any
multiple lower than two, the quantity of seed appears the only
usable index. Assuming fallowing, 100 *modii* of seed should point
to an area of 50 *iugera* (12.6 hectares).[29] But the amount of seed
may still be only a convenient and therefore arbitrary round figure.

VI OTHER LAND IN PRIVATE POSSESSION

A. *The layout of private property*

Since land was the principal source of wealth in Roman society, the
size differentiation of land ownership often coincides with actual
differentiation of wealth. The principal means of transfer of
wealth appear to have been inheritance and, to a lesser extent,
marriage.[30] Inheritance could enlarge landholdings in cases where
owners died without issue and left their property to other landowners, or it could fragment them by dividing a property among
several heirs.[31] Where this mechanism enlarged landholdings, it
was unlikely to do so by adding conveniently adjacent plots. As a
result, large landholdings typically took the form of several non-
adjacent components. A wealthy man whose land lay entirely in one
district would often own a number of farms, like Sextus Roscius
whose HS6 million at Ameria was made up of 13 farms adjoining the
Tiber. The wealthiest would typically own land in more than one
district, like Pliny who farmed on a large scale both at Comum and
Tifernum Tiberinum, or his rival Aquillius Regulus who farmed in
Umbria and Etruria.[32]

The ownership of great wealth potentially conferred cash re-
serves large enough to allow the reconstitution of estates on a
less scattered basis. There are hints that Pliny was alive to the
possibility of enlarging his main holding at Tifernum by buying
adjacent property because it was adjacent (*Ep.* 3.19.2-3).[33] But
the pattern of random location generated by inheritance nevertheless seems to hold good in most cases where any indications are
available.

One result of this fragmentation is that locally based lists
do not properly reflect the scale of the largest landholdings,
which consisted of land in several districts. They will under-
represent both the maximum and the mean size of holdings. But
local lists can illustrate fragmentation as it affected landholdings concentrated in one neighbourhood.

In our most detailed land-register from Italy, the Trajanic
inscription from Veleia, landholdings generally consist of a
series of components whose valuation and position it was found
convenient to specify individually, and which provided security
for individual portions of the loan. The average size of these

components varies relatively little, despite very large differences in the total value of estates (Table 1).[34]

TABLE 1. *Estate-sizes and component-valuations at Veleia*

	Average total	Average component	Average number of components
5 smallest estates (50,000-53,900)	HS 51,050	42,542	1.2
7 intermediate (200,000-300,000)	251,032	42,931	5.8
5 largest (733,660-1,508,150)	1,098,076	69,498	15.8

The total span of variation between the first and third groups in average component-size is only 1.6, compared with a variation in estate-size of 21.5. These figures suggest that at Veleia, however large an estate became, the average size of its constituent parts would remain relatively small. The five largest private estates each consist of holdings located in as many as ten different *pagi* or parishes on average.[35]

B. *Average property-size*

Three pieces of evidence provide some direct information about average property-size.[36] Two come from Cicero's speeches against Verres and refer to Sicily in the first century B.C. The third is a detailed land-register recording holdings in one of the four wards of an Egyptian town in the mid-fourth century A.D.

According to Cicero, at Leontini in Sicily, 84 farmers had been registered in Verres' first year as governor (73 B.C.), but the number had fallen to 32 by the third year. The area under wheat in the third year was 30,000 *iugera* (Cicero, *Verr.* 2.3.113; 116; 120). Since wheat was normally fallowed, the implied cultivable area is not less than 60,000 *iugera*; other crops would almost certainly have increased the total to not less than 70,000 *iugera* (176 km^2). The mean average holding that this implies is 2,200 *iugera* (5.5 km^2). Even if no land ceased to be exploited during the period of Verres' rule, the average holding in 73 B.C., before Verres' exorbitant demands had begun to reduce the number of farmers, would be 830 *iugera* (2.1 km^2), still very high.

Cicero says that 252 farmers were listed at Herbita, another Sicilian town, in Verres' first year. The corn tithe, apparently reasonable compared with other much larger exactions made by Verres and his men, was sold for 18,000 *modii* (Cicero, *Verr*. 2.3.75-80; 120). The tithe figure could imply that the total area of cultivable land was of the order of 14,000 *iugera* (35.2 km^2), in which case the average holding at Herbita would be 56 *iugera* (14 hectares).[37] Though neither estimate can be more than an approximation, the Herbita average is clearly of a different magnitude from the average for Leontini in Verres' third year, apparently lower by a factor of 39. Since Leontini was the prime wheat-growing region in Sicily according to Cicero, it is likely to be the exception rather than Herbita, for which no special economic claims are made.

The register of local land owned by residents of one of the four wards at Hermopolis in Egypt in the mid-fourth century A.D. (*P.Flor*. 71) provides fuller and also more reliable information. 198 owners are named; they own a visible total of 13,883 *arourae* (15,135 *iugera* or 38.1 km^2), though a few area figures are missing.[38] The average holding is thus 76 *iugera* (19.1 hectares), or slightly more. This level is broadly comparable with the figure of 56 *iugera* deduced for Herbita four centuries earlier.

None of these averages takes account of land held outside the neighbourhood to which they refer by any of the individuals concerned. They may therefore under-represent the average total landholding somewhat, even though as far as we can tell only the larger landowners are likely to have held property in more than one city. The average area figure for those farming at Leontini, although already very high, may suffer from serious omission of this kind. Cicero singles out the fact that only one local family farmed any of the land at Leontini (*Verr*. 2.3.109). Since the cultivators in this case virtually all came from other cities, they are likely to have held land at those cities as well in many cases, about whose area we have no information.

However the papyrus from Hermopolis mentioned above gives some indication of the relative scale of the extra-territorial holdings of some Egyptian landowners. Property at Hermopolis held by citizens of the neighbouring town of Antinoopolis is listed in full. It shows 180 landowners with a total of 6,183 *arourae* (6,739

iugera = 17 km^2).[39] The average is thus 37 *iugera* (9.3 hectares),
less than half the average for land at Hermopolis owned by Hermo-
polites (76 *iugera*). Though this of course shows only one of the
possible areas in which external holdings belonging to citizens of
Antinoopolis might be located, it may imply that individually at
least, external holdings would on average be smaller than those held
in a man's native city.

C. Differentiation of property-sizes

Evidence about the distribution of property between large and small
landowners is more plentiful. Six registers will be considered
here. Each register quantifies properties by a linear or broadly
linear measure, either area, value, tax-potential, or water-
requirements. The main details can be summarized in a table
(Table 2).

The first register refers to land at the small south Italian
town of Ligures Baebiani at the start of the second century A.D.
(*CIL* IX 1455). The list appears to be a random cross-section of
local properties of all sizes (9 out of 66 estate-valuations are
missing). Since the parallel register at Veleia evidently omits
estates below a certain size, similar omissions from the Baebian
list would not be surprising. But if there was a threshold for
alimentary loans at Ligures Baebiani, it was set at a low point
(the highest possible round figure for the threshold would be only
HS10,000, since the smallest estate declared was worth HS14,000).
Consequently, it seems that what is visible here is, if not the
whole, at least a very large part of the spectrum of landed wealth
at Ligures Baebiani.[40]

At the top of the scale 3.5% of the landowners own 21.3% of
the land, and the wealthiest single individual owns 11.2% (see
fig.1). At the bottom, the poorest 14% own 3.6% of the land. The
Gini coefficient of differentiation is .435.[41]

The contemporary register from Veleia in northern Italy (*CIL*
XI 1147) lists the values of 47 estates, 46 of which are in private
hands. Though much richer in information than the Baebian register,
this list suffers from an arbitrary omission, the evident exclusion
of all estates worth less than HS50,000. It is thus likely to be
seriously incomplete in its coverage. Yet, despite the high

TABLE 2. *Land-registers illustrating differentiation of property-sizes*

Location	Date (A.D.)	Measure	Nature of measure	Total units	Maximum	Minimum	Mean
1. Ligures Baebiani	101	sesterces	value	57	501,000.00	14,000.00	78,442.0
2. Veleia	102/13	sesterces	value	46	1,508,150.00	50,000.00	264,328.0
3. Volcei	307	M(illenae?)	tax-potential	36	120.00	1.00	24.9
4. Lamasba	218/22	K (?)	water-entitlement	78	4,000.00	48.50	672.6
5. Magnesia	(c4)	iuga (tax)	tax-potential	67	75.15	0.01	5.2
6. Hermopolis	c.330	arourae	area	198	1,370.00	<2.00	70.1

threshold, the range of differentiation as it stands is still
greater than that shown at Ligures Baebiani. At the top of the
scale, the biggest private estate accounts for 12.4% of the wealth,
while at the bottom 23.9% of owners account for 5.1% of the land
(see fig.2). The Gini coefficient of differentiation is .526,
nearly 21% higher than the Baebian figure.

A comparison of the overlapping sections of these two registers
reveals more detailed differences (41 estates at Veleia fall within
the range between HS50,000 and 510,000, while at Ligures Baebiani
there are 36 estates in this range; see figs.3-4). Although the
Gini coefficients are now almost identical,[42] at Ligures Baebiani
83% of the estates in this range are worth HS125,000 or less,
whereas only 54% of Veleian estates belong to this group. The
Baebian list shows a complete lacuna between 201,000 and 400,000,
whereas 22% of Veleian estates belong to this range. 10% of the
Veleian estates fall into the top sector, from 401,000-510,000,
compared to only 6% at Ligures Baebiani. Thus the Veleian distribution is to a large extent even throughout the range, whereas the
Baebian estates are heavily concentrated at the bottom, and less
heavily at the top, with a substantial gap in the middle. If not
merely random, the irregularities of the Baebian pattern might
conceivably reflect changes in the pattern of private landownership
that had occurred with the creation of imperial estates in the
district.[43]

A third Italian land-register comes from Volcei in the south,
in Lucania (*CIL* X 407). The register, compiled two centuries after
the lists from Veleia and Ligures Baebiani, is dated to 307. It is
a list whose surviving portion shows 36 farms, which evidently has
some connection with Diocletian's revisions of taxation. The area
of tax-liability of the farms is defined in a measure abbreviated
as 'M'. Déléage conjectured plausibly that this initial stands for
millena, which is found in Italy as a unit of land-measurement for
tax purposes in legislation from the fifth century onwards.[44] A
piece of land whose area is given as 50 *iugera* (12.6 hectares) is
described as 4 'M'. The *millena* (whose area is otherwise unattested) may thus have been equivalent to 12½ *iugera*.

The chief drawback of the register, apart from the fact that
it is incomplete, is that it does not list units of ownership,

merely individual farms, several of which could have belonged to
the same person. If some units of ownership were greater than
single farms, differentiation of property-sizes is likely to have
been greater than these figures suggest. The Gini coefficient is
.394, 91% of the Baebian figure, and 75% of the figure at Veleia.
The largest single unit accounts for 13.4% of the total area (see
fig.5). If the equation between 50 *iugera* and 4 'M' holds good for
the whole list, the average area would be 312 *iugera* (78.5 hectares)
and the size of the largest unit would be 1,500 *iugera* (3.8 km^2).

A register from another part of the West, Lamasba in Numidia,
shows the water-entitlement of a series of properties under a local
irrigation scheme in 218/22. The list is compiled by locality, and
the names of five owners occur twice. In the surviving section,
which appears to be the major part of the list, 78 owners are named.
Again the unit of measurement is uncertain; it is signified here by
the letter 'K'. This seems to be a linear measure, though its implications for the duration of watering time vary somewhat according
to the point in the irrigation cycle at which a given property received its water.[45] The Gini coefficient is .447, only 3% higher
than the value found at Ligures Baebiani, and 15% below that at
Veleia (see fig.6). The percentage of total assessment accounted
for by the largest unit of ownership is only 7.6%. A complete list
would probably show a somewhat larger number of owners in possession
of several properties, and might thereby increase the degree of
differentiation slightly.

The assessments of three of the four veterans named in the
list are almost identical (600, 600 and 650 'K' respectively).[46]
This is a possible suggestion of standardization, for which the
obvious explanation would be that the three men spent the same retirement gratuity and thus each acquired about the same area of
land. If we make the speculative assumption that this area was
similar to the average landholding for veterans in the contemporary
list from Philadelphia in Egypt, that is about 15 *iugera*, the unit
'K' becomes equivalent to 0.025 *iugera*.[47] If even roughly correct,
this equation implies that the scale of properties in the Lamasba
list is very modest. The average estate-size would be only 17
iugera (4.3 hectares), the maximum 100 *iugera* and the minimum 1.2
iugera. The average is much lower than those discussed earlier.

There is also evidence from eastern areas of the empire. An
incomplete list from Magnesia on the Maeander in Asia Minor, apparently of the early fourth century, shows 81 farms of stated value,
distributed among 67 owners.[48] The measure used is the *iugum*, a
tax-unit. This unit represented an attempt to measure economic
potential by differentiating land according to its fertility and
type of cultivation. Though not a linear measure of area, it is
preferable to such a measure as a means of assessing economic differences (since estates of equal area may differ in productivity).
Differentiation within the surviving part of the list is very
marked (see fig.7). The largest single estate accounts for 21.6%
of the total assessment, and the wealthiest 7.5% owned 49.7% of the
total. The Gini coefficient is .679, 56% higher than the level at
Ligures Baebiani, and 29% higher than that at Veleia.

The alphabetical arrangement of this list allows us to estimate
that the surviving section amounts to as little as 8% of the likely
original length.[49] The listing by farm-name means that owners occur
randomly; hence the overall proportion of owners who hold more than
one farm is likely to much exceed the 12% shown in the small surviving portion. This would almost certainly mean that the actual proportion of very large estates was substantially greater than is
shown, thereby raising the Gini coefficient to an even higher level.

Finally, the fourth-century list from Hermopolis in Egypt which
has already been mentioned yields detailed information about differentiation. The sample is substantially bigger than any from the
West (there are 198 owners) and the list appears to be virtually
complete in its delineation of land owned by the inhabitants of one
of the four districts of Hermopolis. Though the proportion accounted for by the largest estate is not high in comparison with the
other registers (9.9%), the other inequalities are extreme. The
wealthiest 3.5% of owners have 53% of the area, while the poorest
47.5% have only 2.8% (see fig.8). The Gini coefficient of .856 is
very high indeed, not far from the theoretical maximum of inequality. It is 97% higher than the Ligures Baebiani level, 63% higher
than that at Veleia, and 26% higher than the level at Magnesia.
Nearly half the owners have holdings with an area less than 10
arourae (11 *iugera* or 2.8 hectares); Jones points out that a few of
these smallholders in fact have urban occupations such as builder,

potter, fuller, letter-writer or door-keeper.[50]

D. *Conclusions*

Reading the implications of these six registers as a whole involves
certain problems. Do the various registers describe differentiation
within the same sector of wealth? Does differentiation appear
higher in the East because of an inherent regional difference, or
because the eastern registers are later than those from the West?
Does differentiation appear most extreme at Hermopolis because of
agrarian inequalities peculiar to Egypt, or because information
from other areas is too selective to include the smallholder? Does
under-representation of the largest landowners in locally based
lists bias all the registers to the same degree?

Only the most tentative inferences are possible here. It is
worth noticing first that the registers evidently do not all refer
to the same range of landed wealth. Much the smallest average is
that conjectured for Lamasba, 17 *iugera* (4.3 hectares). The Hermopolis average of 76 *iugera* (19.1 hectares) is $4\frac{1}{2}$ times greater. At
a price for cultivated land in Italy *c.* A.D. 100 which we might
estimate at HS500-1,000, the Ligures Baebiani average would be 80-
160 *iugera* (20-40 hectares), and the Veleia average some three
times higher at 260-520 *iugera* (65-131 hectares).[51] The Volcei
average of 312 *iugera* (though this is also uncertain) appears similar to the Veleian range, but the units listed are not necessarily
whole estates. The average area of the Magnesia holdings might be
in the region of 420 *iugera* (106 hectares), from Jones's estimate
of the values of the *iugum*.[52]

If we relate these area estimates to the Gini coefficient
(taking the mid-point where more than one average has been estimated), there is little sign of any linear relation (Table 3). But
in the three cases where cross-comparisons are practicable it
becomes clear that the degree of differentiation apparent in any
one locality can depend heavily on which sector of wealth is under
scrutiny. The degree of differentiation in the Hermopolis data
taken overall is much the highest in the six registers (.856);
while the differentiation in the Lamasba sample is little more than
half as much (.447). But if we take that part of the Hermopolis
sample roughly corresponding in size to the range from Lamasba

TABLE 3. *Area related to the Gini coefficient*

Location	Average estimated area in *iugera*	Average estimated area in hectares	Gini coefficient	Number of estates
Lamasba	(17)	(4.3)	.447	78
Hermopolis	76	19.1	.856	198
Ligures Baebiani	(120)	(30.2)	.435	57
Volcei	(312)	(78.5)	.394	(36)
Veleia	(390)	(98.1)	.526	46
Magnesia	(420)	(106.0)	.679	67

(0-108 *iugera*, N=178, compared with an estimated range of 0-100 *iugera* at Lamasba, N=78), the differentiation at Hermopolis falls to .540. Instead of being 91% higher (as in the overall figures), differentiation at Hermopolis is now only 21% higher than that at Lamasba.

Similarly, if we take the remaining part of the Hermopolis range (109-1,493 *iugera*, N=20), and compare it with the Veleia range (estimated at 50/100-1,508/3,016 *iugera*, N=46), the differentiation at Hermopolis is as little as .390 compared with .526 at Veleia. Thus on a more accurate comparison the Hermopolis figure falls 26% below that for Veleia, instead of being 63% above it. And differentiation at Magnesia becomes much closer to that at Ligures Baebiani if the part of the Magnesia range that appears similar in size to that at Ligures Baebiani is taken in isolation (0.01-8 *iuga* = ?0.8-650 *iugera*, N=54, compared with HS14,000-501,000 = ?14/28-501/1,002 *iugera*, N=57). Differentiation at Magnesia falls from .679 to .469; instead of being 56% more, it is now only 8% more than the figure at Ligures Baebiani (.435).

The dramatic changes that occur when size is taken into account emphasize that comparisons between different land-registers (insofar as they are valid at all) are only practicable within the same sector of wealth. In the few cases where such comparisons are possible, the variations that emerge are unsensational. Most of the East-West contrast inferred from the overall figures now disappears: the relevant ranges of the Hermopolis register show differentiation 21%

higher than that of the register of small farmers at Lamasba in
Numidia, but 26% below that of the register of substantial landowners at Veleia. Differentiation at Ligures Baebiani appears to
be within 8% of that in the relevant part of the much later register at Magnesia. Insofar as the scanty data permit any general
conclusion, it would be that regional contrasts in the steepness
of the distribution-curve of agrarian wealth were probably slight
rather than large. But even this is suggested rather than proven.

There is no direct clue to regional variation in the extent
to which large landholdings are under-represented in local registers because of regional dispersal of property. But it has been
inferred from other evidence that during the later Empire the size
of the largest fortunes was greater in the West than in the East.[53]
The apparent shortage of smallholdings in two Italian registers
(one early, one late), and the greater abundance of such properties
in two late registers from Asia and Egypt is at least a possible
correlation.[54] But the list of smallholders at Lamasba and its
similarities to the corresponding sector at Hermopolis show that we
must still be chary of generalizing in broad terms about the West
as a whole.

The similarities between the Gini coefficients for the same
sector of wealth in different areas should not lead us to think
that local patterns of agrarian wealth everywhere corresponded to
the same basic matrix, varying only in the completeness with which
the matrix was delineated. The measure used is much too crude to
provide any such demonstration. This can be seen from the differences that exist between the histograms for the sector of overlap at Veleia and Ligures Baebiani, despite Gini coefficients
which are within 4% of each other (see p.17 and figs.3-4). But
the variations seem to have been small-scale, rather than large.
The available samplings appear too localized to provide secure
delineation of basic regional archetypes, if these existed. It is
doubtful for example how far the contrast between Veleia and
Ligures Baebiani represents general contrasts between landholding
in northern and southern Italy under Trajan, and how far it is the
product of much narrower local variants.

Insofar as the registers suggest a broader spectrum of agrarian wealth in Egypt and Asia than in Italy, they still do not

demonstrate the presence of greater economic inequality. Even if
smallholdings were rarer in Italy, the need for tillers of the soil
was no less great there; the fact that they might often take the
form of slaves or tenants is certainly no ground for thinking inequality less great than in countries with plentiful peasant free-
holds. Insofar as this pattern was the correlative of very large
landholdings, the potential inequalities that it implies are actually greater than those elsewhere.

Almost all the registers point unequivocally to heavy aggrega-
tion of property in the hands of the rich. Though the total area
of land represented in each register varies very widely, the proportion of that land occupied by the largest single estate is always substantial (Table 4).

TABLE 4. *Overall area and the largest estates*

Location	Estimated total area in *iugera*	Estimated total area in km²	Largest estate as % of total
Magnesia	28,160	70.9	21.6
Veleia	24,318/48,636	61.2/122.4	12.4
Hermopolis	15,132	38.1	9.9
Volcei	11,188	28.2	13.4
Ligures Baebiani	8,942/17,884	22.5/45.0	11.2
Lamasba	1,316	3.3	7.6

Only in the case of Lamasba, where the total area of land represented is minuscule, does the largest estate fail to occupy some
10% of the total or more. In three cases out of the remaining
five, the proportion is more than 12%. Such a distribution would
mean for instance that of the 70,000 *iugera* of cultivable area
estimated at Leontini, the largest estate would occupy between
7,000 and 8,500 *iugera*, or 18-21 square kilometres. When it is
recalled that the largest Roman landowners usually had properties
in several districts, it becomes clear that the likely overall size
of the landholdings of a typical member of this class must have
been very large indeed.

One illustration is provided by the immense wealth of
Symmachus, a senator of the mid-fourth century, which was dispersed

in landholdings all over Italy and parts of the provinces.[55] In
some cases the large landholder could become completely dominant
over a single area, and might own whole villages.[56] Single estates
in Africa could be so large as to engender settlements which became
villages but took their name from the owner.[57]

Land units on this scale could easily become little worlds on
their own, often to the owner's advantage. One of the Agrimensores
has this to say about the separatist character of large-scale Roman
landholding in Africa. 'Legal disputes between cities and private
individuals are especially frequent in Africa, where the domains
(*saltus*) of private individuals can be as big as whole city-
territories and many are in fact much bigger. The owners have a
substantial population on their estates, and there are villages
(*vici*) surrounding the villas as though they were *municipia*. The
cities are in the habit of raising legal disputes about the terri-
torial rights of these estates, by saying for example that one part
of an estate owes civic *munera*, or by trying to levy military re-
cruits from the estate village, or asking to levy transport animals
or supplies from the parts of the estate which they are trying to
claim.'[58]

FIGURES

Fig.1. Ligures Baebiani, estate-values (N = 57)

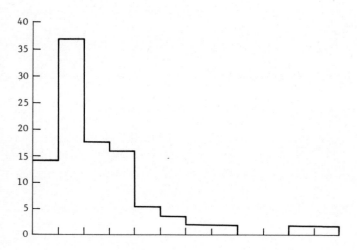

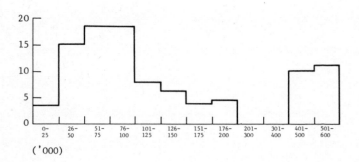

Fig.2. Veleia, estate-values (private estates) (N = 46)

%   I Number of units

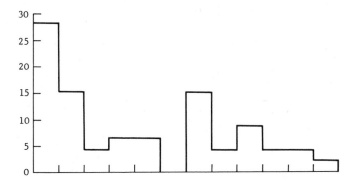

%   II Land-value (sesterces)

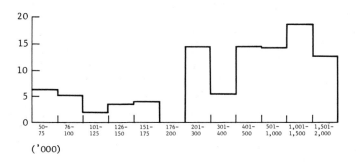

('000)

Fig.3. Overlapping sector of estate-values at Ligures Baebiani and Veleia: Ligures Baebiani

%   I Number of units

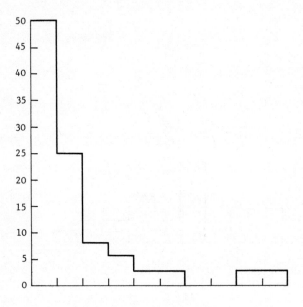

%   II Land-value (sesterces)

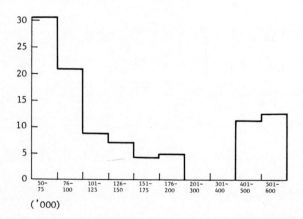

('000)

Fig.4. Overlapping sector of estate-values at Ligures Baebiani
and Veleia: Veleia

%   I Number of units

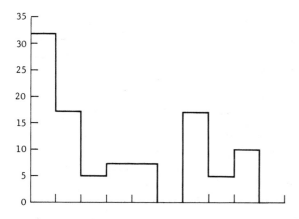

%   II Land-value (sesterces)

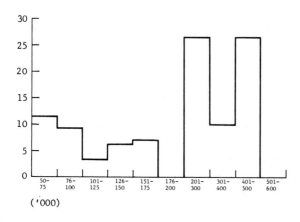

('000)

Fig.5. Volcei, farm-units (*N* = 36)

%   I Number of units

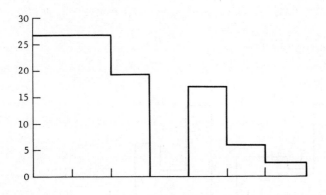

%   II Area (*m(illenae?)*)

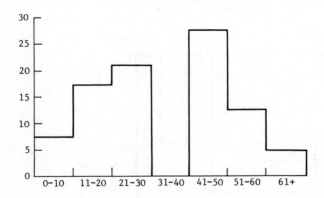

Fig.6. Lamasba, units of water-entitlement (N = 78)

%   I Number of estates

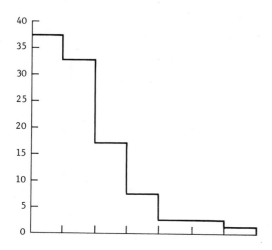

%   II Land-area (K)

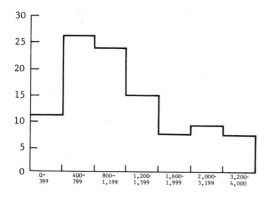

Fig.7. Magnesia, units of ownership (*N* = 67)

%   I Number of units

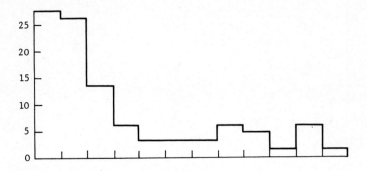

%   II Land-value (*iuga*)

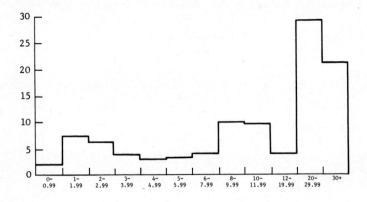

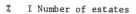
Fig.8. Hermopolis, estate-areas (*N* = 198)

%   I Number of estates

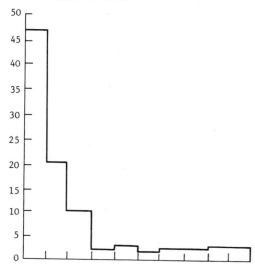

%   II Land-area (*arourae*)

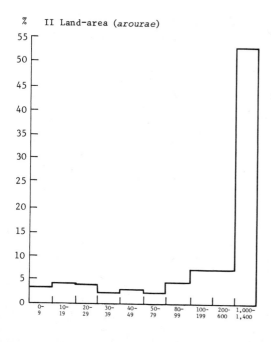

3: IMPERIAL ESTATES

Dorothy J.Crawford (Girton College)

When in A.D. 193 Pertinax was appointed emperor as a senatorial
candidate, he faced the problem presented to each new Roman dynasty
of what attitude should be taken to its predecessor's personal
possessions. Of these land was one of the most important. Pertinax'
reaction, if we may believe Herodian (2.4.1-7), was both novel and
positive. His own name was not to be given to imperial possessions
which belonged rather to the whole Roman people and, in an attempt
to bring uncultivated areas of the empire back into production, he
proposed to offer ten years' tax remission to those who would
undertake their cultivation, to be followed by outright possession
of the land, including that which was previously imperial.

Few emperors shared the scruples of Pertinax and the passage
is controversial (see chapter 8); but the proposals of Pertinax may
be used to illustrate the issues with which I shall be concerned in
this paper: firstly, the definition of imperial estates; secondly,
their movement in and out of imperial control; thirdly, their management, both separately within the estates and more generally on
a provincial level within the overall economy of the empire; and
finally, the involvement of the emperors with their estates. The
main limitation will be that imposed by the evidence, which inevitably gives an incomplete and somewhat erratic coverage by both
period and province. It is nonetheless important to concentrate
on those estates actually attested as imperial and to exclude land
merely thought to be imperial. I have attempted to collect the
chief sources for attested imperial estates in the Appendix but
such a list inevitably remains provisional. I shall also be concerned with imperial estates only down to the accession of
Diocletian.

THE ESTATES

To consider imperial estates is to consider only one of the assets
of the Roman emperors. They had of course many other possessions

- palaces and gardens, villas and hippodromes, mines and quarries, salt pans and brick works - but their landed wealth was probably the most significant.[1] And it was significant not only to the emperor, in the income which it produced, but also, through the emperor's use of his personal funds, to the empire as a whole. For estates paid not only taxes (at least outside Italy) to the central imperial authority, but also rents, and, even if in theory there were distinctions between the different treasuries to which all this income came,[2] in practice it was usually available for imperial expenditure. His estates were also important to the emperor in that, as in the case of Pertinax, they could be used as instruments of imperial agricultural (or fiscal) policy.

At one period or another there seem to have been estates in most provinces of the empire; the actual area of imperial land and its extent in relation to other forms of landholding can however rarely be known. In the northern provinces evidence is often confined to a record of imperial officials or else is archaeological, whereas in the Mediterranean provinces, and especially Asia, Africa and Egypt, there is more extensive documentation. A brief consideration of the different provinces will illustrate the problems met in any attempt to locate the estates.

In Britain an imperial official, recorded in an inscription (*RIB* 179) from Combe Down as initiating a project of rebuilding (*principia ruina oppressa a solo restituit*), has sometimes been seen as evidence for the existence of imperial estates in the area.[3] This may be the case, and the role in rebuilding is a familiar one for such a man, but he might equally well have been involved in quarrying or some other form of imperial interest. Another area which has been identified as imperial is the silts around the Wash. Perhaps there were estates here, but, based on the presence of salt production in the area, large-scale land reclamation and an absence of villas, the identification can only be plausible, never certain.[4]

In Asia there is at first sight a worrying tendency for evidence for imperial estates to coincide with the areas chosen for epigraphical explorations: Anderson in Galatia, Ramsay in Phrygia and Keil, von Premerstein and the Austrians during their '*Reisen in Lydien*' have all produced evidence for fairly extensive estates in the inland valleys of the province.[5] This apparent coincidence,

however, between epigraphical journeys and imperial estates is
likely to be misleading. Many of the large Greek cities of Asia
Minor have been excavated and, apart from Ephesus, an administrative
centre with a sizeable personnel (from procuratores down to secre-
tarial assistants[6]), neither the coastal cities nor the countryside
around them have produced any evidence for imperial estates. In
Asia it seems that imperial holdings were more or less confined to
the inland areas, to the crown land perhaps of the earlier Hellenistic kingdoms, rather than occurring in the territory of the more
independent coastal cities.

Egypt is probably the province which provides the fullest evidence for imperial estates, but in spite of its quantity it is not
always easy to interpret. The area with the greatest concentration
of imperial estates was certainly the Fayum or Arsinoite nome, which
had earlier, under the Ptolemies, been the scene of large-scale
agricultural reclamation and innovation. There is some evidence for
estates also in the Delta, the Memphite, Herakleopolite, Hermopolite
and Oxyrhynchite nomes,[7] but imperial estates are missing entirely
from Upper Egypt, the area earlier dominated by temple control. It
is probably true that the Arsinoite nome is also the area which has
produced the greatest concentration of papyri (the chief source of
evidence for this province) but the comparative absence of imperial
estates from the extensive contemporary records of the Oxyrhynchite
nome does, I think, confirm the picture.

Within the Arsinoite nome there is some evidence both for the
location and for the extent of estate land. One papyrus, *P.Bouriant*
42 of A.D. 167, preserves the survey of an administrative area in
the North Fayum, the *komogrammateia* of Hiera Nesos and its Drumos,
the Drumos of Kerkeesis, the Epoikion of Perkeesis and Ptolemais
Nea, giving details of 12,128 arouras (3,032 hectares). Of this,
39% consisted of imperial estates, or ousiac land as it was termed
in Egypt after the Flavian reorganization of the imperial estates.
Within the *komogrammateia* this land was distributed unevenly; the
whole of the Epoikion of Perkeesis (2,161½ arouras) was ousiac land
whereas at Hiera Nesos (524 arouras) it accounted for only 13%.

Further evidence comes from the neighbouring district of
Karanis, which shows an interesting preponderance of ousiac land
in the outlying parts of the area, those which were the most

difficult to irrigate and the earliest to go out of cultivation.[8]
In the surviving *sitologos* receipts of A.D. 158-9 for Karanis and
neighbouring villages,[9] 335 arouras of ousiac land are recorded,
of which over half (53%) is in the neighbourhood of Psenarpsenesis.
And in *P.Michigan* 372, of A.D. 179 or 211, out of a total of 1,847
arouras of ousiac land, nine hundred, just under half, are from
Psenarpsenesis, with a further 252 arouras from the village of
Patsontis. Both Psenarpsenesis and Patsontis disappear from the
record, presumably sanded over, after the second decade of the
third century, whereas Karanis itself, more favourably placed
between two irrigation systems, continued on into the fifth century.
The evidence then from Hiera Nesos suggests a significant proportion
of imperial land (almost 40% of the total area, both cultivated and
uncultivated) in this part of the North Fayum, and that from Karanis
a concentration of this land in certain outlying villages. What
cannot be known for sure is how typical or significant this evidence
may be.

For Africa the evidence is predominantly epigraphic; from the
area south-west of Carthage comes a series of long inscriptions,
those of Henchir Mettich (*CIL* VIII 25902), Ain el Djemala (*CIL* VIII
25943), Ain Wassel (*CIL* VIII 26416), and Suk el Khmis (*CIL* VIII
10570 + 14464), which give details of some of the conditions of
tenure on imperial estates in this area of the Bagradas Valley.
The estates here were locally known as the saltus Burunitanus, the
saltus Philomusianus, the villa Magna Variana, the saltus Neronianus
and, somewhat to the south, the saltus Massipianus.[10] The use of
saltus for an imperial estate is found elsewhere but the conditions
of tenure on these estates seem due to local conditions and it
would be unwise to generalize on their basis.[11] There were other
imperial estates in the provinces known from the more usual career
or building inscriptions and their overall area must have been
extensive. *In provincia non exiguum possidet* is Frontinus' laconic
description of the emperor (*de Controversiis Agrorum* 2. p.53), and
one modern writer has calculated, though without firm evidence,
that after the Neronian confiscations a sixth of the province of
Africa is likely to have been imperial.[12] In Mauretania imperial
holdings were later concentrated around Sitifis, where earlier
Hadrian's sister-in-law Matidia had extensive estates. On her

death these were apparently taken under imperial control, as is
suggested by the names *territorium Aureliese* (*sic*) and *castellum
Aureliane[nse] Antonia[nense]* by which they were later known (*ILS*
5964; 6890 - A.D. 218). And when the Severans laid claim to their
possessions together with the family name of the Antonines, the
defenicio (*sic*) *Matidiae* in the same area came under the control
of a procurator rationis privatae (*ILS* 5965).[13]

Matidia introduces a further complication in our consideration
of imperial estates. Few could equal her wealth but many others in
her position, relatives of the emperor and members of his *familia*
in its more extended, Roman, sense, owned land in their own right
which was administered separately and privately. Matidia probably
owned land in other parts of the empire besides Mauretania with her
own procurator to administer it.[14] Livia too had had her own procurator, a post once held by Sextus Afranius Burrus (*ILS* 1321; cf.
CIL X 7489), as did Domitian's wife Domitilla (Suet. *Dom.* 17.1) or
Trajan's wife Plotina (*ILS* 1402).[15] Their estates may have been
extensive.

Livia for instance acquired fairly extensive possessions,
ousiai, in the Arsinoite nome of Egypt.[16] At Bakchias in the North
Fayum she held an estate together with Germanicus[17] (a substantial
landholder in his own right[18]) and in the neighbourhood of Theadelphia a large papyrus marsh held by the same two passed to
Germanicus' children on his death.[19] Livia held further land at
Karanis, Philadelphia and Euhemeria; at Tebtunis in the South Fayum
a four-choinix measure of the *thesauros* of Livia is recorded in
A.D. 15, whereas in Lydia at Thyateira an ἄρχη Λειβιανή with its
own procurator was still in use under Caracalla.[20] In Palestine
she was heir to Salome, Herod's sister, in Jamnia, Phasaelis and
Archelais, an area renowned for its palms and their produce.[21]

Other members of the imperial family besides Livia held such
estates. In Egypt again both Antonia minor, the wife of Drusus,
and Antonia the daughter of Claudius held land in the Arsinoite
nome[22] and Claudius' wife Messalina had estates in the Hermopolite
and Herakleopolite nomes.[23] Claudius' freedmen Narcissus[24] and
Pallas[25] acquired enormous estates in Egypt, as did Nero's favourite
Doryphorus.[26] Nero's mistress Acte acquired lands in Egypt,
Sardinia and Italy[27] which were administered by her own procurator

summarum (*ILS* 7386).

The problem raised by these estates is one of definition: to what extent are they imperial? With Matidia they seem to have passed into imperial control on her death and this must often have been the case. But although in some cases a joint procurator might be appointed to look after the interests of the reigning emperor together with those of other members of his family, which suggests a certain blurring of distinctions,[28] estates of other members of the imperial family should I think be excluded from a consideration of imperial estates proper except when by inheritance, either real or assumed, they became part of the emperor's property. The case of Faustina Ummidia Cornificia, the niece of Marcus Aurelius, is instructive. In Phrygia her estates passed to her daughter and on to her grandchildren without, it seems, being taken up by the central imperial authority.[29] These were *not* imperial estates.

ACQUISITION AND ALIENATION

If estates differed from province to province, they also differed from period to period in both composition and extent, being added to by inheritance, confiscation and gift, and diminished by various forms of alienation by the emperors. Hirschfeld examined this process in some detail in 1902 and more recent evidence confirms his picture.[30] The fluctuation is easily illustrated.

Confiscation, acquisition by conquest and inheritance are in practice often closely linked and the legal niceties are not always easy to disentangle. In Egypt the composition of the early imperial *ousiai* raises a problem which may apply to other provinces and which is closely linked to the problem of the definition of an imperial estate. Dio records the confiscations of Cleopatra before Actium which may have enabled the Romans to take over without over-much loss of popularity (Dio 51.5.4-5; cf. 17.6-7). But in bringing Egypt under Roman control did Augustus retain for himself, in a private capacity, any of the land recently conquered, either that earlier confiscated by Cleopatra or indeed any other (such for instance as land uncultivated at the time of conquest)? His personal concern in using the army to clear the sand from the irrigation ditches (Suet. *Aug.* 18.2; Dio 51.18.1) suggests a keen

interest in the province, reflected also in its organization.
There is, however, to date not one documentary reference to any
land in the province held by Augustus personally. What is known
is a well-documented body of estates held by his wife, his friends
and associates, men such as Maecenas[31] or Lurius,[32] who commanded
the right wing of Actium, estates which Augustus will certainly have
inherited on the deaths of their owners. From Tiberius onwards the
Julio-Claudian emperors are all attested as landholders in Egypt[33]
and the process of inheritance added further to their estates.

Gifts of the emperor were a way in which the area of imperial
estates was regularly diminished[34] and the Egyptian holdings
(*ousiai*) of the emperor's family and associates are normally understood as an example of such gifts.[35] It has however recently been
suggested, by G.M.Parássoglou,[36] that Livia and other Augustan and
later estate owners (such as Pallas, Narcissus or Seneca[37]) were
not the recipients of imperial donations but rather acquired their
land on the open market, at a time which certainly witnessed the
increase of private land-ownership in the province. Parássoglou
is surely right in stressing that in terminology at least the
system is other than that practiced by the Ptolemies. The estates
are *ousiai*, no longer *doreai*, and the word *ousia* is also used of
estates with no imperial connections. Yet, although there is no
positive evidence either for this or for the traditional view, I
find it hard to believe that a free market for land ever functioned
for Romans in Egypt, a province which was from the beginning closely
and jealously guarded by the emperor. Could men such as Seneca
really acquire land in such a province without reference to the
emperor? The emperor's interest would seem better served by grateful subordinates.

And in one case at least it may be possible to trace an imperial donation. *P.Ryl.* 171 (A.D. 56-7) is an application made to the
oikonomos of an estate of Nero's favourite Doryphorus, to lease a
plot of twenty-seven arouras. The land, at Heraklia in the Themistos division, is described as 'the *ousia* in the Arsinoite nome'
(presumably he had land in other nomes) 'of (Tiberius) Claudius
Doryphorus, previously of Narcissus'. Narcissus of course survived
Claudius, though driven to suicide shortly after the latter's death
(Tac. *Ann.* 13.1.4; Dio 61 (60).34.4-5), and his land presumably

went to Nero. Nero in turn, I suggest, gave it to Doryphorus. It
is, I suppose, just conceivable that money passed hands in this
transaction though I think it very unlikely; existing evidence
rather shows Doryphorus receiving excessive sums from his master
(Dio 61.5.4). The plot of land which was the subject of the lease
application described (and the favourable terms suggest it was
rather poor quality land) was adjacent to land which had once
belonged to Maecenas (*P.Ryl.* 171.14). This too suggests to me that
the origin of these *ousiai* was land taken over by Augustus and
tactfully distributed amongst his family, his friends and his close
associates. (It might after all be less invidious to put newly
conquered land in his wife's name.) Such land often returned to
the emperor through inheritance and could be redistributed as he
wished amongst a fairly limited circle of associates. The limited
nature of this group may indeed be a further argument for imperial
initiative under the Julio-Claudians.

If after the triumviral period Augustus was careful in his
treatment of conquered land both in Egypt and elsewhere, his
successors were more open in their dealings. Tiberius and Nero
were both remembered for their confiscations.[38] Nero's extensive
African confiscations are still echoed in the Hadrianic inscription
from Ain el Djemala (*CIL* VIII 25943) in the Carthage area, which
mentions a saltus Neronianus (alternatively called a fundus Neronianus) which appears to have subsumed the earlier saltus Blandianus
the saltus Udensis and areas of the saltus Lamianus and Domitianus,
estates most probably named after their original owners.[39] In
Pisidia too a village south-west of Lake Askania was known by the
name of Nero although imperial interests in the area went back at
least to Claudius.[40] The confiscations of Septimius Severus
following the defeat of Niger and Albinus greatly extended his
land, and the fall of Plautianus led to further imperial estates
with a special procurator to organize them.[41]

Inheritance was certainly an important source of new imperial
land and has already been illustrated for Augustus and the later
Julio-Claudians in Egypt, where the separate *ousiai* eventually
underwent a Flavian systematization.[42] During his long lifetime
Augustus acquired extensive property from bequests. In Campania
and the Thracian Chersonese he inherited the estates of Agrippa;[43]

at Coela in Thrace these were still in imperial hands in A.D. 55
(*ILS* 5682). In Asia the Roman emperors seem to have inherited
property which earlier belonged to Hellenistic kings. Amyntiani,
slaves earlier of king Amyntas of Galatia, and Archelaiani, from
Archelaus of Cappadocia, are found in the household of Livia and
Tiberius, the joint legatees of Augustus, suggesting some form of
direct inheritance from the earlier kings which may have extended
to their lands.[44] According to Strabo (12.6.1) Amyntas possessed
three hundred flocks in his kingdom and this pastoral wealth seems
to have passed to the Roman imperial household, since from Karalar
near Antinoopolis in Galatia a second-century dedication (*IGRR* III
153) survives made to the emperors and to the imperial flocks,
their *idia tetrapoda*.[45]

Not all bequests can be traced so easily but the tendency for
the name of an earlier owner to remain attached to a piece of land
sometimes aids the process. This is especially true in Egypt where
the land earlier, for instance, of Lurius and Maecenas was later
known as Λουριανή and Μαικηνατιανή; the same practice has been seen
on the African estates. In Bithynia, which was an area of large
private estates,[46] the appearance in the second century west of
Lake Nicaea of ὁ δῆμος Χαρμιδεανῶν, who honour an imperial freedom
(*IGRR* III 18), suggests an earlier owner of the area called
Charmides;[47] similarly the description of Eutyches as Σεβ(αστῶν)
οἰκονόμος χωρίων Κωνσιδεανῶν in Galatia near Igde Agatch preserves
the memory of an earlier owner Considius.[48]

Large areas therefore accrued to the imperial holdings;
emperors might also alienate these lands in various ways. A new
emperor's ruthlessness was openly illustrated when Augustus persuaded Naples to give him Capri in exchange for Ischia (Suet. *Aug.* 92;
Strabo 5.4.9). The extensive estates, however, acquired by Nero's
mistress, Acte, must I think reflect the generosity of the emperor,
as earlier did the Egyptian estates of Maecenas. Maecenas was
endowed with land in at least seventeen separate villages; Seneca
later held grants in thirteen villages of the Arsinoite nome, with
land also in the Hermopolite, Herakleopolite and Oxyrhynchite
nomes.[49] Other such ousiac grants have already been mentioned.

Under some circumstances the emperors might dispose of their
land in a more profitable way. After the extravagances of Nero,

Galba put much of his predecessor's land up for sale and found many
willing purchasers (Plut. *Galba* 5.5).[50] Nerva too sold land when
he needed to raise cash (Dio 68.2.2) and Pliny mentions with approval Trajan's willingness to dispose of imperial estates by sale
(*Pan.* 50).[51] There is also epigraphical and papyrological evidence
for the sale of imperial estates.[52]

ESTATE MANAGEMENT

An inscription from Rome (*CIL* VI 30983 = *ILS* 3840) dedicating a
shrine to the numen of the imperial house records an interesting
group of people. The place of the shrine was assigned by the
procurator patrimonii Caesaris, and four *vilici* of the praedia
Galbana add their names to the dedication: Felix verna, Aspergus,
Regianus and Vindex verna. These are followed by the names of the
pleps, Actalius Ianuarius, Ulpius Sextianus and Clutorius Secundus,
together with fifty-three others. Four of those named are women
and six (or possibly seven) are specified as *Caesaris vernae*. In
all, sixty members of a religious college are named. The interest
of the dedication, from the point of view of the imperial praedia
Galbana, is the mixture of people named: the procurator patrimonii,
the vilici of the estate together with the imperial slaves whom
they managed, and others who appear to be tenants on the same land.
The picture is complex, suggesting the same mixed methods of exploitation as Pliny's letters show in private land (*Ep.* 3.19). This
document may serve to introduce a consideration of the management
of such estates, firstly on the local level with the vilicus-
managers or the tenants of the separate estates, and secondly, on
the provincial level, within the wider imperial administration.

If the two most common forms of exploitation of land in both
the private and the imperial sector were, firstly by tenants working under lease and secondly by vilicus management with land worked
by slaves, there was still an infinite range of local variations
to these two main methods, depending on a variety of factors: the
type of land - cereal-growing land, orchard land, papyrus marsh,
pasture land, etc. - its productivity potential - good, bad,
marginal - and traditional local labour patterns. The picture may
be further complicated by problems of terminology, especially in
the equivalence of Latin and Greek terms.

Taking leases first, a distinction may be made between short-
and long-term leases and between direct letting and sub-letting.
All combinations of these are possible and all are found on imperial
estates. Short-term direct leasing was, however, the regular Egyptian practice for both public and imperial (ousiac) land,[53] though
the close control of the whole Egyptian system left the peasants
with less freedom than many tenants elsewhere. In the case of
imperial estates the system differed under the Julio-Claudians from
that in the period following the Flavian reorganization. After the
systematization of Vespasian and Titus the income from the imperial
ousiac land continued to be accounted for separately from that of
the existing public or crown land since ultimately its destination
was different. But from the point of view of the tenant farmer
this distinction was not important. The rents were similar (an
average for instance of just under five artabas an aroura on both
ousiac and crown land in the North Fayum area of corn-land covered
by *P.Bouriant* 42 in A.D. 167) and tenants might farm land in different categories indiscriminately.

A more relevant distinction which can be traced from the surviving documents is that between the classes of tenants who farmed
different types of land, corn-land or orchard-land; it is a distinction not confined to the land of imperial estates. The detailed
evidence of *P.Bouriant* 42 may be supplemented by the *sitologos* receipts of A.D. 158-9 from the neighbourhood of Karanis.[54] The
picture here is of peasants cultivating small plots of corn-land
- the average size of holding being seven and a half arouras -
which consisted indiscriminately of ousiac land, public land
(δημοσύα γῆ), crown land (βασιλικὴ γῆ) and γῆ προσόδου. Locally,
seed was all issued at the same collection centre. The names of
these peasants are all either the most common Greek names, hellen-
ized Egyptian or straightforwardly Egyptian. They appear to be the
present indigenous population. In contrast, the second-century tax
rolls from Karanis (*P.Mich.* IV) give a very different picture.
These lists from 171 to 174 record money taxes paid on orchards and
vineyards, some of which are ousiac, by farmers many of whom are
Egyptians but many of whose names show Roman elements: Valerius
Apolinarius, Valeria daughter of Lucius Valerius Secundus, or
Longinia Gemella. Some of these were probably absentee landlords,

immigrants perhaps or veteran families, and they used others,
Egyptians (some of whom are named in the lists), to cultivate the
land for them. So whereas in Egypt there is no real distinction
in the regime of cultivation on imperial land or land in other
categories, there appear to be different sectors of the population
involved in different forms of agriculture.

The earlier Julio-Claudian evidence for Egyptian *ousiai* is a
case of traditional methods of a particular area asserting themselves in a new system. The *ousiai*, whether imperial or in the
possession of Livia, Maecenas, Seneca or the other recipients of
this land, were managed by the personal representatives of their
owners, προεστῶτες[55] or ἐκλήμπτορες.[56] Whereas elsewhere such men
might have managed imperial slaves as vilici, in Egypt the traditional method of leasing was probably used on these estates. The
system is of appointed agents managing leases for the emperor or
other estate owners.

In theory a distinction exists between short- and long-term
leases, yet in practice, when there is no pressure on the land,
consecutive short-term leases by the same people may have had the
same result as leases of a longer term. And very often the evidence does not exist to make the distinction. When for instance
under the Severans the imperial peasants of Aga Bey near Philadelphia in Lydia complain to the emperors of interference in their
agricultural duties by *kolletiones* and their subordinates, and
threaten to leave their ancestral hearths and the tombs of their
forefathers in favour of a private landlord who can protect them
better,[57] we do not know anything of their contractual relationship
with the emperor. They speak of τὸ δίκαιον τῆς γεωργίας, presumably the lease which governed this relationship, and claim to have
been brought up on the imperial estates as were their fathers and
grandfathers (ἐκ προγόνων). But does this mean that the lease
which governed their position was a lease without limit or is this
perhaps a *de facto* rather than a *de iure* comment on their situation?

The farmers of Aga Bey called themselves 'your farmers' (οἱ
ὑμέτεροι γεωργοί) and in making a corporate appeal they show an
identity for which there is evidence elsewhere. In the Latin-
speaking half of the empire *colonus* is the term generally used for
an imperial peasant, and the collective terms such as coloni

Aperienses or coloni Crustisiones from Belgica,[58] or from Mauretania coloni Lemellefenses (*CIL* VIII 8808), coloni domini nostri Pardalari (*CIL* VIII 8425 - A.D. 192) or Kalefacelenses Pardalarienses (*ILS* 6890 - A.D. 213) used by tenants of imperial estates in a variety of activities (especially sending appeals, building and religious activities)[59] suggest, I think, that the Aga Bey picture of tenants associated with one area over a long period may be generally applicable in the second and third centuries A.D.

The use of the word *colonus* can itself cause problems. There are the interesting but puzzling lists on lead from a burial at Pola in Istria which may refer to imperial estates.[60] The first list contains twenty-one names, including two dispensatores, one adiutor coloni (Lucifer) and one man, Anconius, who is a retired vilicus, *qui vilicavit*. The second list, somewhat later in date, has twelve of the same names with three dispensatores, one man, Viator, specified as a colonus, one retired dispensator, *qui dispensavit*, and the same retired vilicus; the names of four *ingenui* are added at the end. With the exception of these *ingenui* it has usually been assumed that the rest are slaves, the personnel possibly of an imperial estate once managed by the vilicus. So, whilst doubtful about other coloni recorded in the area,[61] Degrassi assumed that Viator and Lucifer were also slaves. Without, however, knowing the purpose of these lists certainty is impossible. But given the Italian evidence of the praedia Galbana and other comparable evidence for mixed systems of exploitation there is, I think, no real problem in taking Viator and Lucifer as free tenants,[62] the one with the lease in his own name and the other as an assistant to a lessee, who worked alongside slaves and possibly joined with them for some religious purpose.

In Africa Pronconsularis the epigraphical evidence suggests a two-tier system of leases in practice, with a conductor as head lessor who then sublet to the tenants of the estates. Since the evidence of the big inscriptions is so often quoted in discussions of land management it is perhaps worth looking at them in some detail.

In the Trajanic Henchir Mettich inscription (*CIL* VIII 25902) a letter, from the procuratores, defines the application of the Lex Manciana, possibly a Flavian enactment with widespread appli-

cation in the province. Right at the start there are defined those
who might be responsible for the cultivation of land: *domini aut
conductores vilicive*. The means of exploitation of an estate envisaged here would seem to be direct exploitation by its owner or
dominus, secondly, exploitation by leasing to tenants through a
conductor, and, thirdly, management through a vilicus. In the
present letter conductores and vilici are mentioned frequently,
domini less so, but this may reflect the wording of the original
enactment as much as its present application. The letter concerns
the payment of rents on a share-cropping basis and defines special
rent arrangements for newly planted vines and fruit trees. A money
rent is specified for flocks, as was contemporary practice in
Egypt.[63] The people who farm the estate are termed *coloni*; there
is also mention of *inquilini*, presumably native labour (probably
migrant) from outside the estate, and *stipendarii*, possibly hired
labour. The letter ends with details of corvée labour, work at
ploughing, sowing and harvest time, which I assume the coloni,
otherwise free tenants whose leases were controlled by a conductor,
were to provide on other parts of the estate, possibly the area
which the conductor himself worked and had not sub-let. The coloni
seem to be represented as a group by a *defensor*, Flavius Geminius,
and by Lurius Victor son of Odilo, their *magister*; these men see
to the erection of the inscription.[64]

     In the Ain el Djemala inscription from the reign of Hadrian,
which can be supplemented from the Severan Ain Wassel altar carrying a copy of the same decision (*CIL* VIII 25943; 26416), the petitioners request a ruling on the provisions for the cultivation of
subseciva, marginal lands. In this case some of the land in
question had been taken up by conductores but was not being cultivated. The emperor, ruling through his procurator, made provision
for the petitioners, who were, I assume, coloni, to cultivate on
their own account these lands *neglecta a conductoribus*. Five years
appears to be the normal length of a conductor's lease though the
present provision that the new tenant is to pay rent on cereals for
five years to the conductor named in the lease, and after that to
the treasury, takes no account of a tenancy under the new conditions which starts half way through that already pertaining. It
would appear that the main purpose behind these rulings is an

imperial attempt to encourage the cultivation of marginal land.
These special circumstances may explain the fact that, before the
provisions made in the Ain el Djemala letter, it is only a conductor system which is mentioned in practice in the area; they should
warn against a more general application of this evidence elsewhere
in the province or the empire.

A similar system of conductores controlling a head lease
appears in the Commodan inscription from Suk el Khmis (*CIL* VIII
10570), which also mentions the lease agreement. The coloni of
the saltus Burunitanus complain of the behaviour of Allius Maximus
and other conductores and of their collusion with the procurator
against the coloni of the saltus Burunitanus. They quote a ruling
on corvée requirements which they claim had been put up on a bronze
tablet and was generally available for consultation: *ita sit in*
perpetua in hodiernum forma praestitutum et procuratorum litteris
confirmatum. They make an appeal to the emperor for help as *homines*
rustici tenues, unable to compete for the favour of the procurator
with the *gratiosissimus conductor* with his *profusis largitionibus*.
The lex Hadriana and the *litterae procuratorum* specify their duties
guaranteeing them against constraint by the conductores *contra per-*
petuam formam. This *perpetua forma*,[65] like the *consuetudo Mancianae*
mentioned by the procuratores in the Henchir Mettich text,[66] was
clearly important in defining the rights and duties of these African
coloni.

The conductores, however, seem to have aligned themselves more
closely with the imperial officials than with the coloni, an align-
ment further illustrated by a Hadrianic dedication (*ILAlg.* I 3992)
to T.Flavius Macer, *procurator praediorum saltuum Hipponiensis et*
Thevestini put up by the *collegium Larum Caesaris nostri et liberti*
et familia item conductores qui in regione Hipponi[ens]i consistunt.
A similar dedication (*ILAfr.* 568) to A.Gabinius Datus from the region of Thugga perhaps suggests that these conductores, fairly substantial citizens, formed some sort of informal associations for
common action.[67]

Imperial estates in other parts of the empire might be managed
under a similar system of tenants-in-chief. In Egypt, where some
estate leases are recorded from the reigns of Claudius and Nero
(*BGU* 181.4), under Nero in A.D. 57 a μισθωτὴς ἀπὸ τῆς μητροπόλεως,

probably a conductor-equivalent, leased land at Bakchias in an
estate of the emperor which had earlier belonged to Maecenas.[68]
And in Asia *misthotai* are recorded in inscriptions from Phrygia,
Lycia, Caria and Lycaonia.[69] In two inscriptions from the region
of Cibyra ὁ κατὰ τόπον μισθωτής,[70] clearly an important figure, is
named beside the fiscus and the city of Cibyra as the authority to
whom a fine for tomb-breaking is to be paid. This may be another
tenant-in-chief though details of his role in estate management
are completely unknown.

Besides exploitation by lease, vilicus management was common
for imperial estates in many parts of the empire and, as already
seen from the Italian praedia Galbana and the Istrian evidence, it
often went together with leasing. Italian evidence from the *Liber
Coloniarum* seems to show this double picture and is interesting
also for the imperial initiative recorded. The *Liber* (p.230) records coloni of the emperor Vespasian receiving land at Abella:
coloni vel familia imperatoris Vespasiani iussu eius acceperunt,
and (p.236) under Nola in Campania: *colonis vel familiae est adju-
dicatus ager*. I assume that *coloni et familia* represent tenants
and imperial slaves receiving land here, possibly a further imperial attempt to extend cultivation. Still in Italy, under Lanuvium
the *Liber* records (p.233) that *imperator Hadrianus colonis suis
agrum adsignari iussit*, and the Ager Ostensis also *ab imperatoribus
Vespasiano, Traiano et Hadriano colonis eorum est adsignatus*. In
these two cases tenant-farming only is recorded but the imperial
initiative should be noted. Some emperors appear to have taken a
more active interest than others.

Elsewhere in Italy the evidence is for vilicus management.
Besides the vilici praediorum Galbanorum (*ILS* 3840), a vilicus
praediorum Maecianorum in the mid-second century probably managed
the confiscated estates of the jurist Volusius Maecianus (*CIL* VI
745) and a slave vilicus of Vespasian managed the praedia Peduceana
(*CIL* VI 276). The manager of the praedia Romaniana was called an
actor (*ILS* 1615), but his function is surely that of a vilicus.[71]

In spite of the extensive African evidence for leasing to
conductores, there too the vilicus system was used, at least under
the Julio-Claudians. A slave *vil(ica)* of the emperor Claudius is
known from Calama in Numidia though her duties may not have been

primarily agricultural (*ILAlg*. I 323), and under Augustus, Delius, *vicarius* of the vilicus Abascantus, restored and enlarged a *teloneum* at his own expense on an estate near Bisica (*CIL* VIII 12314).[72] What cannot on present evidence be known is whether the apparent predominance of leasing in the period after the Julio-Claudians in this province represents a real change or merely reflects the random nature of our evidence.[73]

In the Greek-speaking part of the empire three factors complicate the picture of management. The first is the difficulty of knowing what Latin equivalents are meant by Greek terms. I have just suggested that μισθωτής may be used to represent a tenant-in-chief, the man called *conductor* in the African inscriptions. Yet in the papyri from Egypt ἐκλήμπτωρ is probably conductor and μισθωτής is regularly used for tenant with no indication of whether the man is a head tenant who would then sub-let, or a small-scale tenant leasing land on his own behalf;[74] in suggesting that the tenant on Nero's estate at Bakchias was a tenant-in-chief it was his description as 'from the metropolis' which influenced the interpretation. Similarly it has recently been shown that in Egypt οἰκονόμος is used as the Greek equivalent of *dispensator*[75] whereas in Asia and elsewhere it seems rather to represent *vilicus*.[76] The second problem is that of distinguishing between imperial and private estates, since the same vocabulary is applied to both. Unless a man is said to be an imperial slave or freedman, or appointee of the emperors, it is difficult to know whether he is an οἰκονόμος or πραγματευτής on an imperial or a private estate. The third difficulty is that of dating the inscriptions which are our chief form of evidence. When it is a question of appeals made to the emperor, like those of the peasants of Aga Bey or Aragua,[77] an indication of date is generally given. Career records and tombstones generally lack this and it may be that some of the material collected in the Appendix in fact postdates Diocletian.

In spite of these complications there is some interesting evidence for the management of imperial estates in Asia. οἰκονόμος and πραγματευτής are the words used for the Latin *vilicus* and *actor*; these posts might be held by either slaves or free men. Where these officials occur, as for instance in Asia at Blaundos in Lydia (*IGRR* IV 1699), in Galatia,[78] in Phrygia in the Kumbet valley[79] or

in Thessaly at Magnesia (*IG* IX 1124), I assume that they managed a
slave labour force. Such men are notably absent from the appeals
of *georgoi* or tenants, like those of Aga Bey under the Severans.

Asia also provides evidence for what was probably a regular
feature of the organization of imperial estates. With rural estates far from the centres of civilized life protection was necessary
and in Asia as elsewhere estate guards are recorded. These men
might be called *saltuarii*,[80] *orophylakes*,[81] or, in one example from
Egypt, *machairophoroi*.[82]

Turning to consider the organization of the imperial estates
from outside rather than from within, one is faced with a complex
and changing picture. The emperors had a basis for control in
their procuratorial system. At the provincial level it was generally equestrian procuratores who were responsible for the revenues
of the imperial estates. These men had under them large offices
with many under-officials, known to us most fully from the grave-
stones of Carthage.[83] Beneath the provincial procuratores were
other procuratores, more frequently imperial freedmen who might be
responsible for areas, regiones or tractus.[84]

The complex procuratorial system, as seen for instance in the
big African inscriptions, underwent many changes and modifications.
To investigate it thoroughly in its application to imperial estates
would be to write a history of imperial administration. Here I
want simply to look at some points in the development of the management of these estates.

The division of provinces into administrative areas is known
most fully from Africa, where it may have been the work of Vespasian.[85] Regional offices were centred at Hadrumetum, Theveste,
Thamugadi, Thugga and Hippo Regius.[86] There is some evidence for
what may be similar area divisions in Asia. The Latin terminology
used here in a Greek-speaking province is perhaps suggestive of an
administrative reform initiated from Rome. A ῥεγιὼν Φιλαδελφηνή is
recorded in Lydia (*IGRR* IV 1651) which probably included the Aga Bey
estate. It is interesting that in the appeal of these peasants to
the emperor they claim first to have approached the procuratores,
both regional, τῆς τάξεως (? = tractus) and provincial;[87] a similar
hierarchy to the African pattern is suggested. In Lycia a ῥεγεὼν
Οἰνο(ανδικὴ) is found based on Oenoanda (*IGRR* III 1502) and a third-

century regional centurion, a ἑκατόνταρχος ῥεγεωνάριος, is recorded
from Antioch in Pisidia.[88] From Prymnessus in Phrygia an imperial
freedman who was a tabularius regionarius is known from the
regio(nes) Ipsina et Moetana.[89] These regional offices probably
supplemented that at Ephesus as centres of administration, at
least by the third century, which is the main period for which
there is evidence for imperial estates in the province. There is
as yet no evidence to date this innovation in Asia, and Africa and
Asia are the only two areas for which there is evidence for such a
comprehensive regional structure.

Whether or not Vespasian's hand should be seen in this regional
reform and in the Lex Manciana quoted in the African inscriptions,
there is no doubt as to the importance of Flavian reforms elsewhere
in the empire. We have already met Vespasian assigning land in
Campania, and in Egypt it was certainly the Flavians who took over
and organized the Julio-Claudian *ousiai* in the province. Rostovtzeff
argued somewhat perversely that it was Domitian who played a crucial
role in the formation of the *ousiakos logos* and the separate depart-
ment which continued on into the third century to administer this
body of estates.[90] Yet it is the names of Vespasian and Titus which
were attached to the earlier *ousiai* and by which they continued to
be distinguished in the second and even the third century.[91] This
Flavian reorganization was presumably coupled with a financial reorganization; a special fiscus, λόγος τοῦ Καίσαρος, was established
for the revenues of the imperial estates.[92]

In Egypt it seems on present evidence that the next important
development came with Hadrian, the emperor who figures so prominently
in the African inscriptions,[93] who in Italy assigned land in Latium[94]
and who reorganized the procuratores in many parts of the empire.[95]
It is first from the reign of Hadrian that the category of οὐσιακὴ
καὶ δημοσία γῆ appears[96] and the *ousiakos logos* was possibly also
established in its final form in this reign.[97] The ἐπίτροπος τῶν
οὐσιῶν, however, with his own λογιστηρίον, who is recorded in *P.
Amh.* 77.22-3 (139), seems to be a local procurator rather than a
national official. Such men had replaced the earlier προεστῶτες
and ἐκλήμπτορες. The next main change in the province seems to
have come with the Severans, and during the third century a plethora
of new officials occur charged with the administration of the est-

ates. It was Diocletian who was to attempt to control this multi-
plication of office; a *phrontistes*, with two or at the most three
assistants chosen by the *strategos* through the *boule*, was now to
replace separate χειρισταί, γραμματεῖς and φροντισταί; useless expense would thus be avoided and the estates of the treasury receive
proper attention.[98]

THE EMPEROR AND HIS ESTATES

When the *georgoi* of Aga Bey asked the Severan emperors for help
against the *kolletiones*, the reason put forward for imperial interest was the diminution of revenues resulting from the present situation.[99] Such a reason was hardly original but it did nevertheless
indicate a real worry. The main imperial concern in connection with
these estates was certainly the income which they produced and this
concern might operate at various levels and in differing intensity
depending on who the emperor was.

Imperial greed was, according to Tacitus (*Ann.* 14.65), a sufficient reason for confiscation but, if we may believe Pliny (*NH* 18.
94-5), some emperors were also interested in the agricultural potential of their estates. The four hundred-fold grain yield in
African Byzacium described to Augustus in a procuratorial letter
and a similar sample sent to Nero (from his newly confiscated African estates?) are certainly fictitious; the communication at the
basis of the story may have some truth in it.

At the other end of the scale there are Pertinax's attempts to
bring land back into cultivation (Herodian 2.4.1-7) or the lex
Hadriana de rudibus agris quoted by the African coloni on the Ain
Wassel altar (*CIL* VIII 26416.ii 10-13). Indeed the whole context
of the big African inscriptions is of differing imperial attempts
to encourage the continued cultivation of land on estates which was
fairly marginal. In the Henchir Mettich inscription provisions of
the earlier lex Manciana are quoted (*CIL* VIII 25902.i 25-iii 12).
After defining various share-cropping arrangements for arable
crops, for wine, oil and honey, and the arrangements for existing
fruit trees, special conditions are listed allowing five years'
reduced rent on newly planted figs, vines and grafted wild olives
and ten years' on new olive trees. All this suggests a real concern for more extensive cultivation, whether to provide more food,

or, in the long term, to raise more taxes.

Egypt provides evidence of other methods used on imperial estates to ensure their proper cultivation. Both incentives and compulsion appear throughout the period. Under the Julio-Claudians, farmers might be bound to cultivation as appears from a clause in the edict of Tiberius Julius Alexander specifically forbidding this,[100] and in the case of some imperial farmers they were freed from certain obligations and designated ἀπολύσιμοι τῆς οὐσίας.[101] What they were freed from remains unclear. It was certainly not the poll-tax which ἀπολύσιμοι are recorded as paying (*P.Mich.* V 244.6 (43)); it may, as has recently been argued, have been the requirement of holding liturgical office.[102]

Another method used by the authorities in Egypt, both public and imperial, in an attempt to ensure the proper cultivation of land was *epimerismos*, the assignment of poorer land to peasants from more profitable areas.[103] And under Hadrian a new liturgical official, the *epiteretes*, is found in connection with estate land.[104] *Epiteretai* were under the πράκτορες οὐσιακῶν and responsible for the payment of dues on palms, vineyards, pasturage and other types of land which paid a cash rent rather than one in produce. These officials continue until the end of the second century when, with the increase in the number of estate officials, *epiteretai* disappear from view.

It may also have been Egyptian conditions which prompted a Severan innovation. Marcus Aurelius and Verus had earlier exempted *conductores* from *munera municipalia*, and with the upgrading of the Egyptian metropoleis this exemption was extended by the Severans to *coloni Caesaris* (D.50.6.6.10-11). Whereas in Africa, Asia and many other provinces town and imperial estates were generally well separated, in Egypt the two might be much closer together, and the imperial tenants were therefore under greater pressure to divert their resources to municipal ends. As might be expected, this privileged position of the emperors' tenants was not always observed.[105]

One final group of documents suggests a further attempt to attract labour to imperial land in Egypt. An Oxyrhynchite notification of death made to the ἐκλήμπτωρ of an imperial estate of the emperor Claudius in A.D. 50 by Aline daughter of Komon together

with her guardian, describes her deceased husband Mnesithes son of
Petesouchos, as τῶν ἐν τῇ ἀτελείᾳ τῆς προκειμένης οὐσίας (*P.Oxy.*
2837.9-10 (50)). What is this *ateleia*? Then, in *P.Mich.* IX 560.
8-9, a Claudian land lease of A.D. 46, the object of the lease is
described as οὐσί]ας Λιβιανῆς ἐν γῆι [ἀ]τελεῖ. Is it the land that
is *ateles* or could the epithet be transferred to the farmer?
Thirdly an undated bronze tablet from the Fayum (*SB* 4226) bears the
legend, 'Αγρειππιανῆς καὶ 'Ρουτιλλιανῆς οὐσίας τοῦ κυρίου αὐτοκράτ-
ορος ἀτελὴν καὶ ἀνενγάρευτον, 'that which is *ateles* and exempt from
angareia of the *ousia* of Agrippina and Rutilia, now of the emper-
or'.[106] What does this mean? *Ateleia*, whether attached to an individual or to the land, must involve some form of exemption. The
reason why immunity was granted in these particular cases is unknown, as is the nature of the immunity. It may be that like other
privileged groups some imperial peasants in Egypt were freed from
the poll-tax. If they were, the amount involved was small[107] and
would make little economic difference to their position, though the
privilege itself might be significant. Such a privilege however is
unrecorded outside Egypt. But whatever the Egyptian *ateleia* may
have been, it would seem to fit into a general picture of imperial
concern to ensure the smooth working of imperial estates.

Such a concern was not of course confined to imperial estates;
Pertinax's concessions were said to apply equally to public land.
But the personal involvement of the emperor in his land is a constant factor in the history of imperial estates, an involvement
which in the case of Constantine enabled him to use this land to
endow the newly established church on a scale that was then un-
precedented.[108]

APPENDIX

A working-list for the first three centuries A.D.

The order of provinces is determined geographically, starting in the south-west and working round the Mediterranean.

AFRICA

AFRICA PROCONSULARIS

Regio Tripolitana	For procurators see Pflaum (1960-1), no.302; *Les Procurateurs équestres sous le haut empire* (Paris, 1950), 87-8; Goodchild, *Libya Antiqua* II (1965), 24.
Tractus Karthaginiensis	For procurators see Pflaum (1960-1), 1093.
Saltus Burunitanus	*CIL* VIII 10570 + 14464 (180-3), Suk el Khmis; cf. 14451, Ain Zaga.
Saltus Philomusianus	*CIL* VIII 14603 = *ILS* 2305, near Simitthu.
Villa magna Variana	*CIL* VIII 25902 (116-17), Henchir Mettich; cf. *ILAf*. 440, Aquae Traianae (S.S.W. of Vaga), for the same procurators.
Saltus (*or* fundus) Neronianus, Blandianus, Udensis, Lamianus + Thysdritanus	*CIL* VIII 25943 (?117-38), Ain el Djemala, with 26416 (Severan), Ain Wassel; cf. 14428, Gasr Mezuâr.
Regio Thuggensis	*CIL* VIII 12892; *ILAf*. 568, praedia, cf. 569, Dougga; cf. *CIL* VIII 12314, near Bisica, a vilicus; 12892, a verna dispensator; *ILTun*. 1568 (235), near Henchir Mest, fundus turris rutundae; for boundary stones see *CIL* VIII 25988 with *CRAI* (1907), 466-81; *BSAF* (1898), 114.
Regio Thuburbica Maius et Canopitana	*ILAf*. 246.
Regio Assuritana	*CIL* VIII 12879.
Regio [ ]tana	*CIL* VIII 12880.
Saltus Massipianus	*CIL* VIII 587, near Ammaedara; cf. 577-8; 588.
Regio Hadrumetina	For procurators see Pflaum (1960-1),

1094 sometimes with Thevestina; cf. *CIL* VIII 23022, building on the fundus [ ]itanus with imperial dedication.

Regio Leptiminensis

For procurators see Pflaum (1960-1), 1094; cf. *ILAf*. 52-4; 135 for imperial employees.

Tractus Bizacenus

ILAlg. I 2035 = Pflaum (1960-1), no. 245, ratio privata.

Regio (*or* saltus) Hipponiensis

For procurators see Pflaum (1960-1), 1094, with the saltus Thevestinus; cf. *ILAlg*. I 89; 99, a vilicus. From Calama: *CIL* VIII 5384 + 17500 = *ILAlg*. I 323, a vilica of Claudius; *CIL* VIII 5383, a saltuarius of Nero; *ILAlg*. I 325; 476; 477.

NUMIDIA

Tractus Thevestinus

For procurators see Pflaum (1960-1), 1094-5, generally with the saltus Hipponiensis; cf. *CIL* VI 790 = *ILS* 391; *CIL* VIII 16556; 16542; XIV 176 = *ILS* 1484 for imperial employees.

Vicus Augustor[um] Verecundens(is)

Near Lambaesis, *CIL* VIII 4194 cf. 18490 = *ILS* 6852; *CIL* VIII 4192 = *ILS* 6851; *CIL* VIII 4199 cf. 18493 = *ILS* 6850; *CIL* VIII 4205 cf. 18495 = *ILS* 5752; *CIL* VIII 4249 cf. 18503 = *ILS* 6852a.

MAURETANIA SITIFENSIS

For the procurator rationis privatae see Pflaum (1960-1), 1097.

Saltus Horreorum and area

Near Sitifis, *CIL* VIII 8425; 8426 = *ILS* 6890, Ain Zada, castellum Aureliane[nse] Antoninia[nense]; *CIL* VIII 8811 cf. 20618 = *ILS* 5964, Bordj Medjana to the west, territorium Aureliese, bordering ratio privata; *CIL* VIII 8812 cf. p.1946 = *ILS* 5965, Méris, defenicio Matidiae; *ILS* 9382, Kastellum Matidianum; Ain Soltana south of Sitifis, Février (1966), 217-28; Cagnat, *BCTH* (1895), 73, cf. Pflaum (1960-1), no.328, Hammam on line between Sitifis and Tocqueville, vicus Aug. n.; *AE* 1908, 154, Tocqueville, boundary of the ratio privata; cf. *AE* 1907, 158, Ain Roua north-west of Sitifis, dedication to Severan family from a defensio; *CIL* VIII 8808, Lemellef.

Saltus Cu...   *ILS* 5963, Er-Rahel, possibly
                                imperial.

                            *   *   *

EGYPT

For a detailed discussion of the *ousiai* in this province see
Parássoglou (1972). There is also a computer project in hand on
the material, Tomsin and Denooz (1974). The material is arranged
as far as possible in a geographical order.

ARSINOITE NOME
Polemon division

Tebtunis   *PSI* 1028.13 (15); *P.Mich.* II 121.
                                recto i.xii.1; iii.x.1; *SB* 10536.14-15
                                (25-6); *P.Mich.* V 244.3, 13 (43); II
                                123. recto xix.11 (45-7); *P.Mil.R.Univ.*
                                25 (127); *P.Mil.Vogl.* II 75 + *BL*; IV
                                251 (second century); *SB* 10512 (second
                                century); *SB* 10527 (152-3); *P.Giess.*
                                Univ.-Bibl. 52 (222 or 223).

Oxyrhyncha   *P.Oxy.* 986 (132).

Ibion Eikosipentarouron   *P.Mich.* V 274-5 (46-7); *SB* 7742 (57);
                                P.Mil.Vogl. II 98 (138-9).

Theogenis   *P.Mich.* V 312 (34); cf. *P.Mich.inv.*
                                724 = *BASP* VI (1969), 6, both possibly
                                private.

Kaminoi   *SB* 10614.36-8 (167-8).

Kerkesephis   *SB* 10614.41-3 (167-8).

Boukolon Kome   *SB* 5670.6 (second century).

Narmouthis   *SB* 10512 (second century).

Talei and Lysimachis   *P.Tebt.* II 609 (second century).

Themistos division

Andromachis   *SB* 10512 (second century).

Theoxenis   *P.Mil.* 6 (26); *SB* 10512 (second cen-
                                tury); *P.Fay.* 40 (162-3).

Hermoupolis   *SB* 10512 (second century); *SB* 9387.14
                                (second to third century).

Sentrempaei   *SB* 10512 (second century).

Polydeukeia   *P.Leit.* 14 (148) = *SB* 10206;
                                P.Oslo III 91 (149); *P.Berl.Leihg.* 1.

	verso iii.16 (164-5); *P.Col*. 1. verso 4.83-4 (169-77); *P.Ross.Georg*. V 53.ii 8; *P.Strassb*. 67-9 (227-30).
Moeris	*BGU* 1898.358 (172).
Philoteris	*P.Mil*. 6 (26); *P.Fay*. 60 (149); *SB* 10512 (second century).
Theadelphia	*P.Mil*. 6 (26); *P.Giess.Univ.-Bibl*. 12.16 (87-8); *P.Lond*. III 900 = p.89 + Tomsin (1954); *SB* 10218 (98-117); *P.Würz*. 11 (99); *P.Hamb*. 8 (136), ? private; *SB* 10512 (second century); *P.Mil*. 65 (139-49); *P.Wisc*. 34-5 (144) with *P.Mich*. 617 (145); *SB* 10206 (148); *P.Wisc*. 31 (149); *P.Oslo* III 91 (149); *P.Berl.Leihg*. 13 (mid-second century); ? *BGU* 1636 + *P.Berl.Leihg*. pp.246f. (155-6); *BGU* 1894-5 (157); *P.Col*. 1. verso 1a (160), verso 4 (161-80), verso 6 (160-1); *P.Berl.Leihg*. 1 recto and verso (164-5); 4. recto iii (165); *SB* 10614 (167-8); *P.Jand*. 27 (100-01); *SB* 10761 (173); *P.Strassb*. 551 (second century); *SB* 9205 (second century).
Euhemeria	*P.Oslo* 123 (22); *P.Ryl*. 126 (28-9); 134 (34); 138 (34); 140-1 (36-7); 148 (40); *P.Oslo* III 136 (141-2); *BGU* 1893 (149); *W.Chrest*. 363 (second century); *SB* 8972 (156-61); *P.Hamb*. 34 (159-60); *P.Berl.Leihg*. 1. verso (164-5). The following are probably private estates: *P.Ryl*. 166 (26); 128 (*c*.30); 131 (31); 132-3 (32-3); 135 (34); 167 (39); 146 (39); 152 (42); *P.Fay*. 87 (155); *P. Hamb*. 36 (second century).
Berenikis Aigialou	*BGU* 619 + *BL*; *P.Fay*. 82 (145); *BGU* 1893 (149).
Dionysias	*P.Ryl*. 127.26-7 (29); *P.Fay*. 251 (early second century); *P.Leit*. 11 (136-7), ? private; *PSI* 1243 (208).
Apias	*P.Berl.Leihg*. 16 B (161).
Trikomia	*SB* 10512 (second century).
Lagis	*SB* 10512 (second century); *P.Berl. Leihg*. 29, cf. Parássoglou (1972), 72 (164).
Herakleia	*BGU* 650 = *W.Chrest*. 365 (46-7); *P.Lond*. II 280 = p.193 (55); *P.Ryl*. 171 (56-7); 207 (early second century).
Phentumis	*P.Tebt*. 343.76-80 (second century).
Pelousion	*P.Berl.Leihg*. 16 (161); *BGU* 84 (242-3).

Herakleides division

Psenyris

P.Ryl. 207 (early second century);
P.Strassb. 267 (126-8).

Bakchias

SB 9150.4 (A.D. 5); P.Lond. II 445 =
p.166 (14-15); BGU 181 (57); P.
Bacchias 2. 49 (171); P.Gron. 2.87 +
AJP 1942, 303-4 (219-20).

Boubastos

BGU 512 = W.Chrest. 362 (138-61); P.
Ross.Georg. II 25 (c.159); P.Fay. 23
(second century).

Philadelphia

P.Weill inv. 108 (33-4); SB 9224 (50-
1); P.Princeton II 53 (56); P.Hamb. 3
(74); BASP 1975, 87 (26); P.Phil. 1
(103-24); 19 (first to second centuries); P.Hamb. 59 (138); P.Phil. 15
(153-4); ?BGU 1636 (155-6); P.Phil. 9
(158); P.S.A.Athen. 30 verso (178-9);
P.Baden 23 (189-90); P.Ryl. II 383
(second century); BGU 1646 (third
century); P.Gen. 42 (224-5); ? PSI 33
(265-6).

Sebennytos

? P.Strassb. 210.10-11 (90-6); BGU 889
= CPJ 449 (151); P.Fay. 23 (2nd cent.).

Arsinoe

Stud.Pal. XX 1.6, 26 (83-4).

Epipolis

P.Gen. 38 = W.Chrest. 366 (207-8).

Ptolemais Hormou

P.Petaus 43-4 (c.184).

Nilopolis

P.Lond. II 194 = pp.124-5 (first century); P.Ryl. 207 (early second century).

Soknopaiou Nesos

P.Ross.Georg. II 12.iii + Wessely,
DAW XLVII 4 (1902), 13 (48); W.Chrest.
176 (54-68); P.Strassb.inv. 1108 =
APF IV (1908), 142-4 (138-9); P.Amh.
77 (139); BGU 212 (158); 277 (second
century); P.Aberdeen 24 (194); P.Trin.
Coll.inv. 112 = CE 1969, 317 (199);
BGU 199 verso + BL (late second century); Stud.Pal. XXII 120 (194);
SB 4284.12 (207); BGU 653 (207-8);
810 (208).

Karanis

P.S.A.Athen. 32 (39); P.Mich. IX 560
(46); 540 (53); 539 (53); SB 7374
(71); P.Mich. 524 (98); 382 (87-90
and 102-3); BGU 985 (124-5); P.Mich.
inv. 2964 = ZPE X (1973), 57-9 (c.
150); P.Mich.Michael 14 (152); BGU
202 (154-5); Pap.Chic. 5; 7; 16; 27;
32; 35; 42; 52; 53; 57; 62; 63; 65;
67 = SB 4417; 71; 78; 81-2 (158-9);
BGU 104; 172; 206; 262; 280; (+WB)
438 (158-9); P.Mich. 223-5; 357 A

and B; *P.Berol.inv.* 17354 (171-4);
P.Mich. 372 (179-80 or 211-12); *P.
Aberdeen* 50 (? 202); *SB* 7368.20 (third
century); *P.Mich.inv.* 5689 verso.

Kerkesoucha

Pap.Chic. 10; 18-19; 23; 26; 31; 55;
61; 76; 77 (158-9); *BGU* 31 (158-9);
P.Petaus 75; 77; 78 (184); *P.Ryl.* IV
596.20 (204); *BGU* 2101 (209).

Patsontis

P.Mich. 555-6 (107); 557 (116); 223-5
(171-4); 372.ii (179-80 or 211-12).

Psenarpsenesis

SB 4414 (143); *P.Mich.inv.*2964. recto
(*c*.150); *Pap.Chic.* 13; 28; 36; 39; 41;
43; 48; 49; 50; 56; 60; 64; 68; 70;
75; 77; 84; 87; *P.Cairo Goodspeed* 18;
24; *BGU* 105 = *W.Chrest.* 346; *BGU* 160;
204; 210 (now crown land); 211; 284;
438 (158-9); *P.Oslo* II 26a (163-4);
BGU 708 (165); *P.Mich.* IV 224 (172-3);
357 B (173-4); VI 372 (179-80 or 211-
12); *P.Aberdeen* 50 (? 202).

Drumos of Hiera Nesos

P.Bouriant 42 (167).

Epoikion of Perkeesis

P.Bouriant 42 (167).

Hiera Nesos

P.Bouriant 42 (167).

Ptolemais Nea

Pap.Chic. 6; 70; 81; *BGU* 160; 441
(158-9); *P.Bouriant* 42 (167); *P.Mich.*
VI 374. ii 10 (mid-second century).

Unspecified

P.Berol.inv. 8143 ABC + 7397 = *JJP*
1971, 53-61 (after 188); *P.Berol.inv.*
7440 recto = *JJP* 1971, 61-2 (second
century); *SB* 10512. i 6-11 (second
century).

Division unspecified

P.Aberdeen 29 (48-9); *P.Jand.* 26.5
(98); *P.Aberdeen* 151 (first century);
SB 4226; *P.Lond.* II 195 = p.127 = *P.
Ryl.* II pp.254-5 (first century); *BGU*
1047 ii (117-38); *P.S.A.Athen.* 19
(154); *P.Aberdeen* 152; *P.Fay.* 338
(second century); *P.Flor.* 337 (early
third century).

HERAKLEOPOLITE NOME

P.Hib. 279.3 (early second century).

Ankyrona

P.Ryl. 87 (early third century); *W.
Chrest.* 367 (224-5).

HERMOPOLITE NOME

> *P.Ryl.* 684; *PER* = Rostowzew (1910),
> 122 (first century); *PSI* 448 (first to
> second century); *P.Baden* 19b (110);
> *P.Ryl.* 168 (120);? *W.Chrest.* 370 (121);
> *P.Ryl.* 157 (135); *P.Flor.* 40 (162-3);
> *P.Lips.* 96 (second to third century);
> *P.Amh.* 96 (213); *P.Ryl.* 99; *PSI* 1260
> (third century).

MEMPHITE NOME

> *P.Ross.Georg.* II 42. ii 4-5 (second
> century).

MENDESIAN NOME

> *P.Ryl.* 215; 427 (second century); *P.
> Strassb.* 299.17-19 (second century).
> For the Thmouis papyri containing
> information on *ousiai* see Parássoglou
> (1972), chapter 3, 83-8.

OXYRHYNCHITE NOME

> *P.Oxy.* 244 (23); 2837 (50); 2873 (62);
> 3051 (89); 1434 (107-8); *P.Lips.* 115
> (133); *P.Wisc.* 19 (156); 21 (161);
> *CPJ* 452b (possibly Mendesian?); *SB*
> 7173 (second century); *PSI* 1328 (201);
> *W.Chrest.* 278 (242); *P.Oxy.* 3047 (245);
> *P.Giess.* 101 (third century); *BASP*
> 1975, 91 (83).

UNSPECIFIED

> A dedication in the Alexandria Museum
> records a σύνοδος γεωργῶν Καίσαρος,
> E.Ziebarth, *Das griechische Vereins-
> wesen* (Leipzig, 1896), 213 no.64.

*   *   *

JUDAEA

> Pliny, *NH* 12.111-13, *horti regii* pro-
> ducing balsam. Josephus, *Vita* 71,
> Καίσαρος σῖτος which may only imply
> tax.

Jammia, Phasaelis
and Archelais

> Josephus, *Ant.* 18.31, cf. Pflaum
> (1960-1), no.9, Livia's estates from
> Salome passing to Tiberius and Gaius.

SYRIA

Regio Parh[a]l(iae)

> *BCH* III (1879), 270, Ph[a]sis, Aug.

lib.proc.[r]eg.parh[a]1.

Byblos   For Hadrian's control of 'arborum
                                genera iv' and his 'definitio silva-
                                rum' see R.Mouterde, *MUB* XXV (1942-3),
                                41-7; XXXIV (1957), 230-4.

North Lebanon, near Arca   Rey-Coquais *MUB* XLVII (1972), 94-105
                                (hypothetical rather than certain).

                        *   *   *

ASIA MINOR

The approach of Broughton (1934) remains fundamental. There is
much important discussion of both geography and epigraphy scattered
in the works of L.Robert. I omit what have sometimes been identified as imperial estates where the evidence consists only of imperial employees not specifically connected with estates.

LYDIA

Philadelphia   *OGIS* 526, ἐπίτροποι ῥεγιῶνος
                                Φιλαδελφηνῆς; Keil and Premerstein,
                                DAW LVII 1 (1914-15), no.55 = Abbott
                                and Johnson, *Municipal administration
                                in the Roman empire* (1926), no.142
                                (Aga Bey); cf. no.51, πραγματευτής;
                                no.11, σαλτουάριος (possibly private).

Thyateira   *CIG* 3484 = *IGRR* IV 1204; *CIG* 3497 =
                                IGRR IV 1213 = *ILS* 8853 (which reads
                                ἀρχή), with record of earlier read-
                                ings, ἄρκη Λειβιανή; cf. Keil and
                                Premerstein, *DAW* LIV 2 (1911), nos.
                                75-6; Hermann, *DAW* LXXVII 1 (1959),
                                no.12, dedication to Λεβία δέσποινα.

Hermus valley, 15 km NW   Robert, *BCH* LII (1928), 413, οἰκονόμοι
   of Sardis (Assar Tepe)   Σεβ[αστῶν.

LYCIA

Oenoanda   *BCH* XXIV (1900), 337 = *IGRR* III 1502,
                                ῥεγεὼν Οἰνο(ανδικὴ).

PHRYGIA

Aragua   *OGIS* 519 = *CIL* III 14191.

Prymnessos   Ballance (1969), 143-6, cf. *Bull.Ep.*
                                1972, no.456; Haspels, *The highlands
                                of Phrygia* (1971), Appendix, no.31,
                                recording different readings.

PISIDIA/PHRYGIA

Lagbe-Ormeleis

Ramsay (1895-7), no.192 (Lagbe); no. 193 (Ormeleis), ὁ κατὰ τόπον μισθωτής.

Lake Askania

Bean, *AS* IX (1959), no.30, with earlier references, Tymbrianassus; cf. *CIL* III 6872 from Kılıç. In this general area see Bean, *AS* IX (1959), no.49, πρόοικος from Bademli (? = Polyetta); no.63, οἰκονόμος from Akören (? = Macropedium).

PISIDIA/LYCAONIA

Tractus Cillanicus and neighbouring areas

Strabo 13.4.13 (629); Pliny, *NH* 5.147. Robert (1962), 234-5; *Hellenica* XIII, 77-108, especially 99-100 for ὀροφύλακες; 77-87 treat the area of Kireli Kasaba to the east of Lake Bey Şehir. *MAMA* VIII 364, an ἐπίτρο]πος τοῦ Κιλλανί[ου πεδίου; Calder, *JRS* II (1912), 80, a regional centurion from Antiocheia somewhat to the north.

LYCAONIA

Laodicea Combusta

MAMA I 24, procurator of the praedia Quadratiana makes dedication to Julia Mamea; there are a large number of imperial employees from this area.

CILICIA

Coropissus

CIL X 8261, soldier from vicus domini nostri.

CAPPADOCIA

Annexed by Tiberius, Tacitus, *Annals* 2.42.6; 56.4. There were large imperial estates here in the late empire, see W.E.Gwatkin, *Cappadocia as a Roman Procuratorial province* (Missouri, 1930); Just. *Nov.* 30.

GALATIA

Karalar, near Antinoopolis

CIG 4120 = *IGRR* III 153.

Lower Tembrogius valley, north of Germa

Anderson (1937) with Pflaum, *ZPE* VII (1971), 277-8.

BITHYNIA

CIL XIII 1807 = *ILS* 1330, cf. Pflaum (1960-1), no.317, proc.prov.Bithyniae Ponti Paphlagon(iae) tam patrimonii quam rat(ionis) privata[e].

West of Lake Nicea

Robert (1937), 240-3 with *BCH* XVII (1893), 540, nos.16-17; cf. Flam-Zuckermann (1972).

Dacibyza

Keil, *JAO* XXI-XXII (1922-4), 260-70, an ἐπιμελητὴς κτηνῶν Καίσαρος, perhaps connected with the postal service.

THRACE

Regio Chersonesi

For procuratores regionis Chersonesi see Pflaum (1960-1), 1069; cf. A.H.M. Jones, *The cities of the eastern Roman provinces* (1971), 16-18. Dio 54.29.5, inherited by Augustus from Agrippa; *CIL* III 726 = *ILS* 1419, a procurator from Lysimacheia; *CIL* III 7380 = *ILS* 5682 (A.D. 55), populus et familia Caesaris from Coela.

*　　　*　　　*

GREECE

MACEDONIA

Ovid, *ex Ponto* 4.15.15 with Seneca, *de tranquillitate animi* 11.10, property of Sextus Pompeius taken by Gaius.

THESSALY

Larisa

Arvanitopoullos, Ἀρχ Ἐφ (1910), 355, dedication by an imperial *phrontistes.*

Demetrias

IG IX 2.1124, an imperial *oikonomos.*

ATTICA

Philostratus, *Vita soph.* 2.547, estates of Hipparchos; cf. J.H.Oliver, *The ruling power* (Philadelphia, 1953), 960-3; *IG* II-III^2 2.2776.202-3 and 20^{f}

*　　　*　　　*

PANNONIA SUPERIOR

CIL III 4219, silvae dominicae, but for a post-Diocletianic date see A. Mócsy, *Pannonia and Upper Moesia* (London, 1974), 306; also 300-7 for the whole area.

PANNONIA INFERIOR

> *CIL* III 3774; 10694.

NORICUM

> For the patrimonium regni Norici see
> *CIL* III 4800 = *ILS* 4198; *CIL* III
> 4828; 5695, domnica rura. On imperial
> possessions in the province see furthe
> G.Alföldy, *Noricum* (London, 1974), 43,
> 100, 115–16, 175.

RAETIA

> *CIL* III 6002, f(iglina) C(aesaris)
> n(ostri); not necessarily imperial
> estate.

> *   *   *

ITALY

CISALPINA

> For procuratores rationis privatae
> see Pflaum (1960-1), 1036-8.

Tridentum

> *CIL* V 5050 = *ILS* 206 (46), agros
> plerosque et saltus mei iuris
> (Claudius).

near Ferrara

> *CIL* V 2386, dispensator of Claudius;
> 2385 = *ILS* 1509, dispensator region.
> Padan.Vercellensium Ravennatium.

Veleia

> *CIL* XI 1147 = *ILS* 6675 (102-14), emp-
> eror named as neighbour four times.

Praedia Galliana

> *CIL* III 536 = *ILS* 1575 (Severus Alex-
> ander), with saltus Domitianus; for
> location cf. Pliny, *NH* 3.15.116 and
> perhaps *CIL* XI 1147 ii 59, fundus
> Gallianus.

ISTRIA

Polla

> *Inscr.Ital.* X 1.592, second-century
> lead lists (cf. 593); see above p.47.

Abrega, Parentium

> *Inscr.Ital.* X 2. pp.71-9 collects the
> evidence, by no means conclusive, for
> imperial estates in this area.

LIGURIA

> For procuratores rationis privatae
> see Pflaum (1960-1), 1036-8. *CIL* V
> 7752 = *ILS* 1658, dispensator rationis
> privatae.

CENTRAL ITALY

For procuratores rationis privatae
see Pflaum (1960-1), 1039-40.

ETRURIA

Lorium

For Antonine property here see references in *CIL* XI p.549; cf. *CIL* XI
3732, an actor; 3738, a dispensator.

PICENUM

CIL VI 8580 = *ILS* 1497, tabul.reg.
Picen.; for procurator rat.priv. see
references above.

LATIUM

Labicum

CIL XIV 4090.14, praedia Quintanensia;
cf. 2770, res publica Lavicanorum
Quintanensium.

Laurentum; Laurentes
  vico Augustano

Pliny, *Ep.* 2.17.26; Gellius 10.2, ager
Laurens; Herodian 1.12.2; *CIL* XIV pp.
183 and 486; *CIL* VI 8583 = *ILS* 1578,
Claudius' procurator Laurento ad
elephantos; *CIL* XIV 301; 341; 347;
352; 431; 2040; 2044-5; 2047; 2050-1;
J.Carcopino, *Virgile et les origines
d'Ostie* (Paris, 1919), 255, saltuarii;
R.Meiggs, *Roman Ostia*[2] (Oxford, 1973),
343, vilicus saltuariorum. Ager Ostensis, *Liber Coloniarum* 1. p.236; *MonAL*
Ser.Misc. I 5 (1973).

SABINUM

Praetorium Pallantianum

Phlegon of Tralles, *de long.vit.* 4
(Jacoby, *FGH* 257).

CAMPANIA

Tractus Campan(iae)

CIL X 6081 = *ILS* 1483, procurator
tractu(s) Campan(iae).

Abella

Liber Coloniarum 1. p.230.

Lanuvium

Liber Coloniarum 1. p.235.

Nola

Liber Coloniarum 1. p.236.

Capreae

Strabo 5.4.9; Suetonius, *Aug.* 92;
Dio 73 (72).4.6.

Location unspecified

Ovid, *ex Ponto* 4.15.17 with Seneca,
de tranquillitate animi 11.10, estates of Sextus Pompeius taken by Gaius.

SAMNIUM

Ligures Baebiani
CIL IX 1455 = *ILS* 6509, emperor named seven times as neighbour in alimentary table.

Saepinum
CIL IX 2438 (168-72), conductores gregum oviaricorum - passing through the district.

APULIA, CALABRIA, LUCANIA, BRUTTIUM

For a p(rae)p(ositus) tractus Apuliae Calabriae Lucaniae Bruttiorum, a pro-curator s(altuum) A(pulorum) and pro-curator regionis Calabricae see Pflaum (1960-1), 1041.

LIPARI ISLANDS

CIL X 7489, procurator of Tiberius and Julia Augusta.

LOCATION UNKNOWN

Praedia Galbana
CIL VI 30983 = *ILS* 3840.

Praedia Luciliana
CIL VI 8683 = *ILS* 1616.

Praedia Maeciana
CIL VI 745 (177).

Praedia Peduceana
CIL VI 276, vilicus of Vespasian.

Praedia Romaniana
CIL VI 721 = *ILS* 1615, an actor.

Praedia Rusticeliana
AE 1922, 93 = *CIL* XIV 4570 (205); cf. 4553.

SICILY

Ovid, *ex Ponto* 4.15.15 with Seneca, *de tranqu.anim.* 11.10, estates of Sextus Pompeius taken by Gaius.

Panormus and Segesta
Liber coloniarum 1. p.211, assigned by Vespasian.

MELITA and GAULUS

CIL X 7494 = *ILS* 3975.

CORSICA

CIL X 8038, Vespasian's boundary ruling.

SARDINIA

Possessions of Acte: *CIL* X 7640; 7980; 7984; *ILS* 2595; *CIL* X 8046[9];

CIL XI 1414.
Imperial employees (not necessarily
connected with estates) are listed by
Sotgiu (1957), 44-8.

*   *   *

SPAIN

Plutarch, *Galba* 5; *HA*, *Sev.* 12.3.

TARRACONENSIS

For the ratio patrimonii see *CIL* XV
4134-6.

LUSITANIA

For the ratio patrimonii see *Eph.Epig.*
VIII (1899), 366 no.26.

BAETICA

For the ratio patrimonii see *CIL* XV
4111; 4116; 4121-2; 4124-33. *CIL* II
1198 = *ILS* 1659, a dispensator arcae
patrimonii buried in Seville.

*   *   *

BELGICA

For the procurator patrimonii and procuratores rationis privatae (of
Belgica with duae Germaniae) see
Pflaum (1960-1), 1057.
The large Langmauer estate near Trier
including the Welschbillig villa probably dates from the fourth century,
see Rostovtzeff (1957), 690; Wightman
(1970), 170-1, cf. 180; H.Wrede, *Die
spätantike Hermangalerie von Welschbillig* (Berlin, 1972), 6-10.

GERMANIAE

For procuratores see under Belgica.

Saltus Sumelocennensis

CIL XIII 6365 = *ILS* 7100; *CIL* XIII 2.
p.214 = *IGRR* III 70, centred on
Rothenburg-am-Neckar. Civitas and
cives: *ILS* 2334; 4608; *CIL* XIII 6358
= *ILS* 7099; *ILS* 7101; 7101a; *CIL* XIII
2506.

4: CLASSICAL ROMAN LAW AND THE SALE OF LAND

John Crook (St John's College)

To limit disappointment the reader is asked to bear in mind the
genesis of the contents of this chapter. The task set by the
seminar was, in the context of discussions about the movement of
land (or dispersal of land, or the 'market in land'), to see
whether anything in the classical Roman legal sources had any
socio-economic interest or bearing on those discussions. What
follows is the carrying out of that task. It therefore has no
particular thesis or structure; whether it has much or any interest or bearing of the kind sought, the reader must decide. It is
also sternly confined to the subject in hand: it is about classical Roman law and the *sale* of *land*. It does not deal with rules of
conveyance except as related to sale, and it does not deal with
rules of sale except as related to land.[1] There is a rough division
into two parts. Part I examines some sets of legal rules related
to the sale of land: Part II examines the principal Titles about
sale in the Digest and the Code, to see what part land plays in them.

I

The first rule worth a mention is one to whose economic significance attention was drawn long ago by Jonkers.[2] It was a legal
obligation upon guardians not to leave any spare capital of their
wards unproductive: they had to do with it one of two things –
either *faenus exercere* or *fundos comparare*. A corollary of the
rule was that money of a ward might only be put on *depositum*
(that is, be non-interest bearing) if it was being accumulated in
order to buy land.[3] The existence of these requirements presumably
helped to swell the number of potential buyers for land at any time.

Specific to land was also the *actio de modo agri*, going back
to very early days and surviving throughout the classical period.
If an acquirer, when the land was conveyed to him, found the acreage to be less than stated, he had this special action against the
conveyor. The right of action was inherent in the *mancipatio* :

that might seem to be in conflict with the principle of this chapter not to discuss conveyance except in relation to sale, but it is not so, because *mancipatio* was in origin not just a formality of conveyance but an **actual sale** for a real price. The best texts for this *actio* in the classical age are *Pauli Sent.* 2.17.4 and D.18.1. 18.1. The latter concerns a subsidiary point: 'If a slave, on orders of his *dominus*, in demonstrating the boundaries of land sold, has overstated (by error or fraud), only that should be held to have been demonstrated which the *dominus* intended.' On the *finium demonstratio* which was consequently of great importance in sales of land there is a general discussion by Daube.[4]

The *actio de modo agri* is a special case, for land, within the general topic of warranty: the liability of a seller to a buyer for secure enjoyment of the thing sold and for its being free from defects. Another special case, for *res mancipi*, is the *actio auctoritatis*: if the real *dominus* came along and, by virtue of having title, evicted the buyer from what he had purchased, the buyer could sue the seller on his warranty. That action also was inherent in the *mancipatio*. Warranty forms a large chapter in the Roman law of sale; but apart from the above the features of it that apply particularly to land are not of great significance, and it is massively treated in the standard works,[5] so that not much needs to be said here.

As to warranty for secure enjoyment, in the case of *res nec mancipi* – which included non-Italian land – the buyer would have to see that he obtained a separate covenant, a verbal *stricti iuris* contract by *stipulatio*.[6] One might have expected that since sale was a *bonae fidei* contract such a warranty would be inherent in it and not require a special covenant, but that was not so to begin with, though it came to be so ultimately.[7] The sources also state that, as an aspect of providing secure enjoyment, the seller has the duty to secure promises against *damnum infectum*.[8]

Warranty for freedom from defects provides at least an excuse for reminding the reader of some good anecdotes of Cicero's. A seller must not, of course, positively state what is false: but need he refer to defects at all? Cicero takes this up as a moral question in the *de officiis*,[9] and tells the story of C. Canius, who bought a property under the false impression – fraudulently

induced - that it was a marvellous place for fish, that of
Calpurnius Lanarius, who bought a town house subject to an undisclosed augural demolition order, and that of Sergius Orata, who
bought one that had an undisclosed servitude over it. It is clear
that already in Cicero's day sale, as a *bonae fidei* contract, pre-
cluded a man from deliberately concealing faults known to himself
(but the difficulty for the buyer would be to prove that the seller
had known). Also if land was mancipated with the description
optimus maximus, that phrase counted as warranty against a servitude and gave ground for an *actio auctoritatis*.[10] Beyond that,
caveat emptor applied. For slaves and cattle sold in the open
market the aediles from early on enforced a stricter liability -
in effect 'absolute' liability for certain standard defects without
the need to prove knowledge, and giving the buyer a right to hand
the goods back and get his money back. The aedilician liability
began to be extended to private sales and to other commodities
already in the classical age;[11] whether and if so when it was extended to land remains a disputed question.[12]

We turn to a quite different rule, which can be summed up in
the maxim of modern Romanists that 'sale breaks hire'. This means
(in so far as it is relevant to the present subject) that a
tenant of land or housing had no right *in rem* to the land or
house, that is to say no security of tenure against the *dominus*,
but only a right *in personam*, to sue for damages for non-fulfilment
of his contract, against the person who had rented it to him.
Therefore, if I bought the property from you I could turn all your
tenants out at once: against me they would have no legal leg to
stand on. They would, of course, be able to sue you for not being
able to continue their tenancy. It seems, however, worth noting
that Gaius, in adverting to this rule, puts it, so to speak, the
other way round.[13] He does not say 'a tenant has no security', or
'a buyer can turn a tenant out'; he says 'If for any reason a man
who has rented land or housing to anyone sells the land or house,
he should take steps to ensure that the tenant can secure from the
buyer the right to farm the land or live in the house on the same
terms as before; because otherwise the tenant, if baulked, will
sue the seller on his contract of tenancy.' This is by no means
the only piece of evidence that some *coloni*, at least, were persons

of sufficient status to be quite capable of litigating in defence
of their rights.[14]

Since housing has come up, we may note one or two other
features relating to it. *Aedes* on Italian soil were, like the land
itself, *res mancipi*; and *usucapio* of *aedes* took two years, like
land and unlike movables. Cicero twice provides evidence (in
references to *auctoritas fundi*, the antique precursor of *usucapio*
of land) that the decision to count *aedes* along with *fundus* was a
piece of early juristic interpretation, since the Twelve Tables had
referred only to *fundus*.[15] Presumably it was so decided in order
not to fall foul of another principle embodied in the maxim that
superficies solo cedit, namely that ownership of what was built
upon land lay with the owner of that land.[16] Nevertheless, awkward-
nesses could still occur in relation to sale. Suppose, for example,
that I sell you a house, but, unknown to both of us, it has been
burnt down and does not exist at the moment we make our contract.
Sale without a *res quae veneat* is void: but is there, in this
case, no *res quae veneat* at all? There is no house, but there is,
after all, the site, which you would have automatically bought with
the house because *superficies solo cedit* - you cannot own a house
unless you own the site. So the law could have said 'You have acquired the site, and the contract stands as to that, with appropriate modification of the price.' It did not in fact say so. If
the house was totally destroyed the main authorities agreed that
the sale was a complete nullity, *quamvis area maneat*: you could
not keep the site (though naturally you could recover the whole
price).[17]

Houses were subject to legislation, enshrined in the municipal
charters going back to Republican times and in the *senatusconsultum
Hosidianum*, as well as referred to in the Digest and the Code, forbidding their demolition except by permission of the authorities
and for the purpose of replacing them. The subject is discussed
by Dr Garnsey below.[18] Here it is appropriate to reiterate a previously stated opinion[19] that the motives behind the Roman government's insistence on this odd rule were not those suggested by
Homo[20] but are sufficiently implied in the speech of Claudius in
the *SC Hosidianum* and in CJ.8.10.2 and 3: *ne publicus deformetur
aspectus*. Attention may be drawn to the same surprisingly aesthetic

principle being applied in the Digest Title *ne quid in loco
publico*:[21] someone who has put up a structure on public land without being prohibited must not subsequently be required to demolish
it *ne ruinis urbs deformetur*.

The last rule to be discussed in Part I concerns *usucapio* by
a *bona fide* buyer. It is customary to exclaim at the shortness of
time - two years in the case of land and houses, one in the case
of movables - in which full title could be acquired by *usucapio*,
but to add that one difficulty that might have resulted from the
shortness was countered by the rule that *res furtivae*, stolen
property, could not be usucapted - not merely not by the thief
(which goes without saying) but not by a *bona fide* buyer from the
thief either, however long he kept the thing: the true *dominus*
could always recover. There was, however, no such thing as theft
of land,[22] so land was never *res furtiva*. On the other hand,
again, land could be *vi possessus*, and legislation in the late
Republic and the principate of Augustus extended the perpetual ban
on *usucapio* of *res furtivae* to cover also *res vi possessae*.[23]
Finally, however, we have one more swing of the seesaw:[24] 'It is
possible for someone to gain *possessio* of land belonging to someone else without *vis*, if it is lying vacant either through neglect
by the owner or because he has died without a successor or been
absent for a long time; and if that person transfers his possession
to a third party who receives it in good faith the third party will
be able to usucapt.' In Gaius' *Institutes* this passage is followed
by a discussion of *usucapio lucrativa*, a rule that made it possible
to possess and usucapt items belonging to an inheritance lying
vacant, even though you knew you had no right to them;[25] and that
was because the public interest demanded a sharp inducement to
heirs not to delay taking possession of their inheritances. So in
the present case the motive for the rule was probably, in the
public interest, to prevent land from lying neglected by providing
an inducement to owners to maintain possession. Nevertheless, one
notices that it may have been relevant to the well-known accumula-
tions of landed property by the governing class in the second century B.C.

As a brief appendix one further rule about *usucapio* may be
introduced. It stemmed from the Twelve Tables and lasted through-

out the classical period. It was that *usucapio* does not run *intra quinque pedes*: that is to say, between the boundaries of estates there must lie a five-foot space not subject to acquisition.[26]

II

The principal relevant Titles in the Digest are these: D.18.1, *de contrahenda emptione*; 18.2, *de in diem addictione*; 18.3, *de lege commissoria*; 19.1, *de actionibus empti venditi*; 21.2, *de evictionibus*. There is a good deal about land in the biggest Titles, 18.1 and 19.1, and within the scope of this chapter only select reference to matters of interest can be made.

18.1.6.1 displays the situation in which the price of land is paid in instalments, *annua bima trima die*. The arrangement is here coupled with a *lex commissoria*, which is simply an agreement that may be added to a contract of sale that unless the price – or final instalment of the price – is paid by a certain date the seller is entitled to call the sale off. In the present case the buyer enters into possession straight away and so is able to start cultivating immediately.

18.1.7.2 must be taken with 19.1.13.24: they were discussed not long ago by Daube.[27] They concern price. The former displays an agreement 'I will buy it for 100 plus whatever above that I make by resale', and the latter an agreement 'I or my heir will make over to the seller a half of any profit I make by resale.' The puzzle is to grasp the *Sitz im Leben* of such agreements; they appear to have been insisted on by the seller as a disincentive (more acute in the one case than the other) against resale. Daube suggests that the purpose could have been to discourage resale to a speculator who would put up something objectionable, a factory or a block of flats, on the land. Another possibility might be that it was sentimental, to discourage the sale of ancestral acres to total outsiders. Daube very properly notes the analogy of the so-called pacts *de retrovendendo* (D.19.5.12), by which the seller gets the right, under certain circumstances, to buy the land back, and *protimeseos* (D.18.1.75; 19.1.21.5), by which resale may be only to the original seller. They too may have been usually sentimental in purpose - and we shall return to sentimentality later in this chapter.

18.1.75 and 19.1.21.4 refer to yet another possible agreement: I sell land to you on condition that I am granted the tenancy at a stated rent. Perhaps that is the significance of the *exceptio colendi annis x* in *Tabula Herculanensis* no. 31.[28]

18.1.9 pr. takes up the significant theme of error: I think I am buying the *fundus Cornelianus* while you think you are selling me the *Sempronianus*. To this category belongs also 18.1.37, envisaging the immediate sale of inherited land by an heir who knows nothing about its background - he thinks it was bought by the testator whereas in fact it was a gift. Another error is envisaged in 18.1. 62.1: the man who buys *loca sacra vel religiosa vel publica* in the belief that they are ordinary private land. And we have already met in 18.1.18.1 the error as to acreage resulting from survey by a slave and sale evidently in the absence of the principals from the land sold.[29] It all sounds very careless, and implies pretty certainly the absence of professional land agents, who would presumably have obviated such errors.

19.1.13.31 to 19.1.18.1 displays a series of decisions about what counts as belonging to land and houses when they are sold.[30] 19.1. 17.2 will serve as specimen and light relief: '...in the matter of the dung-heap, however, approval must be given to a distinction made by Trebatius. If the dung-heap was amassed for the purpose of fertilizing the farm it should go to the buyer; but if it was collected for commercial purposes it should stay with the seller.'

Lest the impression should arise that these are merely abstract jurisprudential discussions (and without denying that some of them may be just that), it is fair to point out that there is no shortage of constitutions in the Code dealing with the same matters that we have met in the Digest. For example, CJ.3.32.4, of Gordian, confirms that the *bona fide* buyer of land from somebody who possessed in bad faith will be able to usucapt, so that the man who claims to be its true *dominus* will only be able to recover if he steps in

before the *usucapio* has run its term. CJ.4.54.1-3, of Caracalla
and Severus Alexander, refer to standard covenants, the *lex
commissoria* in 1 and 3 and the *pactum de retrovendendo* in 2. (In
that case, incidentally, the purpose looks like mortgage; after
all, it is practically indistinguishable from *fiducia*.)

It is not surprising, given the troubled age, to find three
constitutions of Gordian, CJ.2.19.3 and 4 and 5, about land sold by
people under the compulsion of *vis* and *metus*. The first insists
that the seller's heir can recover even from a *bona fide* third
party so long as the much longer period of estoppel called *longi
temporis praescriptio* has not run its term; the second sets out the
measure of restitution available; in the third there is explicit
mention of what might be inferred in all three cases – that the
sale had been for a particularly low price. We find ourselves here
on the fringes of the topic of *laesio enormis*, the rule that if a
sale has been for less than half the *iustum pretium* of the object
sold the seller is entitled to demand rescission of the contract.
The bibliography about that rule is large,[31] and on few topics is
there such unanimity of modern opinion. It is said to be 'one of
the prime and most certain results of interpolation study'[32] that
the two constitutions of Diocletian, CJ.4.44.2 and 8, that appear
to inaugurate the rule of *iustum pretium* and *laesio enormis* are
interpolated, and that the rule was invented by Justinian's men
under the influence of near-Eastern legal institutions, Christian
notions of just price and so on. In the classical age, we are
told, rescindibility by the seller depended (unless he was a minor)
on *vis* or *metus* and not at all upon inadequacy of price: *caveat
venditor*, in fact, just as much as *caveat emptor*. Without seeking
to challenge this happy unanimity, it might be fair to suggest that
one aspect of the antecedents of the *laesio enormis* principle has
received less notice than it deserves. Are *vis* and *metus* and inadequacy of price such unconnected notions? Surely not. Why should
a man (not being a minor) sell for a ridiculously low price –
apart from the case where he is making a concealed gift? *Dolus*
might so induce him, but apart from *dolus* the most likely causes
would be *vis* and *metus*. And so CJ.2.19.5 of A.D. 239, unless it
too is interpolated, can be seen as a precursor of CJ.4.44.2 of
A.D. 285; and even if the concept of *iustum pretium* and the rule of

dimidia pars are to be held post-classical the train of thought
relating duress and price can be seen evolving in the late classical
age.[33]

   Two of the shorter Titles, 18.2 *de in diem addictione* and 18.3
de lege commissoria, demand attention, because they have to all
appearances a particular relevance to land. In so far as 18.2 refers
to specific situations they are almost all about land, and in 18.3
- admittedly a short Title - they are all so. And as an earnest
that the discussions they contain are not merely theoretical, 18.2.
16 quotes a rescript of Septimius Severus and 18.3.4 pr. refers to
rescripts of Septimius and Caracalla. What a *lex commissoria* was
has already been described: an agreement attached to sale whereby
the seller can choose to rescind the contract if payment is not
completed by an agreed date. *In diem addictio* was another possible
agreement attached to sale, also in the interest of the seller:
sale 'subject to a better offer'. The Title includes such rules as
that if a better offer comes in notice must be given to the earlier
bidder so that he may have a chance to raise his own bid (18.2.8).
The *lex commissoria* is a way of meeting the need for payment spread
over a period, while *in diem addictio* is a way of meeting the need
for auction over a period.

   Unfortunately, on one potentially important detail about these
agreements modern scholars take a great diversity of views.[34] Such
agreements could in principle be construed in either of two ways:
as 'suspensive conditions' to the sale (so that the effects of the
sale are suspended until and unless the condition happens: the
land or house is not conveyed, the buyer cannot enter or cultivate),
or as 'resolutive conditions' to the sale (the whole thing goes
through and is fully valid until and unless the condition happens:
the buyer takes over at once, though he may have to withdraw again).
How *were* they construed in Roman law? As exclusively suspensive,
or exclusively resolutive, or exclusively one or the other at
different periods, or capable of being either according to the intention of the parties? There seems to be some agreement that down
to the time of Salvius Julianus in the second century A.D. they were
both *mostly* regarded as suspensive, and after that both *mostly* regarded as resolutive. Extreme 'interpolationists' argue that the
possibility of choice by the parties was a Justinian development

- a view that entails believing in massive reconstruction of the
texts, as a glance at either Title will show - while others think
that there was choice after Julianus and others that there was
always choice. We have seen in 18.1.6.1 a situation where the
buyer has entered into possession and cultivated: one feels that,
particularly for land and housing, if any long interval was intended to elapse before final payment or in hope of a better offer, a
resolutive interpretation of the agreements would better have suited
their social and economic purpose.

We know how common, well-organized and legally sophisticated
the auction was in Roman society as a means of disposing of private
chattels: to what extent was it used for land and houses? It may
be that our agreements in 18.2 and 18.3, especially *in diem
addictio*, have a contribution to make. Auctions of land occur in
various compulsory situations - when you are sold up for debt or
upon condemnation - and they occur when inheritances are being
disposed of (about which more anon). Apart from that not much is
heard of them, and it may be that in the case of land and housing,
and where there was no hurry, they were not the best procedure
available, and that instead you advertised the property, waited
for bids, and made bargains with potential buyers for them to have
it subject to a better offer. That is, after all, a kind of auction
over time, and one can easily perceive its advantages in disposing
of a major capital asset in an age of slow communications, just as
one can easily perceive the advantage of permitting a costly asset
to be paid for in instalments with a firm terminal date.

There remains the role of the auction in the partition of
joint estates. Two Titles in the Code are relevant to this: CJ.3.
36, *familiae erciscundae*, which relates to the partition of inheritances as between joint heirs, and CJ.3.37, *communi dividundo*,
relating to the partition of common property as between other sorts
of joint owners. Under the Title *familiae erciscundae*, out of
twenty-six constitutions only two (10 and 24) have specific reference to land, and they are not very illuminating; but out of the
five constitutions under *communi dividundo* there are two of importance for our theme. In spite of their appearance in 3.37 and not
3.36 they do in fact relate to partition between joint heirs: that
is because of the rule that if one of a group of joint heirs sells

his share of the estate[35] the buyer is not a joint heir with the
other heirs, to be dealt with under *familiae erciscundae*, but a
joint owner, to be dealt with as a *socius* under *communi dividundo*.

In 3.37.1 Caracalla explains to a petitioner whose brother has
sold his fraction of the landed estate that there is no question of
the sale being declared null: the petitioner must proceed against
the buyer, who now owns jointly with him, under *communi dividundo*,
and 'by that action, if you win in the bidding you can acquire the
whole estate, provided you pay the *socius* his share of the price,
or, if someone has put in a higher bid, you can obtain your own
share of the price'. The emperor adds that if the estate can be
geographically divided into appropriate shares that do not do in-
justice to any of the joint owners the petitioner can simply have
ownership of his own geographical portion adjudicated to him by the
Court. Certainly an auction is envisaged in this text, but nothing
in it would necessarily imply that it was a public auction, as
opposed to being simply a bidding process between the joint heirs
(or their successors in title); and if a geographical division is
possible there need be no auction.[36]

In 3.37.3, however, a constitution of Severus Alexander, there
is clear reference to a public auction.[37] 'But if an estate cannot
be geographically divided between *socii*, then either each of the
several farms is adjudicated to each of the *socii* on the basis of
a full valuation, with mutual financial adjustment, the man who
gets the object of greater value being required to pay the others
accordingly; but sometimes even an outside purchaser may be ad-
mitted to the bidding, particularly if one of the *socii* declares
that he has not the resources to offer a proper price, so as to
defeat with his own money an unreasonably low bid by the other
man.' To make sense particularly of the paradoxical-looking last
phrase of the passage a rather long example must be given. Suppose
A and B are heirs to half shares of an inheritance. It consists
of Farm X, a big one worth three quarters of the whole inheritance,
and Farm Y, a little one worth the remaining quarter. The heirs
decide to partition: how? A simple geographical division will not
give the right fractions. Suppose the total value of the estate to
be £1,000, then they must finish up with the equivalent of £500

Farm X is worth £750, so A must compensate B to the tune of £250
in cash. Suppose, however, as is quite likely, that the total
value of the estate is not yet known: how shall it be ascertained?
One simple answer is 'sell it and see': auction it, if you like,
just between A and B. B says 'I offer £800': A says 'I offer
£1,000'; then the whole is A's but he will have to give B either
Farm Y plus £250 or £500 in cash. If an outsider came into the
bidding and said 'I offer £1,200' then the whole would be his but
he would have to give A and B £600 each in cash or its equivalent.
Now in what circumstances would it make sense for the court to let
outsiders in? Suppose B says 'I've no money: I can't offer a
proper bid for the lot': then A might say 'Fine: I offer £200',
and in the absence of any opponent the whole would be his and he
would only have to give B £100 or Farm Y plus £50. In such a case
as this the admission of an outsider would ensure that the estate
did find its *iustum pretium* and that B's poverty did not tend to
his further disadvantage.

It seems likely and reasonable that the joint heirs or
owners may have had a voice in whether an auction should be public:
they might all be uninterested in the property as such and anxious
only to get the highest cash shares. Auction of an inheritance is
the background of Pliny, *Ep.* 7.11, and the *auctio hereditaria* in
Cicero, *pro Caecina* 12-17 was certainly public: the testator's
mother, a beneficiary, put in her own bid for the particular property which was the part of the estate she wanted for herself for
sentimental reasons, and the potential outside bidders were choked
off by the knowledge that she wanted it badly and was prepared to
go high.[38]

The conclusion seems to be that the partitioning of inheritances did not necessarily lead to a selling-up but might well do
so, and that if there was a selling-up it would be by auction but
not necessarily public auction.

Sentimentality about land cannot be discounted: we have seen
some possible manifestations of it earlier in the chapter, and as
it happens both the texts quoted just above contain examples of it.
Pliny says that nothing would induce him to part with the land
that came from his mother or his father, and the widow Caesennia
wanted to make sure of not losing her late husband's land that

adjoined her own dower estate. But Roman inheritances, or shares
in them, went frequently to people with little connection with the
testator's own family and background: that is the context of situations in the Digest like 18.1.37, where an heir is selling off
inherited land without any knowledge of its provenance, or 19.1.48,
where he is disposing of 'whatever rights in the *fundus Sempronianus*
Sempronius had'. In circumstances of that kind it looks as though
the Roman possessing class thought of land as pretty 'fungible', as
a commodity like other commodities with a realizable cash value.[39]
And so the disposal of inheritances can be seen, like the duty of
guardians with which we began, as another spur to the brisk movement of land (or dispersal of land, or 'market in land') in Roman
society.

5: THE CICERONIAN ARISTOCRACY AND ITS PROPERTIES

Elizabeth Rawson (New Hall)

Much of the information about the real property of the Roman aristocracy in the Late Republic has already been carefully collected
and listed. This chapter does not aim at any sort of completeness;
it attempts to make some points, hitherto insufficiently stressed
or entirely neglected, about the attitudes which the senatorial
class held to its estates, what types of property it preferred (or
was permitted) to invest in, and how it assisted its dependants to
invest; with the little that can be said about prices and their
variations, and about dealers in real property.

From the corpus of Cicero's letters[*] we get an impression of
the Roman upper class as not only deeply concerned with real property, its main form of investment, but indeed feverishly engaged
in property deals. This impression may not be wholly misleading,
in spite of the fact that Cicero and his brother Quintus were, for
most of the period covered by the letters, rising in the social and
economic scale, and thus particularly prone to buying or considering
buying property. One must recognize that there were a number of
reasons for a hectic turnover: one, obviously, the civil wars and
proscriptions of the 80s and 40s,[1] with, in between, the comparative
frequency with which senators succumbed to prosecutions leading to
exile and, if not always to the confiscation of their estates, at
any rate to the need to make new dispositions of their property (or
at long last to pay their creditors).[2] Another reason is, equally
obviously, the frequency with which the ambitious or fashionable
ruined themselves either in the political race or the very business
of building themselves grand palaces in Rome or villas in the
country. Yet more basic, doubtless, is the absence of any strict
system of primogeniture and entail, and the tendency for a man to
leave fractions of his wealth to a number of different persons, in
token of esteem or obligation. The properties concerned were per-

[*]All references to Cicero's letters in this chapter will be abbreviated as *A.* = *ad Atticum*, *F.* = *ad Familiares*, *Q.* = *ad Quintum
fratrem*.

haps often sold up, the proceeds redistributed in cash, and the various legatees would then very likely re-invest in real estate, as the best and safest investment there was. Even if one bought out the rest, these would still have money to re-invest in the same way. The contrast is great with what one may call the classical English system, where property was usually strictly entailed on the eldest son, but was encumbered with charges for dowagers, dowries, younger sons and other dependants; and where, in the eighteenth century at least, it was very difficult to buy land, so firmly did landowning families hang on to their estates, in a politically stable period when agriculture was increasingly profitable and mortgages easy to obtain.[3] Finally, the Romans often preferred to own a number of smaller estates, rather than one great one, and this would tend to multiply the number of deals that took place.[4]

Let us try to illustrate the frequency with which property changed hands. Cicero's grand house in Rome, which he bought from M. Crassus, had belonged to Livius Drusus, and on Cicero's death it passed to Marcius Censorinus, and, perhaps not directly, to Statilius Sisenna (Vell. Pat. 2.14.3). Badian has recently postulated a villa (with farm attached) at Misenum that belonged to Marius, a Cornelia, Lucullus and the elder Curio within at most twenty-five years.[5] Cicero's Tusculanum had passed through the hands of Sulla, Catulus, and a rich freedman Vettius in the quarter-century before Cicero bought it in the sixties;[6] on his return from exile he put it up for sale, but subsequently changed his mind. Another villa there, as *pro Balbo* 56 shows, went from a freedman, Sotericus Marcius, to L. Crassus, thence, via one Vennonius Vindicius (if not others as well) to a Q. Metellus, perhaps Pius, and then to L. Cornelius Balbus: at least five owners in fifty years or so.[7] When the area, in the sixteenth century, again became a favourite place for great villas, for a time, it is true, a number changed hands rapidly among the celibate ecclesiastical princes; but when they settled down in the possession of a family, they remained in its hands for centuries, and passed, if they did pass, only by marriage: the Villa Borghese remained in that family for nearly three hundred years, and they also owned the Villa Mondragone for almost as long.[8] And these were not old family seats, nor did they carry with them feudal titles and privileges which their owners might be anxious to keep.

If Cicero did not sell his villa at Tusculum, he did sell, some time in the fifties, his house (not villa) at Antium (*A.* 10.9. 4), which he cannot have had for very long.[9] Later, he seems to have got rid of some *praedia*, probably farms (*A.* 5.1.2); and in 45 B.C. he was contemplating selling property to pay for Tullia's shrine (*A.* 12.22.3). Others of his friends seem to sell without agonizing over it - Varro for one, a great multiple property owner (*F.* 9.8.2).[10] This readiness to sell is worth consideration from various points of view. One is the rarity, among the upper class, of renting; which may be connected with the unfavourable position at law of a tenant, on which the studies of Roman law remark. The only gentlemen in Cicero's letters who are recorded as hiring houses in Rome are his brother Quintus, temporarily after Clodius had destroyed his own (*Q.* 2.3.7);[11] young Marcus and young Quintus, who both wished to rent houses in order to set up independent establishments, not presumably on a very large scale (*A.* 12.32.2, 13.38.1); and we recall from *pro Caelio* 17 that that gay young bachelor also rented a flat - but one could not in fact buy a flat.[12] We hear in Cicero's invective of L. Piso hiring a house (*in Pis.* 61); and in Velleius Paterculus (2.10.1) of the censors of 125 B.C. objecting to a senator's hired house - though perhaps its cost was the main point at issue here. Sulla was certainly reproached for having hired a cheap lodging as a young man (Plut. *Sulla* 1.2).[13] Thus there was probably something dubious or vulgar about renting. There is no evidence at all for suburban or country properties being rented by the aristocracy; and the fact that Cicero specially remarks in the *Verrines* (2.3.53) that in Sicily the rich rent estates makes it clear that they do not do so in Italy, except of course by renting *ager publicus*.

By contrast, in late eighteenth- or in nineteenth-century England, it was so distasteful and inglorious to sell one's country estate that owners in difficulties would let - mostly, inevitably, to *nouveaux riches* without estates of their own, but still to persons of considerable standing. Conversely, while the really great magnates or those closely attached to a London life would also own a house in the capital, it was perfectly proper for a country gentleman to hire a house for the Season, and this was

even more true of resorts such as Bath or Brighton.[14]   I make no
apology for using the evidence of Jane Austen. It will be remembered that Sir Walter Elliot, Bart., of Kellynch Hall in Somerset,
fell into financial troubles. 'He had condescended to mortgage as
far as he had the power; but he would never condescend to sell. No;
he would never disgrace his name so far.' He is consequently
forced to let Kellynch - to Admiral Croft, an excellent man but not
quite, Sir Walter thinks, his equal socially,[15] and retires to a
rented house in Bath (it is, I am sure, to be assumed that the
annual visits he had made to London with his eldest daughter had
also been spent in a rented house, since we hear nothing of London
property in the discussion of his desperate finances). In Bath the
Elliots were able to make a fine figure; and they found that their
grand cousin Lady Dalrymple, a Dowager Viscountess, 'had taken a
house in Laura Place and would be living in style'. In Baiae, on
the other hand, private villas seem to have been the rule, from
Caesar and Clodia down.[16] It was however in Roman society entirely
acceptable to *borrow* a house; Cicero lends his Cumanum to Atticus'
wife Pilia and is annoyed when Brutus rejects a similar offer (*A.*
14.16.1). The unsatisfactory nature of ancient inns and hotels is
perhaps relevant here, and this also doubtless affects the question
of multiple properties in single ownership, especially the institution of small *deversoria* on frequently travelled routes (of which
Cicero had several, *A.* 12.36.2).

     Sir Walter's emotional identification with Kellynch, and his
convoluted relationship with his nephew and heir, that is in part
a result of it, is not to be paralleled even by Cicero's attitude
to his ancestral property at Arpinum; not even though his family
cults were established on the place: *hic sacra, hic genus, hic
maiorum multa vestigia* (*de leg.* 2.1.3). Doubtless he would not
have sold it unless very hard-pressed; but there is never a word,
as there might be in England, about regarding the estate as a
trust for his descendants. In fact young Marcus is never mentioned
at all in connection with any of Cicero's properties; at one point
Cicero actually says 'it pains me that I have no one to pass
possessiunculas meas on to' - thinking of course of his daughter,
just dead, and not at all of his son (*A.* 13.23.3). And it is clear
that his properties were not envisaged as remaining long in the

family: one of the problems about Tullia's fane was making sure
that the innumerable strange future owners he foresaw would respect
its sanctity (A. 12.36.1). There was some suggestion at one point
that it should be built on the Arpinum estate; but none that this
would keep it longer in the family (A. 12.12.1). In the event, of
course, Cicero's property was sold up after his proscription, and
prominent Antonians are found in his town house and his villa at
Cumae;[17] we do not know if young Marcus ultimately recovered the
Arpinum property or anything else.

Nor do there seem to be references in the case of other families to estates which have belonged to them for generations and are
closely identified with them - even though *pro Balbo* 56 may be to
some extent special pleading: *simul illud nesciebat, praediorum
nullam esse gentem, emptionibus ea solere saepe ad alienos homines,
saepe ad infimos, non legibus tamquam tutelas pervenire* (he was unaware that estates have no family, that they are accustomed to pass
by sale, frequently to strangers, frequently to men of the lowest
extraction, not, like guardianships, by the provisions of the laws).
There are several laments at houses passing from one highly regarded
individual to a less respected one, but that is a different matter![18]

The picture that has been drawn ought not to surprise the
reader; but it does perhaps illustrate in vivid detail a principle
summed up by Crook: 'Ancient families surviving for many generations
in genetic and property continuity are not characteristic of Rome.'[19]

It is also I think clear that the Roman landowner's relation
to his land was much less emotional than that of the English landed
gentlemen. One reason may be that his productive land, and his favourite residence, were by no means necessarily in the same place:
we never hear of Pompey staying in Picenum, where we assume he had
great estates. The pattern of multiple properties will also have
meant that an owner could only pass a short time in each one; Cicero
could not often get to Arpinum - *raro autem licet* (*de leg.* 2.1.3).
His lack of interest in agriculture was doubtless not wholly typical
(though Columella, 1. *praef.* 7, later said that the subject had come
to be despised); but he and his friends do not seem to be interested
in any country pursuits to the extent that was usual even among book-
ish English gentlemen. He once mentions fishing, perhaps not seriously (A. 2.6.1), but it was not highly regarded in antiquity; Sulla

hunted, and Pliny (in very sedentary fashion), but it was not a religion.[20] And when the Cicero boys come to the country, they are kept busy on rhetoric.

Land was also less closely tied up with political power than in England. We know that Cicero took an interest in the local politics of Arpinum,[21] and conversely drew electoral support from it and the neighbouring region; but there is no question of buying estates in certain areas in order to gain political interest in the tribes to which these belong. One could become *patronus* of a community by cheaper means: Cicero was a patron of Capua, Atella, Volaterrae and Locri (and doubtless other towns), in none of which places did he own a foot of land. The Volaterran connection at least went back instead to the fact that he had represented in court a leading man of the town, on an issue which affected all the inhabitants (*pro Caec.* 95–102). Estates, too, were often worked by slaves, who could not vote for their master: though we know of Domitius Ahenobarbus getting advantage from slaves as well as tenants by using both to fight in the Civil War.[22]

The somewhat detached attitude of the Romans, at least of the senatorial class, to any individual piece of real estate, is also reflected in a tendency to concentrate estates at a convenient distance from Rome. Very few senators, certainly, seem to have any sort of property in the provinces, and it is probable that they were forbidden to do so; this is the implication of a passage in the *Verrines*, 2.5.45 (addressed to Verres): *privatim autem nec proficisci quoquam potes, nec arcessere res transmarinas ex iis locis in quibus te habere nihil licet* (privately you are not able to journey anywhere, nor to transport property from overseas, from areas in which you are not allowed to own anything).[23] The only exceptions I can discover are the one or two senators with estates in Sicily mentioned in the *Verrines* themselves,[24] and Q. Lucienus, who had a ranch in Epirus (Varro, *RR* 2.5.22 – but Varro was probably not so scrupulous historically in his dialogues as Cicero, and it is conceivable that the man only entered the Senate after the supposed date of this conversation). All other cases are highly uncertain.[25] The ban, of course, would not apply to senators in exile; they were not senators, or perhaps even citizens, whether because exile meant loss of citizenship in itself, or only made taking another citizen-

ship often desirable; C. Antonius and C. Memmius, both in Greece
as exiles, seem to have owned property there.[26]

Certainly a senator might be left property abroad; *de leg.* 3.
8.18 envisages a senator going overseas on a *libera legatio* to deal
with *hereditates*, and we know that Lucullus and others received
these (*pro Flacco* 84ff.). But they must have sold what they could
not carry to Rome. The argument *ex silentio* is surely, when one
comes to think of it, overwhelming; the most avid and extortionate
governors, or their officers and friends (of all of whom we know a
great deal), did not use the means that must have been open to them
to gain land in the provinces. Slaves, works of art, yes; and their
wealth was sometimes let out at interest to provincials. But surely
if it had been possible to own land, Pompey would have owned half
the East, and the patrician Claudii most of the rest of it. The
rare exceptions to the rule are obscure men, probably *novi homines*;
the evidence surely suggests that new senators from an equestrian
or even provincial background were beginning to flout the law, being
unwilling to cut their established ties in the provinces.[27] Cicero
indeed suggests that the regulations to which he is referring are
not always obeyed in these lax days; but the statement quoted above
is very definite, and the first part correct (though it ignores the
fact that a senator could go abroad on private business if granted
a *libera legatio*); it should not be dismissed as mere rhetoric.

The position was of course entirely different under the
Principate; by Seneca's time the typical rich senator had estates
all over the Mediterranean world, though he still needed permission
to leave Italy.[28] In the Republican era there was naturally no
restriction on travel or ownership abroad for *equites* or humbler
persons (except that theoretically free states might or might not
grant γῆς ἔγκτησις, the right to own land though not a citizen[29])
and many Roman landowners are attested in the provinces. As Dicta-
tor, however, Caesar regulated the travels of senators' sons and
others (Suet. *DJ* 42).

Even the more remote parts of Italy seem to be little favoured
by senators, though there is of course evidence for senatorial estates in the far south, mostly ranches.[30] These were probably rarely
visited by their owners, though we do hear of Cato planning to go
into philosophic retreat on his Lucanian estates (Plut. *Cato Min.*

20.1). When Cicero is travelling to and from the south, on journeys
taking him abroad, the houses he stops in belong to fairly undis-
tinguished men - and even they are sometimes away from home.[31] It
is true that in 51 he visited Pompey in his house at Tarentum, a
place that later became a popular resort.[32] At Velia in 44 he saw,
though he did not stay in, the house of a friend, the clever young
lawyer Trebatius Testa (*F*. 7.20). But Trebatius (in fact it is
doubtful if he ever entered the Senate) was away, and building in
or near Rome; he was thinking of selling his *paternas possessiones*
because they were so far off (admittedly the reference to the house
as *domus Papiriana* might suggest it had not been in the family of
the Trebatii very long). It is inconceivable that an eighteenth-
century gentleman with estates in Cumberland or Cornwall, even if
he had Parliamentary or other duties in London, and was condemned
to a journey almost as long, and probably over worse roads in worse
weather, would have contemplated cutting his roots in this way.
Cicero's advice to Trebatius was not to sell, but only because a
remote property with loyal dependants was useful in uncertain times.
Arpinum, though not so distant as the crow flies, fulfilled this
function for Cicero himself a few months later, when he bolted there
to avoid Antony.

The letters are not a wholly accurate guide on this point,
since naturally they refer most often to properties near those owned
by Cicero himself; but it does seem that his more prominent friends
tend rarely to own estates further north than Arretium or further
south than Pompeii - both, incidentally, themselves places very
easily accessible by major roads.[33] It should be remembered, of
course, that at this time only a limited number of senators came
from the more recently enfranchised parts of Italy, and these alone
would have, or have had, old family estates in these areas.

Estates in the close vicinity of Rome itself were especially
popular and convenient. 'You take most pleasure in those of your
estates that are close at hand', says Cicero to the senatorial jury
of the *Verrines*; and Sulla's freedman Chrysogonus, according to the
pro Roscio Amerino 133 - who though no senator was as rich and
powerful as one - is described as having a house on the Palatine, a
suburban pleasure villa, and farms, 'all excellent and near the
city'; with him are contrasted those who own property in the region

of the Sallentini or Bruttii (in the far south), who only get news
from Rome three times a year.

Another reason for the concentration of estates in certain
areas is noted by D'Arms: *de lege agr.* 2.78 mentions *fundi* in
Campania as desirable for the support of the *familiarum multitudines*
of Puteolan and Cuman villas. Cicero will be thinking primarily of
foodstuffs, but possibly also of rents: it would be convenient to
have a source of cash at hand - we recall that Cicero and his
brother were caught short of money when proscribed (Plut. *Cicero*
47.2). To be self-supporting in food and drink was a matter of
pride; Horace speaks of those who buy estates near Rome, sometimes
for HS 30,000 or more, so that they can have their own grapes,
chickens, eggs, wine, vegetables and firewood (*Epist.* 2.2.160)[34]
- a good reason also, no doubt, for the popularity of mixed farming
in Latium and Campania.

It was not only the really rich, led by the *civilis ambitio*,
on which Columella comments, to spend much of their time in Rome,
who wanted properties in the neighbourhood. A letter of Cicero's
to his brother in Gaul mentions persons, probably freedmen (the
only one named has a Greek name), who if they join him in the province will expect as rewards 'the price of a suburban farm', *munus
fundi suburbani instar* (*Q.* 3.1.9). This points us, I think, to a
class of small proprietors which is often overlooked. We tend to
think of the small owner in this period as the primeval Italian
peasant, struggling against the expansionist tendencies of his rich
neighbours; or else as the beneficiary of the agrarian laws, a veteran, or one of the urban or rural proletariate. But what of the
client, often a freedman, whose patron helps him, directly or indirectly, to a small property, often as the best way of pensioning
him? This property will doubtless be preferably not too far from
Rome or the Campanian coast, so that the man can still be useful
on occasion. The case of Tiro springs to mind; on his acquisition
of a farm, probably near Puteoli, young Marcus Cicero writes apo-
logising for not having contributed financially, and promising to
do so in future 'especially as the estate will be held in common
for us'.[35] One thinks also of Volteius Mena, the *praeco* of Horace
Epist. 1.7, whose new patron Philippus helps him to a Sabine farm:

                    dum septem donat sestertia, mutua septem
                    promittit, persuadet uti mercatur agellum.

(Giving him seven thousand sesterces, and promising a loan of seven
more, he persuades him to buy a little farm.) Notice the very small
sum involved; the property was clearly much smaller than that of
Horace himself, whose Sabine farm or farms (there were five subor-
dinate small-holdings) was bought for him by Maecenas (Horace,
Epist. 1.14.2). The intellectual's farm indeed is a phenomenon
recognized by literary scholars; one notes that of Catullus (*O funde
noster seu Sabine seu Tiburs*) mortgaged for HS 15,200, not a large
amount (Catullus 26.44); the Tusculan villa which the grammaticus
Valerius Cato had to give up owing to debt;[36] near Naples (or Nola)
the small property of the philosopher Siro, which tradition made
Virgil inherit (*villula, quae Sironis eras, et pauper agelle*);[37]
probably in the same area, the 'simple cottage' to which another
Epicurean, Philodemus, invited his patron Piso on Epicurus' birth-
day (*Anth. Pal.* 11.44 - unless this is a mere poetic convention).
Pliny, *Epistles* 1.24, tells us that Suetonius was trying to buy an
agellus, ideal for an intellectual since there was very little land
attached.

        Many, although not all, of these men will have been helped
directly like Horace by a patron. They form of course only one
section of a much wider class; Pliny (*Epist.* 6.3) pensions off his
old nurse, probably a freedwoman, by presenting her with a property
worth HS 100,000 (generous, surely).[38] Some of these owners will
not have been very interested in farming - Catullus, one would
guess; but most needed to exploit their estates and were probably
often intelligent and enthusiastic farmers. The ideal industrious
smallholder described by the late second-century historian Piso was
a freedman, C. Furius Cresimus; and Treggiari observes that all the
improving farmers mentioned by Pliny the Elder were freedmen.[39]
Adam Smith in the eighteenth century said that the best of all
improvers were merchants turned country gentlemen.

        Being, as they were, mostly in Rome and Campania, such small
estates will have exploited the neighbouring luxury markets and
gone in for various forms of market-gardening or for *pastio
villatica*, which was clearly more developed by Varro's time, at
least near Rome, than it had ever been before (he claims to be the

first writer, Greek, Roman or Punic, to treat it systematically,
RR 3.2.13). He mentions a tiny estate in the *ager Faliscus* of only
one *iugerum*, the honey from which brought in HS 10,000 a year –
clearly in the right area the most minute properties could be
viable. (Compare the very poor farmer of the pseudo-Virgilian
Moretum, with no meat to eat, whose sole surplus for sale comes
from his garden; the small properties of *Priapea* 2 and 3 include
gardens; Valerius Cato, according to Furius Bibaculus the poet,
subsisted in his impoverished old age off his garden; and so did
Virgil's Corycian pirate in *Georgics* 4.125ff.)

The strong concentration of demand round Rome and in Campania
will surely have forced land-values up in these areas, and this is
one of the reasons why it is hard to make useful remarks about
prices. The general applicability of Columella's statement (3.3.8)
that seven *iugera* cost HS 7,000, or twice that if planted with
vines, has recently been doubted, though possibly it is to land
near Rome that it applies. Conceivably a usual price for a good
fundus, attractive to a rich man, was between HS 100,000 and HS
500,000. Cicero buys a *fundus* near Arpinum for Quintus for 100,000
– at a time when prices were probably high, but Arpinum was a bit
out of the way (*Q.* 3.1.3). Horace rhetorically expects a good
property near Rome, able to provide its owner with produce, to
cost up to HS 300,000 (*Epist.* 2.2.160). Sex. Roscius' thirteen
farms, near Ameria, mostly well placed for transport down the
Tiber, average out at perhaps considerably under 500,000 (*pro Rosc.
Amer.* 6 and 20).[40] How large any of these were it would be rash
to say, but about 200 *iugera* seems to be regarded as the limit for
a single *vilicus* to cope with, and properties of this size are
mentioned by Columella (2.12.7) and Varro (*RR* 3.2.15), the latter,
at Reate, bringing in HS 30,000 p.a. Within very broad limits this
would fit Columella's formula. Where *horti*, suburban parks, or
fine villas are concerned, obviously taste and grandeur help to
determine price, and there is little point in listing again the
huge sums that we are told were given for these.[41] But it is perhaps interesting to observe, when considering the prices of villas
at Tusculum, that a passage in a letter to Atticus may suggest that
building costs were twice as high at Tusculum as at Rome, something
perhaps believable in terms, especially, of the laborious transport

thither of heavy and valuable materials such as marble (*A*. 13.29.1).

The strong demand for land in certain areas will also have
meant a tendency for properties there, even those owned by senators,
to be fairly small. Even in England, where the aristocracy was not
so bent on owning estates near London, Essex and Surrey had a markedly larger proportion of small estates than other counties did.[42]
But this does not seem to have been a rule for the whole of Latium;
Cicero tells us *agrum Praenestinum a paucis possideri* (*de leg. agr.*
2.78), and Horace (*Epodes* 1.1.29-30) refers to an imaginary villa
stretching from Tusculum to Circeii, exaggerated doubtless, but
still indicative.

The pleasure villas, even if not attached to mixed farms producing various foodstuffs, often went in for *pastio villatica*.
Varro tells us of great sums made especially by the intensive raising of birds for the table - for example by his aunt through the
sale of field-fares.[43] Cicero tells us little about the economic
aspect of his villas; but he does show that he let some ground at
Tusculum to *holitores*, vegetable-growers (probably freedmen again,
from their Greek names), and perhaps some land, there or elsewhere,
to a flower-gardener. If we are to read *itaque abutor coronis* and
translate it 'and so I am extravagant with wreaths', he is perhaps
getting some rent in kind.[44] The Elder Pliny reminds us that
flowers and honey are conveniently combined (*NH* 21.70). (At the
Tusculanum, also, tiles appear to have been made, for private use
if not for sale, *CIL* XIV 4090.66; this, of course, was regarded as
a reputable side-line for a land-owner.)[45] There can be no doubt
that at this time, with Rome expanding fast, all these lines were
profitable; a little later Strabo (5.3.5) notes that Latium was
fertile and prosperous.[46] No wonder that corn, which does not have
to be eaten fresh and sells for less, was little grown near the
city and Rome relied largely on imports.

Some sorts of *pastio villatica*, it is worth noting, were
practicable even in Rome, as some gardening must still have been.
In particular, pigeon-breeding: Varro tells us that it could
bring in a good deal of money, and suggests it was common, for
pre-fabricated pigeon-houses for the roof-tops could be bought
(*RR* 3.7.11). (For pigeons on the roof of an *insula* later on, see
Juvenal 3.202.)

The income of Cicero and his family seems to have come from properties of remarkably varied character as well as location. Apart from the garden or gardens just mentioned, Cicero drew rents from his tenant farmers at Arpinum (he once had to go there to fix *mercedulas praediorum*, A. 13.11.1).[47] What kind of farming the Arpinate properties supported is uncertain; it was probably mixed. There is much corn, with olives and vines, and the remains of woodland, in the area now; but a reference to fifty *iugera* of *prata* on Quintus' land, with the name of the Via vitularia on which his estate stood, suggests the importance of grazing (Q. 3.1.3).[48] It is conceivable that the fulling establishment which Cicero's enemies accused his father of running really existed, and was still part of the property (Dio 46.4.2, Plut. *Cicero* 1.1).

de off. 2.25.88 suggests that it was possible to prefer town property to agricultural land as more profitable (also more risky, owing especially to the danger of fires, adds Aulus Gellius (15.1. 3), and Cicero (*Parad. Stoic.* 51) tells us that, not surprisingly, clever valuers preferred some locations, both rural and urban, to others on grounds of safety). Even before he inherited highly remunerative shops, *horti* and other property at Puteoli from the rich banker Cluvius, a letter shows him playing with the idea of owning real estate there, as the orator Hortensius did; while he once refers in a dialogue to the wealth that possession of granaries there would bring in.[49] Puteoli was of course a rapidly developing port and industrial town. We do not in fact hear of rich Romans anxious to own urban property anywhere else than at Puteoli and Rome in this period; Ostia was still only a place for villas, and if Cicero at one time owned a house in Antium, and thought at another of buying one in Naples, it was because both places were quiet and pleasant resorts (F. 9.15).[50]

Terentia owned woodlands, unfortunately we do not know where (A. 2.4.5). The agricultural writers indicate that *silva caedua* can be very profitable,[51] and we remember that the Romans liked heating and hot baths. Terentia also rented *ager publicus*, perhaps pasturage (or conceivably identical with the above-mentioned wooded *saltus*) but was unwilling to pay dues to the *publicani* (A. 2.15. 4);[52] she is also mentioned as possessing a *vicus*, which can mean either a village or town property (F. 14.1.5, A. 7.3.6); if the

latter, perhaps it was hence that the *mercedes Argileti et Aventini*
were drawn, that were used to support young Marcus at Athens; they
seem to have been part of Terentia's dowry. *Insulae*, apparently
hers and part of the same property, are also recorded.[53] We know
of course from archaeological evidence that shops were often included on the ground floor of residential buildings: this might
be true of the *insulae*, but probably not of Cicero's palazzo on
the elegant Palatine. Many of his acquaintance owned valuable
property in Rome.[54]

About Quintus Cicero's rural possessions we learn a good deal
from *Q*. 3.1, in which Cicero reports to his brother, then in Gaul,
after a tour of these estates near Arpinum. It looks at first
sight as if there are three of them, plus a *fundus* just bought by
Cicero for Quintus at HS 100,000, as we saw above (prices were
probably high at this point, with the influx of precious metals
from Gaul, where Quintus himself was obviously doing well); but it
is possible that we can reduce the basic number of properties to
two.[55] Cicero cannot unfortunately tell us anything about the
agricultural side of what he sees – after repeating the remark of
a local friend that Quintus will be able to make irrigated pasture-
land, he turns rapidly away to architectural matters, 'which I
understand better'. Each of the two estates seems to have, or to
be in process of acquiring, a thoroughly *signorile* residence. The
new farm, the Fufidianum, seems to have been bought so that its
abundant water supply might be diverted to make a *piscina* and
fountains at the Manilianum (which I would identify with the
Arcanum), and so that its woods should also be attached to the
latter. Quintus thought of keeping the *fundus* thereafter, but
Marcus advised against it, saying that it could still be sold for
the price paid for it. At the Laterium the house and portico are
overgrown with ivy, to which the numerous statues point like
fashionable gardeners, but building is going on which will make
the villa lose its philosophic simplicity. In the Manilianum the
contractors have still to build *balnearia et ambulationem et
aviarium*, though the *pavementata porticus* is grand and there are
columnae politae (*Q*. 3.7.7). Elsewhere the Arcanum is described
as worthy of Julius Caesar or of anyone else. Why should Quintus
want two (or conceivably three) elegant villas a few miles from

each other? He is not likely, as we saw, to have been intending
to let. He may have had an eye on ultimate sale, though systematic
improvement would not perhaps be profitable in that remote area, or
proper for a man of praetorian rank. Perhaps he just wanted to be
able to get away from his irritable Pomponia on occasion; or was he
proposing a seasonal progress, a *peregrinatio inter sua* as Pliny
(*Ep.* 3.19.4) terms it[56] - on a smaller scale than, for example, his
brother's? (The aviary, we might note, may or may not have been
purely decorative; probably it was, so far from a good market.)

   We are often told that the Romans were not much interested in
developing property, and that legal rules (for example those concerning usufruct) tended to inhibit it. But certainly the Cicerones
did improve their properties to some extent, though in a senator any
kind of greed was theoretically base (however no doubt *Paradoxa
Stoicorum* 43 on the subject is philosophically and rhetorically in-
flated). Quintus clearly had capital from his Gallic booty, and
Marcus perhaps used the legacies that seem to have been his main
external source of funds. Quintus is told of the opportunity of
making fifty *iugera* of *prata irrigua*: the agricultural writers will
assure us, if we need assurance, that these are much better than
prata sicca (Cato, *de agric.* 8 and 9). His brother apparently spent
a lot of money on improving the vegetable garden at Tusculum to get
a higher rent, introducing an *apricus hortus* (whatever this is and
if the reading is right), drainage, a wall, and a *casa*, hut or
cottage.[57] When his shops at Puteoli fell down, his architect
planned to restore them so as to bring a better rent - but this was,
interestingly, the idea of a practical business friend and agent,
Vestorius (*A.* 14.9.1, 14.11.2), whose unusual enterprise was shown
by the fact that he introduced a new form of manufacture to Italy,
as we are told by Vitruvius (7.11.1). Some planting was done on
Cicero's own estate at Arpinum, for there is a reference to
novellis arboribus in a fragment of *de leg.* 5; it might be merely
decorative.

   One notes from the interesting letter to Quintus already discussed that two of his neighbours, fronting on the same road, are
absentees (Varro is hardly likely to be the famous Varro), to be
got in touch with at Rome; though Quintus' new farm was bought
from a man of local origin at least, and perhaps residence. One

also hears a good deal about Quintus' staff, including a *vilicus*,
bailiff, who undertakes to double as building contractor, and a
somewhat inadequate builder-cum-architect (local? but with a Greek
name, Diphilus). It is clear that there is not much specialization,
compared with England in the late eighteenth or early nineteenth
century, where the great estates at any rate generated complicated
hierarchies of agents, bailiffs, building and drainage officers,
and a good head agent might earn the very considerable salary of
£1,000 a year. Columella says that any slave can be a *vilicus*,
even if he is illiterate (Varro demanded literacy at least), and
complains that there are no schools of agriculture (1 *praef*. 6 and
12); Horace's *vilicus* had been a *mediastinus*, a common servant, at
Rome, for which he pined (*Epist*. 1.14.14-15). On the other hand,
Cicero's villa at Cumae seems to have had *vilicos* and *procuratores*,
both in the plural; probably there were one or more *fundi* attached
(*A*. 14.16.1).[58] There were of course professional architects and
builders, who could also act as surveyors; when Atticus went to
look at one of the properties on which Cicero thought of building
Tullia's shrine, he took the architect Chrysippus with him, who
wrote a report proposing to turn the small baths into a winter
suite (*A*. 13.29.1); on another occasion *fabri* were to see if the
structure was sound in a house at Naples that Cicero thought of
buying (*F*. 9.15).[59]

Next, an aspect of the buying and selling of property. The
nearest approach to property dealers seems to be represented by two
interesting figures, who both deserve some discussion, and whose
activities are revealed primarily by Cicero. Earliest in time is
C. Sergius Orata, whose activities in Campania fall into the nine-
ties B.C.; he built extensively on the hitherto empty shore of the
Lucrine Lake, though perhaps in part for his own use. He is said
to have invented commercial oyster beds and *balneas pensiles*, possibly shower baths, and to have sold villas tarted up - *ita mangoni-
catas* - with the latter. We may guess that he was hand-in-glove
with the most fashionable physician in Rome at the time, Asclepiades
of Prusa, who is implied by Pliny (*NH* 26.16) to have recommended
balneas pensiles for the health; both men were friends of the great
orator L. Crassus. Campania, and especially Baiae, formed a health
resort for wealthy Romans.

We know that Orata sold a house to Cicero's cousin Marius
Gratidianus, and a few years later bought it back again - for resale? His social origin is not to be precisely established (it has
been suggested that he was from Puteoli) but he was or became extremely rich, *praedives*, and according to Cicero the chief of all
the epicures of history; and he could get L. Crassus, the leading
advocate of Rome, to represent him in a law-suit.[60] His cognomen
probably, as Varro (*RR* 3.3.10) says, means goldfish, and perhaps
refers to his wealth as well as his fondness for *auratae*, gilt
bream.[61]

Secondly, and perhaps yet more interesting, Damasippus. The
man of that name whom Cicero mentions in 45 B.C. as splitting up
some *horti* on the Tiber and selling the lots at a fixed price,
presumably for building (*A.* 12.29 and 33), is certainly the
Damasippus of Horace, *Satires* 2.3, by the dramatic date of which he
has lost all his money. He is usually described as a connoisseur
or art dealer; certainly he was an expert on ancient statues and
Corinthian bronzes, but he also says

hortos egregiasque domos mercarier unus / cum lucro noram.
Horace shows that he was primarily a business man, known apparently
as Coctio, the haggler, or Cerdo, the profiteer;[62] clearly a dealer
in various forms of luxury property. There were probably numbers
of his kind; Cicero, anxious to get rid of some statues, anticipates
no difficulty in finding a pseudo-Damasippus if the original fails
him (*F.* 7.23.3).

The man's social position is interesting. Münzer points out
that a scholiast to Horace calls him Junius,[63] and he is thus probably the son of the praetor of 82, L. Junius Brutus Damasippus,
killed by Sulla; and presumably forced into business by the loss of
his estate and the impossibility (till 49) of going into political
life. He retained enough position in society to be able to have
Cicero to dinner, as an anecdote in Macrobius shows (*Sat.* 2.3.2).[64]

What these two figures have in common is that dealing in property is not their sole activity, that they do not act as agents
for others, and that they are on the fringe of aristocratic society;
also that they sell directly to clients rather than by means of the
auction so common in the Roman world. It is by no means surprising
that the society of the time, when there was such a vast amount of

luxurious building, should throw up such profiteers, but it is
interesting to catch them at their work. Whether there were such
semi-professional property-dealers lower down the social scale it
is impossible to say.

6: PRIVATE FARM TENANCY IN ITALY BEFORE DIOCLETIAN

M.I.Finley (Jesus College)

I

The delimitation of subject expressed in the title requires comment.
There were many tenants on public land as well, some under legal
and economic conditions comparable to those of tenants on private
holdings. But the public hand introduced an additional element, at
least *de facto*, that can only confuse the discussion, and on many
imperial estates (which are examined in an earlier chapter) there
were tenancy arrangements for which private parallels are unattested
and, in the nature of the case, impossible. The most obvious example is the 'Mancian tenure' in North Africa, which, as it happens,
constitutes the bulk of what we know today about tenancy on imperial
estates, apart from Egypt. My concern is with one of the two ways
that Roman owners of large landholdings exploited them - the other
was of course 'direct' exploitation by slaves under a *vilicus* - and
that can be studied only by exclusive concentration on private
owners.

Restriction to Italy has a double explanation. First, the
conditions and the rules in various parts of the empire differed
greatly, chiefly because the Roman conquerors did not normally over-
throw existing institutions, so that Roman Egypt, for example, was
in this respect more like Ptolemaic, or even Pharaonic, Egypt than
like Italy.[1] Egypt provides by far the fullest and most detailed
documentation, but for extremely short leases, one to three years,
within a legal system which, however one chooses to label it, was
not Roman, and within an inexorable irrigation system wholly alien
to Italian, or European, experience.[2] We cannot study Cicero's tenants or Pliny's tenants from the papyri.

Second, the available *Roman* sources refer almost exclusively
to Italy, or at least to the forum of the Roman law. Columella is
the apparent exception, with his references to various provinces
and to older writers, including Hellenistic ones, but when he is
talking about farm organization or labour, as distinct from

agronomy, I find nothing which is not Italian. About the others,
Cato, Cicero (apart from the Verrine orations), Varro, the younger
Pliny, there is no possibility of doubt. A few texts of Gaius and
in the Digest relate to the provincial edict, and there are a handful of imperial rescripts addressed to provincials, but no more until we reach the fourth and fifth centuries, which have been ruled
out by definition: 'before Diocletian' is shorthand for 'before
the emergence of the later colonate, the system of tied tenants'.

The paucity of the evidence is well enough known. The jurists
had no interest in farm tenancy as such. In consequence, their
references, under *locatio conductio* (in which they were also not
much interested), for example, or inheritance, are tantalizing in
the uncertainty they generate, from their own unconcern, about the
actual practice on the land which induced a particular rule of law,[3]
and never revealing about the practical importance of a situation,
whether it was exceptional or not, whether it most commonly occurred
under one set of conditions rather than another, and so on. This
last point is so banal that one would not bother to make it, were
it not that scholars continue to offer such unwarranted arguments
as that the mere existence of juristic texts about tenancy from the
late Republic and the reign of Augustus 'demonstrates the presence
of tenants *in such large numbers* that it had become necessary to
deal juristically with their activity and position' (my italics).[4]

Yet the majority of the texts, in purely arithmetical terms,
are juristic. Epigraphical evidence is virtually non-existent (in
contrast to the rich material in Greek inscriptions from the fifth
century B.C. on). I can find nothing in the *alimenta* inscriptions,
for example, which throws any light on the subject. As for the
literary sources, the three 'agricultural writers' say little, and
that largely in the nature of sweeping value judgements; we are
otherwise reduced to one speech by Cicero, the *pro Caecina*, letters
of Pliny about his own estates, and a handful of miserable scraps
from here and there. That no quantitative generalizations can be
drawn from such a body of evidence is obvious, but it must be said
explicitly that there is also no justification for deducing 'trends'
from the absence or presence of a statement in Cato as compared
with Columella,[5] or in Augustan jurists as compared with Severan.
That there were trends, changes, developments between the second

century B.C. and Diocletian is undeniable, but a mere count of
passages will never reveal them and may in fact invent them.[6]

To be sure, the word *colonus*, the normal Latin for 'tenant'
(though *conductor* is of course possible), occurs much more frequently than my melancholy quantitative assessment of the evidence
might suggest. Unfortunately, *colonus* is used with absolute indifference to mean either 'farmer' or 'tenant'; only if the context
is unequivocal, which it often is not, can we know the meaning.
When Martial, cataloguing various ways in which one lives in the
country inexpensively, writes, *uilica uel duri conpressa est nupta
coloni, incaluit quotiens saucia uena mero* (4.66.11-12), the usually
sober Heitland sees 'a touch suggestive of almost medieval relations'
and composes half a page on this 'vivid side-light on the position
of some at least of the *coloni* of the first century A.D.'.[7] He
leaves no doubt that he takes *colonus* here to be a tenant-farmer,
which is possible but not assured, and, further, that he is being
mesmerized by the post-Diocletianic connotation of the word. But
then, the entry in the *Thesaurus Linguae Latinae* reads as if a coin
were tossed in order to assign each text to one or another definition.

II

The *fundus in agro Tarquiniensi* which made up the bulk of the large
fortune at stake in Cicero's advocacy of Caecina had been let to a
single tenant, who remained in possession throughout the various
deaths, legacies and manoeuvres mentioned in the oration (sect. 94).
That takes us back to the beginning of the first century B.C. We
do not know who the tenant was, but it is at least possible that he
was one of the *coloni urbani* against whom Columella inveighed (1.3-
4), partly on the explicit authority of the Sasernas, whose *de agri
cultura* cannot be dated precisely but must have appeared before 57
B.C.[8] There is no way of our knowing how common a practice this
was for large holdings - like most scholars I suspect it was rare -
and the phenomenon is not otherwise interesting. It merely shifts
all the problems from A to B, whether B then sub-lets or works the
estate himself through a *vilicus* and slaves.

The normal practice when a large unit was leased, I infer from
the sources, was to divide it into smaller lettings. That is the

implication not only of Columella (1.7.3-4) but also of the jurists,
as when Paul writes, in a legacy context, 'sed quo facilius conduct-
orem inueniret, per duas partes locabat...' (D.31.86.1). That is
what Cicero did in Arpinum (ad Att. 13.9.2; 13.11.1), Pliny in
Comum (5.14.8),* the owner of the estate in Umbria which Pliny once
thought of buying (3.19), and generally the *mancipes* who leased
large blocks of public land and then sub-let sections (Hyginus, ed.
Thulin 79.22-24). The number of subdivisions is not usually indicated, but Horace's Sabine farm, a gift from Maecenas which enabled
him to live in Rome properly, though, by the standards of high
society, modestly, was divided into one sector exploited directly
by a *vilicus* and eight slaves (*Sat.* 2.7.118) and another leased to
five tenants (*Ep.* 1.14.1-3).[9]

It is with tenancy on that scale (including the tenants of
small *fundi* leased as single units) that this analysis will be
chiefly concerned.

III

Although five-year terms were apparently the norm, they could be
varied. The details need not detain us, for the variations did not
upset the practice (barring the inevitable possibility of an occasional exception) of short-term tenancies, some implications of
which will be considered later.

It was probably also the most common practice to let for a
fixed annual rental in money, but recognized alternatives were
available in both Republican and imperial times. There was straightforward share-cropping (Pliny 9.37.3; D.19.2.25.6), and there was
the possibility of an agreement to pay the rent in a fixed amount
of produce at fixed prices (D.19.2.19.3). References to such alternatives are scarce, but I shall say once again that I should hesi-
tate to draw conclusions about the frequency or infrequency of the
practices from that fact. Cato (136-7) was already familiar with
share-cropping in the middle of the second century B.C., at least
for the harvesting; Gaius uses *partiarius colonus* in D.19.2.25.6 as
a term requiring no explanation; Pliny, thinking aloud about his
tenant problems, considers going over to share-cropping in language

*All references to Pliny are to his letters and I therefore cite
numbers without the title.

which implies – admittedly this is a subjective reaction – that the alternative is the less common, but not an unfamiliar, procedure.

There is no conceivable way of our estimating the average or normal or typical ratio of rent to acreage or purchase-price or anything else. No doubt Roman landowners made calculations, of greater or lesser accuracy, against which they had to set a number of unquantifiable considerations, such as the availability of tenants, local customs or their own predilections. But the source-references to the existence of such calculations can be counted on one's fingers; they refer to income, not to rent as such; not one gives a ratio.[10] That is why modern calculations of the 'rate of yield on investment in land' are so speculative.[11] On the rents paid by tenants, one cannot even speculate intelligently.

IV

Cato was already familiar with detailed lease agreements (e.g. 146-50). We are unable to say how much older the practice was, but the inference seems solid that it was henceforth the normal procedure, and that it was the landlord who laid down the terms. Agreements could be brief or elaborate. The range of detail one might include was considerable; in principle, it extended to any undertaking which was not expressly illegal.[12] But, then as now, any agreement, no matter how carefully and fully drafted, lent itself to differences of opinion when a dispute arose; hence juristic interpretation began to play its part at an early date, exemplified among surviving quotations from late Republican jurists. There was, over the years, considerable development and refinement in the law respecting landlord-tenant relations, perhaps accelerated under the Severi. Unfortunately, the juristic texts in this area have been severely mauled by the interpolation-hunters,[13] so much so that it would be folly in a brief essay to attempt a developmental account. Even such simple propositions of early second-century jurists, that the landlord has a lien on the produce *tacite*, 'even if not expressly agreed to' (Pomponius, D.20.2.7 pr.), and that in rural property, unlike urban, the tenant's personal possessions (the *illata*, *inducta*, etc.) are free from seizure by the landlord unless the tenant has specifically agreed to pledge them (Neratius, D.20.2.4 pr.), have been challenged. I shall therefore restrict myself in

this section to the more important problems and 'standard' rules,
with some indication of *interpretatio* and imperial interference,
but with no attempt to put a date to anything unless there are
grounds for doing so.

The landlord had the general obligation of giving the tenant
full access to the property, in good condition, with tenure and the
right of enjoyment for the period of the lease.[14] A *fundus* was
defined as an *ager cum aedificio* (D.50.16.211), but it was common
for the landlord also to supply *instrumentum*.[15] How common we cannot say; it was not obligatory (Ulpian's *soleat* in D.19.2.19.2
makes that clear[16]), and both the juristic discussion of what is
and what is not counted in the *instrumentum* (see e.g. the lists in
D.19.2.19.2; 33.7.8, 12.10) and the problems arising over the landlord's right to seize the tenant's personal possessions indicate a
wide variation in practice. Slaves, for example, are regularly
mentioned in both contexts. Pliny (3.19) implies that the sitting
tenants of a run-down estate he is thinking of buying had had their
own slaves sold off because of arrears; he will therefore have to
supply them with slaves himself if he decides to go ahead with the
purchase. That there was a correlation in the practice with the
economic and social status of the tenant is obvious, but the evidence does not permit us to flesh out that banal general statement.

Both the condition of the estate at the time of entry and the
practical meaning of 'full enjoyment' could lead to disputes between the parties. Of the former, it is sufficient to mention the
tenant's right of action if the farmhouse or stables were not
handed over in good repair (D.19.2.15.1). 'Full enjoyment' was a
much more complicated concept. To begin with, the landlord could
sell the property while the lease still had time to run, in which
case the rule that 'sale breaks hire' normally applied, giving the
tenant an action *in personam* against the seller (who had let the
property to him) but no right against eviction by the buyer.[17]
Then there were all the accidents that may befall the farming
industry – flood, landslide, storms, blight, fire, robbers, enemy
action – which led to complex juristic debate and distinctions,
chiefly in allocating the financial loss between the parties, in
assessing whether there was liability for the whole rent or for a
portion of the rent. The complexity is sufficiently revealed by

two long passages from Ulpian *ad edictum* (D.19.2.9 and 15), which
include quotations from five jurists, ranging in time from Servius
Sulpicius to Papinian, and two Severan rescripts. Any or all of
these possibilities and risks, furthermore, could have been dealt
with in the lease-agreement with binding force (D.19.2.9.2).[18]

The tenant was required to carry out the provisions of the
lease-agreement, to pay the rent and in general to give due care
and attention, or, as Gaius specifies it (D.19.2.25.3), to cultivate at the proper times of the year (so as not to cause deterioration in the farm) and to maintain the villa in good order. He
might also be obligated under the contract to make specified improvements, such as new plantings (D.19.2.24.3). If he improved
the land or buildings on his own initiative, without instruction
or authorization from the owner, that was his affair, unless a
neighbour's property was damaged in consequence or the landlord
tried to deprive him of the benefits. In the latter case, he could
claim return of his expenses if evicted and sued for arrears of
rent, but nothing more (D.19.2.61 pr.).[19] That the law did nothing
to encourage improvements by tenants is not surprising: five-year
leases were in themselves a sufficient deterrent. 'It was agreed
by all writers' during the agricultural revolution in England 'that
one of the major instruments of agrarian change was the long
lease.'[20] In the world of the Roman Empire, special devices, such
as *emphyteusis*, were introduced where reclamation or genuine improvements were sought, but they played no part in the private
tenancies in Italy under consideration.

V

The tenant was liable for the whole of the rent for the full term:
for example, if he should abandon the farm before the expiry of the
lease (D.19.2.24.2). That obligation included interest on unpaid
rent (19.2.54 pr.), the value of improvements specified in the
lease-agreement, if any (19.2.24.3), and, presumably, the value of
the *instrumentum* provided by the landlord - they were evaluated in
the agreement at times, perhaps usually: 19.2.3 - if he took them
off with him. However, another text in the Digest (19.2.55.2)
qualifies the general obligation by adding the words 'sine iusta
ac probabili causa' to the verb meaning 'to abandon'. It therefore

became a defence that the tenant had good reason to leave. Whether
this clause is an interpolation or not, the implication is that at
some, perhaps relatively late, date the law intervened to mitigate,
under certain conditions, the unqualified responsibility for the
full rent of a tenant who had decamped.[21]

The practical value to the landlord of his right in such cases
is another matter. There were tenants, like the man in Cicero's
pro Caecina, whom it would have been possible and worthwhile to
pursue at law, but the economically weaker tenants, who made up the
great majority of this class, lacked the resources with which to
pay up even if they were condemned in court. It is therefore noteworthy that the sources make little reference to the taking of
sureties; it gets little mention by the jurists in a private tenancy
context, and, far more significant, it is wholly absent in our fullest non-juristic source, the letters of Pliny.[22] I suggest that,
given the difficulty of securing enough tenants and the economic
stratum from which they were drawn in large part, insistence on
sureties would have defeated the main objective, that of finding
labour for the land. If the owner then had the bad luck of a tenant who decamped, he could usually recover only to the extent that
there was *fructus* on hand, which served as a pledge by law,[23] or
that the tenant left behind possessions of his own which were
pledged in the agreement. That this added up to poor compensation
can scarcely be doubted.

Nor, I believe, can it be doubted that the decamping tenant
was not the serious problem, so much as the sitting tenant who was
unwilling or unable to pay the rent in full. He alone concerns
Pliny, and the most decisive text is 9.37.2: the tenants are ruin-
ing the estate because they have no hope of paying despite reductions
already conceded to them in the past. Such tenants could of course
be evicted (D.19.2.61 pr.), but frequently they were not, for the
same reason I have already suggested in connection with the absence
of sureties. The physical (or geographical), if not economic, stability (or inertia) of this class of the Italian population was
therefore a large element in the situation. The contrast with the
unstable and mobile urban lower classes is reflected in the legal
distinction, that the latter's possessions were automatically
treated as liens for the rent in a lease, whereas the possessions

of rural tenants had to be positively pledged in the agreement.[24]

That such pledges were common is clear, and the landlords sometimes seized and sold them against arrears in rent payments (e.g. Pliny 3.19.6). Unless the *illata* (or *introducta* etc.) were itemized in the agreement, the opportunity for disputes was unlimited, and the jurists had a field-day with the problem of definition (though even more so, judging from the Digest, with *instrumentum*: D.37.2). For example, was a child subject to seizure if born to a slave woman (among the *illata*) after she had been illegally sold (D.43.33.1 pr.)? It is hard to believe that these elegant distinctions found much application in practice. In the letter just mentioned, Pliny goes on to make the obvious comment that seizure of a tenant's goods merely decreases his chances of paying up, and in the end increases his arrears. Practical considerations counted for more than their formal rights under the law with prudent landowners concerned with regular income from estates they exploited through leases, and so they reduced the rents when tenants were in difficulties. That was already the practice in Cicero's day: he selects it as the model (against Cato) for correct treatment of the tax-farmers (*de off.* 3.88).

Pliny expresses his boredom and annoyance with the *querelae* of his *rustici* whenever he visited one or another of his estates. Their complaints could have been about anything involved in these complex farm-lease situations, but demands for a reduction in the year's rent surely ranked high on the list. Two letters, in particular (9.37.2 and 10.8.5), indicate that this was a recurring problem, after a succession of bad harvests, for example, and that much haggling went on, regardless of the rent fixed in the lease. What this meant either in the number of reductions in any area in any given period, or in the rate of reduction, is of course totally unanswerable.

At some point the jurists intervened, and then the emperors: *sterilitas* was accepted as a valid ground for a reduction in rent, with the inevitable consequence of difficulties in definition. It was ruled, for example, that the fact that the vines were old did not count as *sterilitas*, nor did the small size of the *fructus* (D. 19.2.15.5). More important, it was also held that abatement for a bad year could be reclaimed by the landlord if the following year

were a good one, unless the reduction occurred in the final year of
the lease (19.2.15.4). In general, the tenant was expected to bear
a share of the loss: his claim was for a reduction in the rent,
not for compensation (19.2.15.7).[25] We cannot date the beginnings
of this intervention by the law, but rulings by Servius on *vis maior*
(19.2.15.2) invite the suggestion that the first decisions about
sterilitas also went back to the late Republic.

From this kind of evidence, compounded by the fact that *reliqua
colonorum* were included in wills in the enumeration of the property
bequeathed (e.g. D.33.7.20.1, 3) and occasionally in other contexts
where a similar enumeration was made (e.g. *once* in the Veleian tablet, *CIL* XI 1147, sect. 43), it has been concluded that 'all these
difficulties, and others, suggest no great prosperity in Italian
agriculture of the period'.[26] This seems to me wholly false. The
language of wills reflects no more than lawyers' caution, familiar
enough in modern instruments which enumerate all possibilities as a
matter of prudence.[27] For the rest, tenancy appears in our sources
only when there is a dispute. One could draw the same conclusion
for any society, including our own, if the evidence were restricted
to cases in the Law Reports and a small selection of grumbling
letters to *The Times*. For the reality, one should look not at
Pliny's irritations but at Pliny's wealth. In 98 or 99, Pliny,
then prefect of Saturn, wrote to Trajan, who was on the northern
frontiers, requesting a month's leave in order to attend to matters
on his estates in Tifernum Tiberinum in Umbria, rented to tenants,
which, he said, normally brought him more than 400,000 sesterces a
year (10.8.5). His overall income exceeded (perhaps by a substantial amount) one million sesterces annually, the bulk of it from
his land-holdings. And his benefactions, the largest in Italy by
a private individual in his period, reveal that he 'enjoyed quite a
high level of liquidity'.[28]

VI

Who were, or rather, who became tenants? Two factors which, in
other societies, drove people into tenancy and greatly affected
their economic condition as tenants can be ruled out in Italian
society of this period, namely, primogeniture and demographic pressure. At certain moments, quite long ones, a special source of

supply was available which was presumably very important: I refer
to those who lost their farms during the great periods of confiscation, when the *ager publicus* was created and when there was active
establishment of colonies in Italy and Cisalpine Gaul (to *c.* 150
B.C.). We guess that many became tenants on their 'own' land,
though we cannot put any figure to the guess. However, these were
not permanent phenomena: they could have no relevance to Columella
or Pliny, for example. And the same can be said of the peasants
who lost their holdings while serving abroad in the Roman armies or
in the course of the civil wars.

Some tenants were the freedmen or slaves of the owners of the
farms they leased. We know that from the jurists, but there is no
literary evidence worth mentioning and we cannot assess their relative significance. My own guess is that they were not very important, and that the tenants in the main were free men, largely from
the countryside. We are still left with the question of who they
were, and I see no answer other than an enumeration of possibilities.
The majority, I presume, were country people who were unable to acquire their own farms, whether from lack of sufficient funds or from
a shortage of land for sale at their level. Whether their ancestors
had once been landowners or not, or freedmen or anything else, is
neither discoverable nor immediately relevant. Some in this group
had the means to equip themselves with the requisite *instrumentum*,
including slaves, others did not. Then there were the smallholders
who helped make up the harvesting gangs (and similar special task-
forces) which the agricultural writers took for granted. It seems
probable that some of these, whose own holdings were insufficient
to keep themselves and their families fully occupied, took tenancies
when they could as an additional source of family employment and
income. If they had the bad luck of a large family, their sons
would also have been in the market for a lease. Then there were
the peasants who were compelled to dispose of their holdings and
were able to find buyers who would, as a condition of the sale,
lease the farms back to them. That was the case with Horace's
Ofellus (*Sat.* 2.2) and almost certainly with the Herculaneum document which reads: *Chirographum L. Comini Primi / fundi uenditi ei
HS LXX M / et exceptio colendi / annis X.*[29] It is also allowed for
by the jurists (D.18.1.75; 19.1.21.4).

I might rephrase my question: Where would one expect to find, in Italy, and especially in peaceful Italy, large numbers of skilled free men (I stress 'skilled': farming is not an occupation that the *plebs urbana* could turn to whenever the spirit moved them) willing to engage themselves in the 'draconic' *locatio-conductio* agreements of Roman law and practice?[30] The oblique answer to my (rhetorical) question is Pliny's *penuria colonorum* (3.19.7). It is a false inference from the silence of earlier writers that this was a new problem in Pliny's day, that there was some sort of trend in evidence.[31] We have allowed ourselves to be bemused by one bit in Columella (1.7) that is promptly belied in his own treatise, which proceeds throughout, after this one introductory paragraph about tenants, on the premise that slaves are the standard labour force in agriculture. And, as we know from other sources, tenants on larger leased units themselves used slave labour.

The agreements were 'draconic' because, drafted by the landowners, they were offered to men who were normally in a weak position economically and therefore unable to haggle over terms. It was the tenants, not Italian agriculture, of whom one can properly say, with Heitland, 'no great prosperity'. Five-year leases were crippling enough, but the one-sidedness of the relation was further underscored by the landlord's absolute freedom of choice, under the law, on termination of the five years. He could re-let to the sitting tenant, or he could let to someone else at the same or a different rent, or he could put in a *vilicus* and slaves. Were the sitting tenant displaced, there might be complications, if for no other reason because in mixed farming different crops were harvested at different times of the year. The claim of the old tenant to crops he had sown but could not yet reap or the liability of the new tenant for actions of his predecessor could lead to disputes. So could improvements (as we saw above).

However, these details need not detain us. The landlord's actions were also restricted by practical, not legal, considerations. *Penuria colonorum* meant that sometimes, perhaps more often than not, he had to accept, and retain, such tenants as he could get. Continuity of tenancy was the ideal, said Columella (1.7.3), and I believe he was speaking for the whole class of absentee landowners, not only for his own day but also for earlier times.

No doubt they hoped for continuity of ideal tenants, but they often settled for less. By A.D. 260 at the latest, tacit renewal of the lease (and the pledged *illata*) at the time of expiry, without a formal declaration, became an accepted procedure (CJ.4.65.16), and I do not share the interpolation-hunters' doubts that *relocatio tacita* was in fact already recognized at a much earlier date for farms, though not for urban housing (D.19.2.13.11 and 14). Indeed, I see no reason why the practice of *relocatio tacita* should not have been familiar in the late Republic, as it presumably was for leases of public land.[32]

Without this search for continuity, it is not easy to understand Pliny's behaviour, or Cicero's more than a century earlier. Not only are they willing to be annoyed year in and year out by complaints and demands for abatement, but Pliny, who alone provides enough relevant information, does not normally take the 'obvious' and permissible step of removing bad tenants, or even contemplate it. Tenants who have proved to be a consistent 'failure' remain in place (9.37), and when he is thinking of buying an estate, he assumes that the sitting tenants will stay on, despite the fact that their possessions had been sold up and he will have to make good the lost *instrumenta* himself (3.19). Such behaviour requires explanation, and I suggest that it lies not in Pliny's kind heart but in his rich purse, which was regularly replenished from his estates in the face of *penuria colonorum*.

The question then arises as to why tenants did not take advantage of the chronic labour shortage on the land to improve their terms. Why did tenants of Pliny's, who had lost hope of ever paying up - so he says (9.37.2) - and simply consumed what they could of the *fructus*, not clear out? Or why, in a different, Republican, context, should the *coloni* of Ahenobarbus have joined his private fleet along with his slaves and freedmen (Caes. *B.C.* 1.34.2, 56.3). Are we to believe that Ahenobarbus' tenants shared his political views and willingly joined in the fight, or that they were under some constraint? I suggest we should revive the old view of Fustel de Coulanges, and the remainder of this section follows his arguments closely.[33]

The legal principle was that a tenant 'nostro iuri subiectus non sit' (Gaius 4.153). However, Pliny's delinquent tenants had become debtors *ipso facto*, hence his precise and technical phrasing, 'inde plerisque nulla iam cura minuendi aeris alieni'. Therefore, writes Fustel, 'la terre les retient, non pas encore à titre des colons, mais à titre des débiteurs'. Debtors were subject to *addictio*, in effect to compulsory labour because of their default.[34] Though magisterial authority was required in strict law, no one will seriously argue that due process of law had been applied to all the bondsmen involved in the conspiracy of Catiline (Sall. *Cat.* 33), to the *obaerati* of Varro (*de R.R.* 1.17.2) or to the staffs, disapproved of by Columella (1.3.12), with which wealthy landowners filled those holdings they 'occupatos nexu ciuium et ergastulis tenent'.

I do not suggest that a Pliny haled his tenants before a magistrate, much less that he kept them under restraint illegally. He had no need to. The threat of *addictio* was in the air, so to speak, and the Roman law was never gentle with debtors. I therefore assume that tenants in arrears remained in place as a matter of course, so long as the landlord wished to keep them there, which he did as a rule. When the jurist Scaevola held that the *reliqua colonorum* bequeathed in a will did not refer to those tenants who, though still in arrears, had left the estate after providing a surety, the implication is that those who were unable to find a surety were still on hand (D.33.7.20.3). 'Neither unwilling tenants nor their heirs', said a rescript of 244, 'are to be retained after the completion of the period of the lease' (CJ.4.65.11) - and then added three sinister words, 'saepe rescriptum est' ('it had often been ruled in rescripts'). The rescript was addressed to a provincial, but I see no reason to think that the situation in Italy was qualitatively different. A century earlier Hadrian had already condemned the 'inhumanus mos' of retaining tenants on public land against their will (D.49.14.3.6; cf. D.39.4.9.1). Daube's comment on the Biblical six-year limit on servitude for debt comes to mind: it was 'a social programme rather than actually functioning law'.[35]

In the late Empire, tied tenants, who were clearly less free than Pliny's, and even slaves escaped by 'fleeing' illegally from one landlord to another.[36] The society with which we are concerned had not reached the situation in which the aristocracy would play that game. No one can say that it never happened, of course. Nor am I suggesting that these debtor-tenants constituted a majority,

or even a large portion, of the tenant class as a whole. Continuity was in their interest, too, and no doubt the normal practice
came near to Columella's ideal. But the threat of debt was, in the
nature of things, ever present, and that strengthened the already
powerful advantage on the side of the large landowners.

VII

One other dictum of Columella's has had a bemusing impact, namely,
his assertion that tenancy is less profitable to the owner than
direct personal supervision. Columella's excursions into account-
ancy are demonstrably untrustworthy.[37] More to the point, if he
were right, late Republican and early imperial Italy would have
been remarkably exceptional, if not wholly unparalleled, in this
respect.[38] Nor am I persuaded that, *for absentee landowners*, tenancy offered much relief from 'managerial' concerns. When a landlord 'rationes a colono accepit' (Cic. *pro Caec.* 94) or when Cicero
writes to Atticus that he must go to Arpinum, because his properties
need his attention, and that only after he gets there and sees what
there is to be done can he say when he expects to return (*ad Att.*
13.9.2), one begins to wonder about the need for 'attention' and
accounts if land leases were a matter only of an annual fixed rent.
Pliny specifically mentions a procurator and *actores* in one letter
(3.19.2), *exactores* in another (9.37.3), both with reference to
tenant-run holdings, and he not infrequently makes the rounds, once
even requesting a month's leave from official duty (10.8). I therefore find no significant managerial difference, for absentees, between tenancies and slave-operated estates under *vilici*. The reason,
I have tried to argue, lies in the complexity of the operation,
which was in practice nothing like the simple picture of recurrent
five-year leases for fixed money rents.

The upper strata of Italian society were rich, some very rich,
throughout this period. A substantial portion of their incomes –
to put it no more strongly than that – came from the land. Their
choice of methods of organization was essentially restricted to two.
Which they preferred, I conclude, depended primarily on the availability of either slaves or tenants, perhaps on local or family
tradition (habit), not on notions of comparative profitability, of
the comparative quality of the two types of work-force, or of

greater freedom from care for themselves.

APPENDIX

Columella (1.7.1-2) on opus and accessiones

'Comiter agat cum colonis facilemque se praebeat, et auarius opus
exigat quam pensiones, quoniam et minus id offendit et tamen in
uniuersum magis prodest. nam ubi sedulo colitur ager, plerunque
compendium, numquam, nisi si caeli maior uis aut praedonis incessit,
detrimentum adfert, eoque remissionem colonus petere non audet.
(2) Sed nec dominus in unaquaque re, cui colonum obligauerit, tenax
esse iuris sui debet, sicut in diebus pecuniarum ut (uel: Lundström)
lignis et ceteris paruis accessionibus exigendis, quarum cura
maiorem molestiam quam impensam rusticis adfert; nec sane est
uindicandum nobis quicquid licet, quam summum ius antiqui summam
putabant crucem.'

Ash, in the *Loeb Classical Library*, translates as follows:

'He should be civil in dealing with his tenants, should show
himself affable, and should be more exacting in the matter of work
than of payments, as this gives less offence yet is, generally
speaking, more profitable. For when land is carefully tilled it
usually brings a profit, and never a loss, except when it is assailed
by unusually severe weather or by robbers; and for that reason the
tenant does not venture to ask for reduction of his rent. But the
master should not be insistent on his rights in every particular to
which he has bound his tenant, such as the exact day for payment,
or (reading *uel*) the matter of demanding firewood and other trifling
services in addition, attention to which causes country-folk more
trouble than expense; in fact, we should not lay claim to all that
the law allows, for the ancients regarded the extreme of the law as
the extreme of oppression.'

This could be an important passage, if we could be certain of
what it says. The banal message is obvious: well cultivated land
is more profitable than land not so well cultivated. Even the mis-
application of the maxim, *summum ius summam iniuriam*, is comprehen-
sible in the context. That *coloni* here are tenants is also clear;
not even so careless and inelegant a writer as Columella would have

spoken of *pensiones* and *remissiones* if he did not have in mind
tenants paying fixed annual rents. But what are *opus* and
accessiones?

Max Weber thought it improbable that *opus* referred only to
work on the tenant's own parcel, and preferred the alternative that
what was meant was additional labour, at harvest-time, for example,
on the 'Herrenland' (and he went on to further feudal language when
he called them 'frohenende Coloni').[39] Heitland wavered: Weber's
view is 'tempting' though 'perhaps rash', the alternative is
'safer'.[40] Both cited as their one parallel the inevitable North
African 'Mancian tenure', which is irrelevant, and were seduced by
the manorial system (Heitland writing 'Home Farm' for Weber's
'Herrenland'), for which there is not a shred of evidence in any
ancient text of this period known to me. Neither was troubled by
accessiones: Weber ignored it, Heitland translated 'perquisites',
Ash (as we have seen) 'services in addition'.

This is all too loose. Compulsory labour services were always,
so far as I know, *opera*, not *opus*, as in the relevant North African
inscription (*CIL* VIII 10570) or throughout the Digest titles, 7.7
(*De operis seruorum*) and 38.1 (*De operis libertorum*). *Opus* either
means 'work' in the simplest sense, e.g. 'ut...bouem commodaremus
ut opus faceret' (D.19.5.17.3), or, in an agricultural context, it
could mean 'improvements' (D.19.2.24.3), which is not really possible
in the Columella passage. I see no choice, therefore, but to take
opus here as simply 'work' and to accept the 'safer' interpretation
of Columella's meaning, namely, that the owner should make certain
that his tenants give the due care and attention which was their
basic obligation under the law. That this was more important than
the rent is a conceit, which Gummerus glossed as follows: the rent
is the 'Hauptsache'; insuring it by keeping the tenants on their
toes is the 'Hauptzweck'.[41]

That still leaves *accessiones*, for which I can find no translation that is not forced. Columella is quite specific that these,
whatever they are, are obligations, not 'perquisites', not 'extras'.
They are obligations, furthermore, to which the landlord, not the
law, has bound the tenant (assuming that Columella has not carried
carelessness to a degree of inexactitude which permits any interpretation one chooses). Hence they must have been specified in the

lease. No surviving juristic text mentions such things; for the
jurists, an *accessio* was an external or contingent increment, as
distinct from *fructus*, a natural increment (D.21.1.31.24; 47.2.62.2).
I suppose firewood could be forced into such a sense, as distinct
from the rent, and, since Columella gives no other example, we cannot carry the analysis further.

If my interpretation is correct, it confirms my text both on
the suggestion that lease-agreements were often full of details,
some very minor, and, more important, on the conclusion about the
extent of the landlord's 'managerial' interference in land he had
leased.

7: URBAN PROPERTY INVESTMENT

Peter Garnsey (Jesus College)

When historians of the Roman economy write of investments in land,
they normally have in mind rural property. The role of investment
in urban property in the economy is seldom discussed. Moreover,
what little has been said on the subject suggests that its significance is inadequately understood.

The standard works on economic history might be expected to
place urban property firmly in its economic context. Tenney Frank
recognizes the following sources of income for wealthy Romans in
the late Republic: commerce and trade, provincial investment and
moneylending (Pompey, Brutus, Atticus), managing and enlarging an
inheritance (Atticus, his landowning and industrial concerns,
inter alia), dealing in real estate, the legal profession, acting,
and provincial government.[1] Urban rents are not on the list.
Rostovtzeff writes of the local aristocracy of Italian cities in
the first century B.C. in the following terms: 'Most of them were
landowners, some were owners of houses let at rent, of various
shops; some carried on moneylending and banking operations.'[2] Here
acknowledgement is made of the relevance of urban property to the
matter of the sources of wealth of the propertied class. But the
reference is an isolated one. When, for example, Rostovtzeff enu-
merates those investments supposedly favoured by the new rich, the
items mentioned are rural property, moneylending and Italian industry. Either it is by a mere oversight that urban property is
omitted here, or we must conclude that in Rostovtzeff's view urban
property was not taken at all seriously as an economic investment.
For that matter, I know of no work of economic history which attempts to assess the scale of the urban investment of the Roman or
Italian rich, or to estimate what proportion of their income came
from this source.

We have some knowledge of the financial interests of at least
a few members of the Roman propertied class, and it is of interest
to see how the available information has been handled. I discuss

here, *exempli gratia*, two leading Romans of the late Republic, Atticus and Cicero.

Several texts illuminate Atticus' attitude to property, both rural and urban, and reveal that his holdings in each were extensive. To facilitate the interpretation of these texts one may usefully distinguish several possible functions of urban property. A city residence or country villa might be viewed primarily as an item of consumption, a source of status or of political power. One need only refer to *de officiis* 1.138 on the kind of house a man of rank should have, and to Cicero's own adventures in house-purchase which led to his taking up residence on the Palatine deeply in debt (*ad f*. 5.6.2). Atticus was not attracted by this aspect of property, which we might call its non-economic use. Nepos his biographer thought it noteworthy that a man with such wealth should have showed so little interest in buying or building: his house on the Quirinal, inherited rather than purchased, was tastefully, not luxuriously, ordered, and subjected to no unnecessary remodelling. And he goes on to assert that Atticus 'owned no gardens, no sumptuous villa in the suburbs or on the coast' (*Atticus* 13.1; 14.3). Next, urban property might be seen as an economic investment, and in two distinct senses: it might be valued chiefly for its capacity to yield revenue, or as a capital asset. Atticus was primarily concerned with the revenue-earning aspect of property, rural or urban. Cicero did not bother to notify Atticus about a property at Lanuvium which had come on to the market, because it was not a productive investment (*ad A*. 9.9.4);[3] while Nepos claims that Atticus did not accumulate country estates: in Italy he had but two, one at Arretium and another at Nomentum. He continues with the bold, and erroneous, assertion: 'his entire monetary income was derived from his possessions in Epirus and his urban holdings' (*Atticus* 14.3). Nepos was obviously unaware of the multiplicity of Atticus' financial concerns. At the same time, there is no reason for doubting that urban rents made a substantial contribution to his income.

Neither Cicero nor Nepos suggests that Atticus speculated in property. Speculation is, typically, the purchase or sale of land or a commodity with the object of realizing a profit from fluctuations in its price. Damasippus, who subdivided pleasure-grounds on the Tiber bank for redevelopment, and Crassus, who purchased

houses gutted by fire at knockdown prices and sent in his slave
architects and builders to construct replacements, are well-known
representatives of what must have been a fairly populous band of
property-speculators.[4] Martial's Tongilianus may perhaps be conceded the status of a fringe number of the group: 'You bought your
house for 200,000, Tongilianus. A disaster such as happens all
too often in this city snatched it from you. 10,000,000 in contri-
butions came in. Don't you think, Tongilianus, that you may have
given the impression that you set fire to your own house?' (3.5.2).[5]
Atticus' attitude to property might be called that of a 'conservative investor' rather than 'speculator'. This distinction between
speculation and conservative investment seems to me valid, even if
the two categories overlap to some extent in practice.

It is instructive to see how the subject of urban investment
has been treated in relation to Atticus.

Salvioli regarded investment in urban property as speculative,
discussing it briefly beside usury in a chapter entitled 'le
capital mobilier'.[6] His two prime examples of housing-speculators
were - Atticus and Crassus. The chapter that follows, 'les place-
ments fonciers', does not discuss capital investment in land in
general, but only investment in rural property.

The conceptual confusion recurs in Feger's article on Atticus.
In a short section on 'Landwirtschaft', Atticus' suburban house,
the two Italian estates, the ranch in Epirus, are all registered.
Feger goes on to mention Atticus' concern with profitability, and
to refer to Nepos' statement on his sources of income, which, in
Feger's words, 'identifies revenues from his properties as his only
source of wealth'. Nepos, as we saw, writes of property in Epirus
and in the city (*urbanis possessionibus*). We might be excused for
supposing, on the basis of Feger's version of this text and the
preceding discussion, that the reference in Nepos was to *rural*
properties. Feger goes on to assert, in a section headed 'Speku-
lation und Geldverleih', that Atticus speculated in property. The
two texts cited show no more than that Atticus was interested in
purchasing a house either in the city or in the country (*ad A*. 1.
6.1; 4.8.1).

Urban rents do not appear among the sources of wealth attributed to Atticus by Frank. He refers to Nepos, but has not noticed

the crucial clause. Frank may have been following Nepos less
closely than a modern biographer of Atticus, Byrne. She notes
Nepos' statement on the revenues of Atticus, dismisses it as
'incorrect', and has nothing more to say of the urban holdings.[8]

In discussing the income of Cicero, Frank juxtaposes two
texts, *Philippics* 2.40 and *Paradoxa Stoicorum* 49. The first of
these is used as the basis of the argument that Cicero's income
came to about 600,000 sesterces annually, while the second is cited
for Cicero's opinion there expressed that an income of these dimen-
sions would enable one to live a life of luxury.[9] However, Cicero
says in the next breath that his own estates brought in only
100,000 sesterces. One wonders, therefore, whether the passage in
the *Philippics* has also been misread. This proves to be the case.
What Cicero there claims is that he has received some 20,000,000
sesterces in legacies from friends and kinsmen; it is Frank's de-
duction that Cicero's annual income over thirty years would have
been more than 600,000 sesterces (and his assumption, equally
erroneous, that the money came exclusively from clients at law).[10]
It surely needs no demonstrating that Cicero did not have such a
sum of money to dispose of annually from the beginning to the end
of his legal and political career. Moreover, even if Frank had
been able to show that Cicero was equipped to live lavishly
throughout his active public life, it does not follow that he did
so. Cicero is not likely to have regarded the legacies as a source
of regular spending-money. The bulk of them probably consisted of
immovable property, and were best left in this form. *Some* of the
property made over to him would have been productive and furnished
him with income. Thus the shops at Puteoli left him by Cluvius the
banker brought in 80,000 sesterces a year despite their dilapidated
state. But part of the legacy consisted of *horti* and other unspecified property, which could only be designated *possessiones volup-
tuariae*.[11] Incidentally, this was one legacy from which Cicero
derived little benefit, as it arrived in the second-last year of
his life.

In addition to *Paradoxa Stoicorum* 49, there are passages in
letters which contribute information on Cicero's income. It is
known that from the time of his marriage to Terentia shortly before
77 B.C. Cicero had the use of an annual income of 80,000 sesterces

in rent from apartment blocks, *insulae*, in Rome.[12] This figure is
more reliable than the 100,000 sesterces from rural properties (if
indeed *praedia* stands here for *praedia rustica*), which derives from
a highly rhetorical passage. (The figure of 20,000,000 sesterces
has been rejected by some scholars on the same grounds.) But an
income of 100,000 sesterces from country estates may not be very
wide of the mark. This level of income presupposes a holding in
productive land worth somewhere between one and two million sesterces, depending on the kind of farming carried out.[13] Carcopino,
who was not prone to underrate the wealth of Cicero, opted for the
lower figure, on other grounds.[14] (It might, I suppose, be charged
that Carcopino's dislike of the man may have led him to exaggerate
the value of Cicero's non-productive property as against his productive property.) The numerous texts which relate to Cicero's
financial standing and dealings do not prepare us for a much higher
figure. It therefore seems a safe conjecture that urban property
contributed almost as much to Cicero's income as country estates.
We might have been prepared for this significant result by *de officiis* 2.88, where the choice between urban and rural rents, *vectigalia*, is put on the same level as that between *gloria* and *divitiae*,
or *bona valetudo* and *voluptas*, or *vires* and *celeritas*.

There is some evidence, then, that the subject of urban property investment has been mishandled. Why should this have been so?

There appears to have been a reluctance among scholars to con-
cede that the typical Roman aristocrat regarded the activity of the
rentier as respectable. Writers of agricultural treatises and moral
discourses have reinforced this belief by giving the impression that
involvement in only a very few income-producing activities was
countenanced. Thus, for example, in *de officiis* 1.150-1 only agriculture, trade (under certain conditions) and the liberal arts are
designated honourable revenue-earning occupations. Such passages
must be recognized for what they are, statements of an antiquated
value-system with only limited relevance to contemporary economic
behaviour.[15]

The conceptual confusion referred to earlier has played its
part. The category of speculation has been broadened to include
the activity of the *rentier*; and speculation is viewed as the
characteristic activity of the capitalist, whose outlook is

branded as unmistakably plebian.[16]

Again, there are relatively few texts that bear on urban
property, and their numbers are reduced markedly if we discard
those relating primarily to non-economic aspects of house-
ownership. This in itself might feed the supposition that Romans
did not regard urban property as a serious investment. But the
paucity of texts might be explicable on other grounds. As I have
already implied, ownership of productive rural property was the
cornerstone of the ideology of the ruling class. A senator writing
for a public audience if not for posterity would not fight shy of
identifying himself or a peer as a rural landowner. But residential
rents were a proper subject mainly for private correspondence with
agents or friends. It is because Martial thought nothing of divulg-
ing confidences that we know of the finances of the mysterious
Afer: 3,200,000 out on loan, 3,000,000 coming in from apartment-
houses and country estates (*ex insulis fundisque*), and 600,000 from
grazing (Martial 4.37). There was nothing degrading about being a
rentier, but this was thought of as a purely private affair, having
no relevance to a man's public image or political stance.

Finally, the message of a number of literary texts seems to be
that urban property brought in a higher return than rural property,
but was in two respects less secure: it was more vulnerable to
damage or destruction, not the land itself, but the capital addi-
tions required to make it revenue-earning; and its greater destruct-
ibility rendered it more liable to suffer sudden loss of market
value. There is an explicit text in Aulus Gellius (15.1). A member
of a rhetorician's entourage looks down on a fire from the Esquiline
and comments: 'The returns from urban property are great, but the
risks are far, far greater. If there were some remedy, something
to prevent the houses of Rome burning so readily, I assure you I
would have given up my estates in the countryside and purchased
urban property.' On the basis of this and other passages a generalization might be formulated to the effect that the greater
profitability and insecurity of urban as compared with rural property investment diverted aristocratic funds from the urban to the
rural sphere.

But could such a generalization be defended? Its validity
would have to be tested with reference to Republican Rome, Imperial

Rome, and the cities of the empire. The outcome of the investigation (which cannot be undertaken here) is not as predictable as
may seem.

Is the thesis valid for the late Republic? What indications
are there that the average senator or equestrian was deterred from
investing in *insulae* by considerations of risk? And how great were
those risks? The house built with walls of wattle work of which
Vitruvius writes was highly inflammable, a real death-trap, but its
loss would have been borne lightly by a wealthy owner. In any
case, rich men were more likely to invest money in a more solid
structure with concrete walls. This was the typical multi-storied
tenement house of Cicero's day, and though less durable than one
built of brick, was officially judged to have a life-span of eighty
years (Vitruvius 2.8.8; 17; 20). Cicero's sang-froid in the face
of his collapsed and cracking buildings is notorious (*ad A*. 14.9.1;
11.2).[17] Can we assume that it was also unusual?

Is the thesis valid for Imperial Rome, and in particular for
the new Rome constructed by Nero and other emperors out of materials
superior to those used in the lifetime of Vitruvius and earlier?
The Ostian evidence is relevant. Ostia became virtually a suburb
of Rome, and was architecturally a Rome in miniature. The Ostian
insulae were secure and lucrative investments. They were well-
planned, brick-faced and vaulted. Most had shops on the ground
floor. A high proportion of Ostians lived in them. Rents must
have been an important constituent of Ostia's gross city income.[18]

Is the thesis valid for the cities? When the inquiry is extended beyond the capital, as it must be, archaeological evidence
leaves no doubt that many house-owners put their property to productive use. Rooms or apartments were rented to lodgers, houses
or parts of houses were made available for commercial enterprises,
in some of which the house-owners appear to have participated
directly. At Volubilis in Mauretania, the economic functions of
urban property can be appreciated at a glance, thanks to the
excellent publication of Etienne. The houses of the north-east
quarter, which date from the first part of the third century, are
ample, even sumptuous. Ten of the twenty-three have oil-producing
establishments, seven have bakeries. There are a great many shops:
only two houses have none, and one of them has an apartment for

rent. House no.19 is left, very rich in mosaics, and owned, according to Etienne, by 'un propriétaire éloigné de toute pré-occupation de lucre'.[19] It would be safer to say that the man did not wish commercial activity to interfere with his domestic tran-quillity; for how can we be sure that he did not own buildings elsewhere which housed commercial or industrial operations? Un-fortunately, names and statuses cannot be assigned to any of the houseowners. We might be tempted to suppose that the higher an individual stood in the social hierarchy, the less deeply he was involved in commercial operations. This would probably be a mis-taken assumption, as is suggested by an analogy from another Afri-can town, whose economy was also basically agrarian. Of the three most luxurious houses in Timgad, Algeria, in the early third cen-tury, the one with most shops, and the only one with shops communi-cating with the house-interior, was owned by M.Plotius Faustus, equestrian army officer, local magistrate and priest.[20] It is of course only at Pompeii, where the names of a large number of house-owners and prominent persons are known, that a division between 'politicians' and 'businessmen' can be seen to be artificial. It is strange that no satisfactory analysis of the economic behaviour of the richer and more important Pompeians has yet been made. A first step might be to assemble all the information relating to the income-producing activities of urban proprietors. One fact that would immediately become apparent is that only a small minority of the better quality houses so far excavated were untouched by any degree of commercial enterprise.[21]

    To sum up the argument so far: neglect of the subject of urban property investment can be explained but not justified. There is room for a study of the relative levels of investment in urban and rural property, and the relative contribution made by these and other forms of investment to the income of the wealthy. The literary sources have not been fully exploited and may serve as a starting-point. We should, however, be prepared to extend the inquiry to include cities where, thanks to the archaeologists, private housing can be studied more profitably than at Rome. An investigation of this kind would not dethrone agriculture, but would reveal that investment and income patterns were very varied, and that by no means all those prominent in politics and society,

in Rome and the cities, would have been able, or would have wanted,
to state with the younger Pliny, *sum quidem prope totus in praediis*
(*Ep.* 3.19.8).

I will conclude by placing the argument in a wider context, that
of the economy as a whole.

Though they seldom make it explicit, historians writing about
the sources of wealth of the aristocracy have some kind of conceptual scheme of the workings of the economy. In emphasizing the
predominance of rural property as a source of income, they are,
indirectly, making a statement about the balance of trade between
the rural and urban sectors of the economy. They are stressing
the flow of goods from the rural to the urban sector. The cities
are viewed as markets for agricultural produce. There was also a
trickle of goods, consumer goods, back to the countryside from the
cities. But on the whole, rural landowners pocketed the returns
from sales of agricultural produce either directly in their capacity
as agricultural producers, or indirectly through the rents they
charged producers. I doubt whether anybody would dispute this as
a general account of the balance of trade between town and country
in a primitive economy.

But it is also necessary to recognize that there were income-
generating transactions taking place in the 'internal' urban economy, as a result of the division of labour within the cities, that
is to say, in consequence of the fact that urban residents were
providing employment for one another. Property-owners participated
indirectly in those activities. For example, they took a rake-off
from transactions between private producers and retailers on the
one hand, and retailers and urban consumers on the other, through
rents charged on premises. Again, as producers themselves - one
thinks of the oil-manufacturers of Volubilis, or Veranius Hypsaeus
the Pompeian fuller and magistrate[22] - they took part in and drew
profits directly from the commercial life of the city.

The purpose of this chapter then, has been not to deny the
importance of the flow of income from the rural sector, but to focus
more closely on income-generating activities that took place within
the cities. Ownership of urban property provided access to, and in
some cases control over, these activities. This other source of

income should not be ignored or defined out as of marginal significance, unless it can be shown that the Roman aristocracy and the
aristocracy of the cities as a class turned their backs on it.

APPENDIX

Demolition of houses and the law

The evidence that the Roman authorities placed restrictions on
house-demolition is familiar but confusing. It consists of legal
enactments that are often brief and uninformative, or decidedly
ambiguous, and of extracts from juristic commentaries which focus
on strictly legal points and in large part ignore the social, economic and even political background. In practical terms this means
that it is seldom possible to probe in any depth into the attitude
of the political authorities, the activities they are seeking to
curb, and the impact of such activities on the community.

The municipal charters may be considered first. A clause in
the late-Republican charter of Tarentum ran as follows:

> nei quis in oppido quod eius municipi erit aedificium
> detegito neive demolito neive disturbato nisei quod non
> deterius restiturus erit nisi de s(enatus) s(ententia).
> sei quis adversus ea faxit, quanti id aedificium fuerit,
> tantam pequniam municipio dare damnas esto, eiusque
> pequniae quei volet petitio est.

In other words, anyone who unroofed or pulled down a building was
liable to a fine equal to the value of the building, unless restoration was made to a state no worse than before. At Spanish Urso,
the Caesarian colony, a security was forfeited if rebuilding did
not take place, while the Flavian law for Malaga required restoration of the building concerned within the following year.[23] It is
hard not to believe that some such regulation was published at Rome
in the late Republic.

The charters are silent as to the motives of either legislators
or those whose activities were being legislated against. The un-
roofing of a building (*detegere*) suggests the practice of *distractio*,
which in this context means the breaking up of a building with a
view to salvaging the materials;[24] demolition that was not followed
by rebuilding might in theory have been aimed at forcing up the
prices of lands and rents.[25] The legislators, for their part, might

have been principally interested in preserving the physical aspect
of the city. This may be implied in the stipulation that a building
should be replaced by a structure 'no worse' (*non deterius*). A
subsidiary motive might conceivably have been to keep the stock of
residential housing at its existing level.[26] But all this is conjecture; the texts themselves do not fill in, or even hint at, the
background of the legislation.

The so-called Senatus Consultum Hosidianum of A.D. 45 is somewhat more explicit.[27] The inspiration for the decree came from the
emperor Claudius himself.[28] Eleven years later its main points are
summarized in the S.C.Volusianum issued by Nero's senate in settling
a case involving housing in an abandoned community in the territory
of Mutina. The Claudian decree, as restated, emended and interpreted, remained the basic statement of the Roman authorities on
the subject of the demolition of houses until the Severan period at
least.

Several differences between the decree and the charters are
evident. The range of the decree is wider; it applies to Rome and
apparently also to Italy, both rural and urban.[29] The decree is
concerned with house-demolition following sale. A profit motive
is supplied for the first time; moreover, the phrase *negotiandi
causa* may even imply that the decree was directed against regular
trafficking in buildings, rather than merely single acts of demolition for profit. The penalty is higher: the buyer forfeits
double the price of the house, the seller is reprimanded, and the
sale is voided.[30] In the final clause exemption is given house-
owners who sell off parts of a house while intending to retain the
bulk of it in their possession, provided that they do not make a
regular business of it (*dum non negotiationis causa*).[31]

The prolegomenon contains a bitter denunciation of 'this most
cruel form of profiteering', which leaves behind a scene of destruction more appropriate to an age of war than of peace.

The language seemed to de Pachtere too strong to have been
employed against professional wreckers of houses.[32] He held that
Claudius was in fact attacking creditors who took over the property
of bankrupted farmers and turned it over to ranching instead of
agriculture, and that the decree was nothing less than an attempt
to arrest the decline of agriculture and the depopulation of the

countryside.

This theory, which won wide acceptance, is not supported by
the text of the decree.[33]   There is no reference in it to agriculture. The emperor's preoccupation throughout is with buildings,
in the first place urban buildings.[34]   In addition, one may wonder
how a decree outlawing trafficking in buildings could have affected
absentee-landlords and *latifondisti*, who would have escaped its
jurisdiction simply by leaving farmhouses intact.

On a superficial reading of the text, Claudius was protesting
at the despoliation of his cities for profit. This might indeed
be a sufficient explanation of his anger. All emperors were concerned about the physical aspect of the cities, Rome above all.[35]
Fine buildings were thought to enhance, and decrepit ones to tar-
nish, the image of a reign. Both the Claudian decree and the
Neronian decree complain that the unsightliness of ruined buildings
has presented a direct challenge to the ruler.

There is just a possibility that Claudius was aware that
profiteering of this sort might have a further consequence. The
words he uses to describe it, *cruentissimo genere negotiationis*,
might allude obliquely to the plight of Rome's tenants. In this
connection it is worth noting that Claudius, unlike many emperors,
did not sacrifice residential areas to wasteful and grandiose
building projects; he did not, in effect, aggravate Rome's perpetual
housing shortage. His public works policy was primarily utilitar-
ian; it aimed at bettering living conditions in Rome through reduction of the risk of flooding, and improvement of supplies of food
and water.[36]   We need not believe that Nero inherited any of his
predecessor's humanitarianism;[37] yet his senate in A.D. 56 might
have accurately interpreted Claudius' intentions, in requiring
Celsilla to show that the buildings she owned and wished to demolish
in the ghost town of Campi Macri were uninhabited, uninhabitable,
and that no one could conceivably be desirous of living in them.[38]

The argument from 'cruentissimo' is not of course conclusive
- the most that I would claim is that it merits consideration.
Meanwhile we should be on our guard lest we exaggerate the extent
of Claudius' sympathy for the plight of the poor. For example, the
decree is not a manifestation of hostility to the practice of
pulling down slum dwellings prior to replacing them with better

quality and more profitable *insulae*. It was the spectacle of houses left in ruins by wreckers which roused Claudius to anger, and the wreckers are accused simply of making money out of their destruction (*diruendo*).[39] The assumption, made here as in later texts, that demolition was a profitable enterprise,[40] together with the emphasis given to aesthetic considerations,[41] indicate that the destruction of sub-standard housing was not at issue.

Similarly, though we may suspect that the house-wreckers included speculators who kept land idle with the purpose of forcing up its market price and the level of rents, there is no hint of this in any of the texts. Explicit reference is made only to the short-term profits obtainable from demolition. Either hoarding was not a serious problem, or the authorities were unwilling or unable to attack it directly and effectively. The Romans were not known for any bias against *rentiers* or profiteers, or in general for protecting the poor against exploitation by the rich.

In the last resort, the texts must be allowed to speak for themselves. The municipal charters apart, they show that money was being made out of dismantling houses for the purpose of salvaging materials, and that the emperors intervened with the aim of preserving the aspect of their cities. This may not be a complete explanation of the legislative and judicial activity we have been considering, but it is as much as can be discerned with certainty.[42]

C.R.Whittaker (Churchill College)

Whatever one's view of the ultimate cause of the fall of the Roman
empire, land and more specifically the decline of productivity on
the land always figure more or less prominently within an assessment
of the social and political changes that were taking place.[1] Even
Jones, who has expressed far more reserve about general theories of
decline than most, gave as his opinion that the devastation of the
land and its subsequent desertion grew worse from the third century
A.D. to the sixth.[2] In other words, *agri deserti* are to be regarded as a malignant growth of the later Roman Empire, with a
datable origin into the bargain.

      The problems involved in making objective judgements about
this, as about so many other subjects in the period, are too well
known to need much repetition. But they are essentially methodological. That is to say, the sources are atrocious and there is a
constant temptation to generalize from inadequate data - a limitation which applies with particular force to the third century
during which the decline is supposed to have begun and with which
this chapter is chiefly concerned. So it is worth stating clearly
at the outset a few observations on the nature of the evidence.

      I

What one quickly discovers in any attempt to generalize from the
literary sources is that they present almost insuperable problems
of perspective and ideology. For instance, Libanius in the fourth
century (e.g. *Or*. 2.32) or Theodoret in the fifth (e.g. *Ep*. 43)
were complaining that taxes were causing desertion of land around
Antioch and Cyrrhus at the very time when we know that the economy
of Syria was booming. Unless there was a deliberate falsification
of the evidence, which there is no reason to suppose, we must conclude that both authors restricted their observation to a narrow,
local level. Both Christian and pagan writers were in any case
inclined for different reasons to perceive the onset of doom with

more enthusiasm than reality. Many Christian writers were committed to a theme of the Second Coming which distorted their interpretation of disasters, while among pagans there was what Martin calls
a 'defeatist' theory in regard to agriculture which can be traced
back to the Republic and which was denounced by Columella in the
opening words of the *Res Rustica*.[3] It is this same outlook which
can be detected in the 'old Roman' views of Symmachus. Panegyrists
on the contrary, upon whose testimony one leans heavily for conditions in the earlier part of the fourth century, were paid to pro-
claim that cities had been the haunt of wild beasts before the
glorious restoration – *tot urbes diu silvis obsitas atque habitatas
feris* (*Pan.Lat*. 9(5).18.1). Can they therefore be taken seriously?

     A good deal of the case concerning *agri deserti* rests upon
provisions in the various law codes. How one should interpret
these regulations is a problem which I must confess I regard with
uneasiness. Few provisions in the codes, it is true, refer to the
third century, but they are not unreasonably quoted as evidence
from the fourth century of a cumulative state of disorder which
began in earlier generations. Certainly there are many references
to *agri deserti*, particularly in relation to *emphyteusis* or to fu-
gitive *coloni* and slaves.[4] Nevertheless legislation concerning
absentee landlords and derelict land – *quae...ex neglegentia domini
vacet* – was not, as this quotation from Gaius makes clear (*Inst*.
2.51), a phenomenon of only the later Empire. The real difficulty
is to discover the context, effectiveness and extent of these often
haphazard collections of regulations. Can we be sure that the
legislation was intended to cover more than a temporary emergency?
In 422, for instance, when large tracts of imperial estates in
Africa and Byzacena were declared by legislation *in removendis*, it
was the very year in which Count Boniface, recently created *comes
Africae*, came from Spain, where he had been fighting the Vandals,
in order to prepare the defences of Africa (Prosper Tiro; *Mon.Germ.
Hist*. I.469). There must therefore be at least a strong presumption
that the legislation was less concerned with emphyteutic land development than with granting tax concessions to keep the province
loyal.[5] The various legal pronouncements on the colonate tell us
more about Roman taxation and fiscal problems than about the condition of the coloni and the same is probably true *mutatis mutandis*

of emphyteutic regulations.[6] Neither therefore provides a particularly useful guide in tracing the shifts of population and rise or
decline of productivity. Even if we suppose that an aggressive
Roman fiscal policy could produce a marginal stimulus to productivity, surely no one believes that this pressure was ever relaxed
in any way?

Another class of evidence concerns the effects of wars or
natural disasters upon agrarian economies; and obviously some note
must be taken of such events. But many of the invasions must have
been like that of the Quadi described by Zosimus (3.7); that is,
small marauding bands who broke into farms and drank the liquor,
clandestine night raiders from the woods, where they hid by day,
who were quite easily countered by private citizens banding together with the aid of a professional adviser. In Cyrenaica, in
spite of the gloomy letters from Synesius, c.400, the enemy usually
turn out to be little more than glorified cattle thieves, and agriculture was far from stagnant.[7] On one occasion in Thrace in 376,
Ammianus (31.6.5-7) describes how barbarian settlers who had been
ill-treated showed the invading raiders where to find the
conditoria frugum occulta. From which we must assume that often
the grain store was not found by invaders. Invading armies with
horses kept to the major routes where there were water supplies.
It takes a long time to cut down an olive tree and most raiders were
primarily concerned to surprise the cities where the main wealth was
stored. Barbarians, too, had their problems. The Franks, says
Zosimus (3.6), on one occasion feared to raid North Germany in case
they provoked a Roman counter-raid - raids which were used to re-
stock farms in Gaul.

In short, there is a danger of overestimating the permanent
consequences of short-term fluctuations in human fortunes. And
never more so than in the political chaos of the later Roman Empire.
Isolated texts or occurrences make bad building bricks with which
to construct any sort of reliable edifice. One of the ways in which
we might achieve a more balanced view, Rémondon has suggested, is
to set the sparse and thus overweighted literary evidence against a
more detailed investigation province by province.[8] Even this will
produce not a statistically more reliable result, but simply a
shift in perspective. But I have taken it as my cue, encouraged by

the belief that in any age voices of gloom and despondency in contemporary or near contemporary sources are rarely as credible as
their volume or stridency would suggest.

II

Investigations of *agri deserti* usually begin with Herodian's report
of the reforms proposed by the emperor Pertinax in A.D. 193. The
programme supposedly aimed, 'To make over all land in Italy and the
provinces which was unfarmed or completely idle in any quantity to
whoever was willing and able to farm it, even if (?) it was imperial property - the man who cultivates it to become the legal owner.
To these farmers he granted tax immunity for ten years and security
of tenure' (2.4.6).[9] If this is the correct translation, it is
impossible to believe that a law could have been seriously contemplated in 193 which would have applied to *all* land in every province, much less to land in Italy where many of the senatorial
class who had acted as Pertinax' staunchest sponsors would inevitably have lost some of their own unworked property. If on the
other hand Herodian's words apply only to imperial estates - which
seems a possible interpretation of the phrase εἰ καὶ βασιλέως
κτῆμα εἴη, meaning 'if indeed the land was imperial property' - then
the scheme becomes at least conceivable but much less obviously a
solution to the problem of deserted land.

Pertinax' proposals are linked by Gabba with the speech of
Maecenas which Cassius Dio purports to report. The proposal in that
speech, which Dio certainly intended to be of relevance to his own
age in the early third century, was to sell off all fiscal property
not χρήσιμα or ἀναγκαῖα in order to set up a land bank whose interest would pay the sudden and rapacious demands of the soldiers
(52.28.3f.).[10] To sell off land is not, of course, the same as to
make tax-free grants of land, as Pertinax planned. But both passages are assumed by Gabba to be concerned with what he calls a
crisis of 'the small and medium landowner'.[11] The difficulty is
that if we accept this interpretation of Herodian, the implication
of the two passages is contradictory. For Pertinax's proposal
would mean that tax relief was needed to encourage any sort of
occupancy, while Maecenas' suggestion would have been pointless
unless the land had been valuable enough to attract buyers and

investors. We can probably discount Dio's evidence as a rhetorical
topos, also found in Pliny's Panegyricus (50.2f.), which laid down
that an optimus princeps sells off or returns imperial estates to
the nobiles. But in any case, as Gabba himself points out, Dio was
obviously more concerned with sparing senators the burden of military exactions than with agricultural economics.

But this still leaves us with Herodian's evidence. Should it
be taken as good evidence of widespread dereliction? The answer is
that, whichever way the passage is interpreted, it could not possibly be true as it stands, since Italian land was already tax free.
Antonine regulations compelling senators to hold a certain measure
of land in Italy were almost certainly still in force (HA, Marc.
9.8) and it therefore seems unlikely that it was necessary to encourage tenure of land in Italy by giving it away. But if, on the
other hand, Pertinax' legislation was intended to apply to the
provinces only, it begins to look remarkably like the Hadrianic
lex de rudibus agris, which was known to have operated on the imperial estates of the Medjerda valley in Africa (CIL VIII 25943).[12]
Since Severus found it necessary to repeat this legislation (CIL
VIII 26416; cf. 10570), it is not unreasonable to think that
Pertinax, too, had reached the same conclusion. But, equally,
since the Severan legislation is not known to have been enacted
for anywhere else than Africa, the probabilities are that this was
the limit of Pertinax' intention also. If this is true, the problem was neither specifically one of agri deserti nor, probably,
was it of empire-wide proportions.

Gabba based his opinion in part upon a belief that much land
in the empire was still deserted and depopulated after the plague
epidemic during the Marcommanian wars twenty-five years earlier.
But this assumption concerning the extent and lasting effects of
such disasters has been seriously called into question.[13] For
what it is worth, Ammianus Marcellinus says that the recovery from
the plague was rapid - mox post calamitosa dispendia res in inte-
grum sunt restitutae (31.5.13). Marcus Aurelius' settlement of
Marcommani and Quadi within the empire, which is often adduced as
a symptom of the increase in deserted land after the plague in
Dacia, Pannonia, Moesia, Germany and Italy (where they were mostly
settled) (Dio 71.11.4; HA, Marc, 22.2), was in reality a practice

long established in Roman foreign policy and not necessarily related to crises.[14] Spread over five or more territories, these displaced barbarians tell us little or nothing about quantities of
previously abandoned lands. How many, for instance, were given land
which had never previously been occupied – as we happen to know to
be the case with the 5,500 Sarmatians Marcus settled at Ribchester
in Britain, or with the colonists he established in the *Hiulca palus*
near Mursa in Pannonia, who took over newly drained land that had
not been under cultivation?[15] Aquileia, centre of the plague and
subjected to ravaging attacks by the Quadi in 169-70, was by 238
described as the major wine producer for Illyricum in a *territorium*
teeming with farming communities (Herod. 8.2.3-5; 8.4.5).

It is difficult to assess the effect of the widespread and
well-publicized Severan confiscations of senatorial estates in the
period between 193 and 197, particularly in the western provinces
which had supported Albinus and where (in Gaul and Spain, at least)
the *vita* notes the demise of *proceres multi* (*HA, Sev*. 12.1; cf. 12.
3). But there is no good reason to believe that imperial appro-
priation of estates *per se* reduced their efficiency or productivity,
as Frank believed,[16] when in most cases it was simply a case of
substituting one absentee landlord for another. Salway conjectures
that the village estate of Hockwold in the Fen skirtlands of Britain
came into Severus' hands in this way.[17] If he is right, then we
should note that the event coincided with a productivity drive in
the area and does not support the notion of *foeda vastitas* which
senatorial ideology attributed to all confiscated land.

Productivity and a concomitant increase in the efficiency of
tax collection are indeed the hallmark of the Severan administration. A high proportion of the dated legislation in the papyri and
law codes is concerned with taxation matters,[18] and one strongly
suspects that the new *boulai* to replace the old nome councils in
Egypt were set up for exactly the same reason; that is, in order to
make a more rigorous application of taxation on uninundated land,[19]
to reinforce the commands which were always necessary in Egypt after
periods of weak central government in order to ensure the repair of
canals and dykes for marginal productivity,[20] and perhaps to apply
some new taxes that appear at about this time.[21] But none of this
proves very much about deserted land. Taken in conjunction with

Severus' reiteration of the *Lex Hadriana de rudibus agris* on the
Tunisian estates,[22] with his stated desire to have *conductores*
idoniores in fiscal estates (D.50.6.6.11), and with some direct
intervention to cadastrate land in southern Numidia (discussed
below), they are indications of the temper of a reign which produced *horrea* in Rome full enough to equal *septem annorum canon* by
211 and an olive-oil surplus equal to five years' worth of distribution in Rome and Italy, even after free distributions had been
made in Rome (*HA, Sev.* 8.5; 18.3; 23.2).

These same surpluses continued to be available to Elagabalus
and Alexander, if we can believe the *vitae* (*HA, Elag.* 27.7; *Alex.*
22.2) - and I cannot see why we should not. What is rather more
difficult to accept is the report of extensive agrarian relief
described in the notorious *vita* of Severus Alexander, which apparently included loans to the poor *ad agros emendos* either at the
lower interest rates of 4% or for repayment in *fructus* (*HA, Alex.*
21.2).[23] Since part of this information is coupled with a regulation which supposedly restricted senatorial *faeneratores* to a rate
of 6% (*HA, Alex.* 26.1), there has been some justifiable suspicion
that this passage is a mere reproduction of later rates laid down
in the Theodosian Code (2.33.4). But even a charitable scheme for
the provision of cheap loans does not in itself prove that land
was undercultivated; on the contrary, it might imply that there was
too much competition from richer buyers. Low investment rates,
says Gabba, were a sign of sluggish investment. But in the case of
Pliny's survey of Bithynian finances (*Ep.* 10.54), he recommended a
lowering of government interest rates simply because there was no
land to be purchased. All in all therefore it is difficult to
agree that these measures reported in the *vita* constitute as strong
a case for the crisis of deserted land as Gabba would have us believe.[24]

It is the appalling pentacontaetiad of the wars of succession
from 235 to 284 which provide the real fuel for arguments of agricultural decline and disastrous desertion of the land, and I have
no wish to argue away the dislocation that was caused by an extensive breakdown of the frontiers, compounded by secessionist movements such as those in Gaul and Palmyra and exacerbated by a series
of fierce plague epidemics which lasted for twenty years. These

are the plagues that caused Dionysius, Bishop of Alexandria, even
at their outbreak in 250 during the Decian persecution to cry out
that 'the human race on earth was constantly diminishing and being
consumed' (Euseb. *HE* 7.21.10). For the same date Zosimus says (in
suspiciously similar language) that the plague had destroyed whatever of the *anthropeion genos* had been spared by war, although the
hyperbole is somewhat blunted when less than ten years later he is
found describing another plague 'the likes of which had never before
occurred' (Zos. 1.26; 1.37). Zosimus furthermore insists that conditions were as terrible in the countryside as in the towns and
equal throughout every province of the empire, but this is in contrast with Zonaras who refers only to the cities (Zon. 12.21). It
is also in this period, whose nadir was reached in the reign of
Gallienus, that the celebrated and doom-laden voice of Cyprian was
heard proclaiming universal catastrophe on land and sea (*ad Demet.*
3).[25]

Alföldy is no doubt right in saying that the variety of sources
offers a guarantee of a widespread belief in the crisis among the
intelligentsia.[26] But that is mere tautology and far from a guarantee that what they believed was true. It is self-evident from
the kind of exaggeration displayed in Zosimus that we cannot accept
the literal truth of what is said. And if not the literal truth,
then how much can we believe? In political and military terms one
cannot question the perilous crisis of the Roman empire in the mid-
third century. But it does not follow automatically that there was
a commensurate economic crisis and decline. Cyprian's evidence,
which is that most frequently quoted as proof of declining agricultural productivity, was part of the standard polemic against
those who persecuted Christians as being responsible for all mis-
fortunes. His reply is to explain the inexorable *Dei lex* of a
world which was growing old. Christian interpretation had already
before Cyprian and Dionysius transformed cyclical theories of bio-
logical growth and decay into a linear concept of decline from the
incarnation to the Parousia. Taken literally Cyprian's words
ought to mean that signs of soil exhaustion were universally apparent. Yet the very fact that Cyprian was forced to change his mind
about the *ultionis dies* so many times must make us question the
validity of the data upon which he founded his prophecies.[27] That

would be true even if Cyprian did not fit into a Christian hist-
oriographic tradition - and more specifically into a western
Christian tradition - of 'providential' history which 'ransacked'
and exploited every incident of the present and the past for an
ideological defence of the faith.[28] One may be sceptical therefore
about the weight which is put upon the passage of ad Demetrianum
by Boak and others as evidence of a long-term trend.[29]

    We are on solider ground with the case of Autun, the civitas
Aeduorum whose derelict and overgrown land is referred to in one of
the Panegyrici Latini delivered before the emperor Constantine, in
an explanation of why the city deserved not to be assessed for full
tax on the formula communis of the Gallic census because of the
disastrous sack of the city in 269 by the secessionists of the
imperium Galliarum. Much is made in this speech of the pathetic
state of the city's territorium before Constantine's remissions.
Claims for tax rebates of course bring out the orator in all of us,
but this particular pleader lets slip the fact that the city's
labour force was still intact, even if it had been smitten with
segnitia (Pan.Lat. 5(8).6.1).[30] From which presumably we must conclude that the economic crisis was of no very long standing. This
impression is confirmed by the fact that we happen to possess two
earlier panegyrics delivered from the same city before Constantius
in the 290s in which derelict land is not presented as a pressing
problem.[31] So this evidence, too, is at best slightly suspect.
Even if we grant Autun's condition due to her special problem of
transport,[32] the orator makes it clear that the neighbouring Remi,
Nervii and Tricassini were getting good returns on their land -
quorum reditus cum labore contendunt - and no general state of
dereliction can be made out from this one example.

    Nevertheless the period up to Gallienus obviously witnessed
widespread damage on the land in a number of different areas. We
hear, for instance, of a breakdown of law and order in Sicily
(HA, Gall. 4.9); there are a number of references to so-called
latrones in various provinces; and soon after Gallienus occurs the
first mention of the notorious Bacaudae in Gaul. Caves in the
Rhône valley, not used since the Stone Age, now show signs of re-
occupation and coin hoards dating from this period testify to the
fact that many owners never came back after leaving their homes.[33]

Yet even with this evidence a note of caution must be sounded.
Coin hoards of the same period are also found in Britain which
suffered no serious dislocation that we know of.[34] It is a mis-
take to assume that barbarian raiders always drove local farmers
before them and that the land was thereafter ruined. In Pontus in
the 260s Gregory Thaumaturgus says that many stayed to endure the
raiders without losing their lives (PG 10.1021,1025,1037,1041,
1044f.), while both our literary sources and the law codes make it
clear that prisoners and booty were often recovered (e.g. CJ. 8.51.
4(290); 8.51.8(294)). Farmers returned with postliminial rights to
their property and the vita Probi makes the interesting observation
that after the defeat of the Alamanni there was an attempt to compensate farmers with exactly what they had lost in the way of grain,
cattle and sheep at the hands of the raiders, tantum...praedae
barbaricae tulit quantum ipsi Romanis abstulerunt (HA, Prob. 13.8;
cf. 14.6). 'The barbarians' oxen now plough the farms of Gaul'
(HA, Prob. 15.6; cf. Claud. 9.6).

The sources are unanimous in proclaiming that Aurelian and
Probus staged a recovery of political control by the central government from 270 onwards, and with this control a rehabilitation of
the land. Of course, the very measures for remedy can be produced
as symptoms of the ailment and depicted as a sort of desperate
attempt to stem the creeping rot of decline, unless one has some
means of proving the results. Most often quoted is the evacuation
of Dacia's Roman garrison in 274 along with its pro-Roman population
to devastated territory formerly contained in the two Moesias. This
was the consequence, says the vita, of massive dereliction in
Illyricum and Moesia (HA, Aurel. 39.7).[35] We have no notion of
previous population densities in these regions, nor of how many
civilians from Dacia chose to abandon their homes. But we may well
ask why, if there were so many agri deserti, Probus felt it necessary just ten years later to begin a huge drainage operation in the
marshlands at Sirmium on the Moesian border in order to bring new
land into production.[36] And why did Galerius a few years later
carry out a similar project in northern Pannonia at Lake Pelso
(modern Balaton), cutting down trees and draining the lake to provide agrum satis rei publicae commodantem (Victor, Caes. 40.9), an
effort that apparently killed him?

This period has also produced the first reference we possess
in the legal codes to direct imperial intervention *pro desertis
possessionibus*. What we find is a measure of Aurelian, later quoted
by Constantine, which lays the burden of care for deserted property
upon the *civitatum ordines* in return for three years' tax concessions (CJ. 11.59.1).[37] The measure was then extended by Constantine
with an extra provision for *agrorum onera* to fall upon private
possessores also. Can we assume that Aurelian's measure was a
piece of general legislation applicable to the whole empire, and
thus evidence of a widespread phenomenon? The most important
feature to note is that by the time the statute reached the
Justinian Code there was not the slightest trace of the circumstances or the extent to which it had originally applied, much less
that it had some mysterious connection with Aurelian's plan to provide free wine for the Roman populace, as Groag and Homo inexpli-
cably believed.[38] In fact, as we saw earlier in the case of
Pertinax' legislation, the measure could not have applied to Italy
which was tax free at this date. And if not to Italy, what means
have we of deciding to which territories it did apply?

To this question, of course, there is no way of giving an
answer with any certainty. But there is a perfectly plausible
context into which such an imperial edict can be fitted; that is,
as a remedy for Egypt. Rostovtzeff long ago demonstrated that
adiectio sterilium or *epibole* was standard practice in the Fayum
in order to keep up cultivation of *abrochos* (uninundated land) and
productivity, just as *epimerismos* laid similar burdens on village
communities[39] - a kaleidoscopic pattern of shared responsibility
which Poethke's recently published lists prove to have been almost
normal throughout the period of the Roman Empire.[40] Such measures
were particularly necessary after periods of administrative chaos,
largely because of the neglect of essential irrigation channels.
There is good reason to believe that in the mid-third century this
is what had indeed happened in the Fayum, particularly as a result
of the Libyan invasions, the usurpation of Egypt by Palmyra and
the secession of Firmus which was brought to an end in 274.[41] It
was doubtless to combat this state of neglect that Probus made a
Severan-like effort to restore decrepit irrigation channels and
dykes (*HA, Prob.* 9.4; *P.Oxy.* 1409). And it would be in line with

this sort of effort that Aurelian should have issued instructions
for the cultivation of marginal lands by *epimerismos* - an *ad hoc*
order which eventually found its way into the Justinian Code. This
is no more than an hypothesis. But if it is plausible, it demonstrates that as a piece of evidence for widespread *agri deserti* the
legislation is wholly unsatisfactory.

Another measure of Aurelian, which is also claimed to reveal
the extent of *agri deserti* is his plan, recorded in the *vita* (48.2),
to settle prisoners of war along the Aurelian Way on *loca inculta*
in order to produce wine (once again) for the *annona* distributions
in Rome. But the *vita* specifically says that it was doubtful if
Aurelian ever carried out his scheme, and, in any case, Aurelian
was going to buy the land from the *domini, qui tamen vellent*. So
the story - if true, which I doubt - would suggest that suitable
imperial estates were already committed to agriculture and is no
more a sign of extensive desertion of land than Pliny's record of
praedia agris meis vicina atque inserta (*Ep.* 3.19).

Every source notes Probus' encouragement of viticulture in
Gaul, Pannonia, Moesia, Spain and Britain, including his personal
hand in the task at Mt Alma near Sirmium.[42] But if Probus gave
official encouragement to viticulture, there was by implication
hardly likely to have been *frumenti inopia*.[43] One of the ways in
which production was restored in devastated northern provinces was
by extensive settlement of *gentiles* - Goths and Franks, Bastarnae,
Scythians and Alamans.[44] But was this all to restore land previously under cultivation? In some of the many examples it is explicitly stated that the settlements were limited to frontier
zones, and therefore to land long set apart as *agri vacui et mili-
tum usui sepositi*,[45] in which we know farms and *vici* were encouraged to grow in the third century, thus producing a dramatic rise
in the prosperity and productivity of these zones.[46] Away from the
frontiers, we may note the example given by Hallam of the rapid re-
population and rising prosperity of the north Wash Fenlands of
Britain, which she dates to the period between Probus and Carau-
sius.[47] Not so much therefore a restoration of destroyed property
as a new imperial initiative similar to the work ordered in Egypt.

So far only passing mention has been made of the individual
records of *anachoresis* or threats of *anachoresis* recorded on papyri

and inscriptions in this century; and of the related question of
latrones. Both phenomena must have contributed to some extent to
desertions from the land, and there is a fair amount of evidence to
show how common it was. MacMullen notes that there is a 'cluster-
ing' of references to brigandage in the Digest dating to the Severan
period, although he immediately weakens his case by pointing out
that this was also the great age of the jurists.[48] So the legal
references may not indicate a particular increase in brigandage so
much as an increasing number of government regulations to deal with
the problem. The anonymous writer of *de rebus bellicis* in the
fourth century says that many poor were driven to crime and 'they
often inflicted the most severe injuries on the empire, laying
waste the fields' (*de reb.bell*. 2.3), and Salvian in the fifth century describes the Bacaudae *qui domus suas deserunt* as a result of
oppressive taxation (*Gub.dei* 5.21, 28, 38). The well known series
of inscriptions recording the complaints of the *saltus Burunitanus*
workers in Africa, the Scaptopare villagers of Thrace, the farmers
on the Aga Bey imperial estates near Philadelphia in Lydia and the
Aragüeni in the Tembris valley of Asia Minor are all celebrated
examples of illegal tax exactions by rapacious imperial soldiers
and officials in the period from Commodus to Philip, which can be
multiplied from almost any period.[49]

But what are we to make of all this in any cumulative sense?
There is a formulaic quality about the letters of complaints in
phrases such as 'we shall be forced to leave our ancestral hearths'
(καταλυπεῖν ... ἑστίας πατρῴας) which are repeated and perhaps
should not be understood too literally. But in any case, desertion
from these sorts of causes was certainly not a new feature of the
third century. In Egypt, for instance, Calderini and Poethke show
that on extant imperial evidence flight from the land was an endemic
problem from A.D. 19 to the seventh century and reached a peak not
in the post-Severan empire but in the period of Claudius/Nero, although one always has to add that Egypt is never a good guide for
the rest of the empire.[50] But even though there is no way to
quantify this sort of evidence, in the case of the Aga Bey tenants
in Philip's reign, they threaten to go to estates of private
possessores and thus the example does not reveal a rise in total
quantity of unworked land.

As for brigandage, the term covers a multitude of totally unrelated phenomena. The Maratocupreni near Apamea in Syria, described by Ammianus a century later, fell upon towns and rich estate
owners and then abandoned their vagrant life for comfortable enjoyment of their ill-gotten gains in houses of some luxury - *ambitiose
...construxerunt* (Amm. Marc. 28.2.14). This presumably means they
worked their own land, as indeed the Bacaudae did in the *tractus
Amoricanus* (Rutilius 1.21.3-6) and the Isaurians did in northern
Cilicia (*HA*, *Prob*. 16.5-6). Whether or not the frontier-baron
Proculus with his rich farm of cattle and two thousand slaves is
fictitious or not, he was at least conceivable in the late third
century.[51] What these examples show therefore is that if the
imperial treasury lost the revenue temporarily, the land did not
necessarily revert to scrub.

The last decades of the third century saw the military and
political recovery of Diocletian and with it a system of taxation
which Jones has convincingly demonstrated was not excessive enough
to drive land out of production.[52] I have no wish to add to his
discussion, except to point out that this did not prevent Lactantius
from shrill denunciations of the (by now dead) emperor, alleging
that the resources of the *coloni* had been exhausted, fields abandoned and cultivated areas transformed into wilderness (*de mort.
persec*. 7).[53] Frend has charitably suggested that *de mortibus
persecutorum* and the conditions there described were written by
Lactantius with the vivid recollection of the devastation caused by
the Quinquegentani rebellion in Mauretania and Western Numidia
(289-97). For it was during this time that the *passio Tipasii*
describes the destruction of landowner and peasant - *universis
possessoribus incolisque prostratis*.[54] Both accounts however fall
within that tradition of pessimistic virulence which only a persecuted Christian could summon (as we saw in the case of Dionysius
and Cyprian earlier) and which ultimately had a literary pedigree
that went back to the roots of historiography and utopian litera-
ture. No one can suggest that North Africa suffered irreparable
damage to her agrarian economy as a consequence of the Quinquegentani. Even Lactantius thought Africa the richest part of the
empire when he wrote (*de mort.persec*. 8.3).

III

Against the background of this mélange we must now put the detailed evidence from the provinces. It is not the intention of
this chapter to survey every single province, nor indeed to claim
exhaustive treatment of any single province. For the facts would
still be random and without quantitive value. All one can hope is
to gain a new perspective to set against the mainly literary portrait which is, as we now see, far from unambiguous. From Greece,
for instance, where literary pessimists had long done their worst,
there is little of substance to pick upon. True, there is the late
but undated Thisbe inscription dealing with encouragement given to
the cultivation of urban *territoria* (SIG^3 884); and there is Dio of
Prusa's *Euboeicus*, which must surely be regarded as suspicious if
not worthless economic evidence.[55] But not much else. Otherwise,
as far as the facts go, most of Greece, with the exception of a
few prosperous districts like Patras, showed significantly no more
or less life in the third century than it did in the second or the
first. The damage of the invasions of the third century and
coastal raids upon cities like Corinth did not apparently prevent
a sort of prosperity returning in the early fourth century. And
even the terrible disasters of Alaric did not prevent Paulinus of
Pella in the early fifth century having many farms in Greece and
Epirus worked by *numerosi coloni* which were abundantly productive
even for an extravagant landlord, he says (*Euchar.* 414-19).

    In Spain it is difficult to resist the conclusion that the
Moorish invasions of the late second century and the successive
disorders of the Severan period had destroyed the corner in
Italian oil which had been the basis of the prosperity of Baetica.
That, at least, is a possible conclusion from the haphazard evidence of potsherds on the Monte Testaccio. The *figlinae* (and no
doubt the oil) of Spain were transferred to fiscal hands about 200,
but exports seem to have declined in quantity until they finally
came to an end perhaps with the *imperium Galliarum*, since 257 is
the latest dated potsherd to have been found so far on the rubbish
dump in Rome. But if this led to extensive desertion of the land,
as one might expect, Thouvenot could discover no obvious sign of
it.[56] In spite of the evidence of Avienus in the late fourth century describing the *deserta tellus*, *orba cultorum sola* and the

ruins of Gades,[57] the *expositio totius mundi* in the same century
gives a very different picture of a land *omnia bona possidens et
praecipua in omnibus bonis* (59). Fiscal cargoes were still being
exported from Spain in Constantine's reign and Genseric found
enough ships in Baetican ports in 429 to take his Vandals and
baggage to Africa.[58]

Egypt we have already examined to some extent. Rostovtzeff's
assertion that a new category of entirely unproductive land –
aporōn or *aporōn onomatōn* – began to appear in the fourth century
is now shown by Lewis to have been true much earlier, perhaps already in Trajan's reign, when *merismos aporōn* as a shared burden
of taxation was placed on various communities.[59] As was said
earlier, there may also have been some breakdown of the 'communauté
hydraulique' before Aurelian defeated Palmyra, as was not uncommon
in periods of weak central government. This could have been one of
the causes of the 'terrible state of neglect' of the vineyards in
Galienus' reign at Hermopolis,[60] although it may equally have been
simply a poor flood year. The termination of papyri records at
Socnopaiou Nesos and at a number of other towns in the Fayum from
the 220s and 230s certainly does not indicate the final desertion
of most or even of many towns of the Arsinoite nome, as has sometimes been suggested. A closer analysis of the evidence upon which
the argument is based shows that it was really only the towns de-
pendent on one particular canal system of the Bahr-Wardan in the
northern part of the Fayum which seemed to suffer from acute water
shortages. Other Fayum communities, such as Karanis, Theadelphia,
Philadelphia and Dionysias, which were served by alternative irrigation channels, continued to produce records well into the fourth,
fifth and even sixth centuries. The correspondence of Heroninus,
a local land agent at Theadelphia, which covers a period of fifteen
years in the mid-third century (collected in *P.Flor.* II, nos. 118-
277), reveals not a trace of agrarian crisis in the petty transactions concerning things like wine, grain and camels which are discussed. Even at Socnopaiou Nesos the discovery of a late coin of
Constantius I (305/6) makes one wonder whether the archaeological
levels can really be dated by papyri – or rather the absence of
papyri – as the University of Michigan Report of 1924-31 wishes us
to believe. At Karanis, for instance, Hayes is now convinced that

some of the red slip ware is to be dated as much as two hundred
years later than the latest dated papyrus from the town.[61]

Perhaps the restoration work carried out by Probus and (as I
believe) by Aurelian did not fully rehabilitate the marginal lands
of the North Fayum, but if so, there is no way of discerning from
this what was happening in the rest of Egypt. After all, the Fayum
was the most delicately balanced and most susceptible to breakdown
of any land in Egypt. Even if we can produce examples to prove
that the *epimerismos* cultivation carried out by the town of Karanis
at Ptolomais Nea had dropped from 859 arouras in 167 to 515 arouras
in 216, we are not entitled to project these figures to all areas
under cultivation without any notion of local year-by-year fluctuations.[62] Hermopolis, whose vineyards in Gallienus' reign were overgrown with rushes and surrounded by much uncultivated land - *cherson*
pollēn kai thruon - appears at the same time to have been in the
middle of a period of conspicuous spending on public buildings and
to have been paying out sums as large as seven talents of silver in
a single year (266/7) from the treasury for athletes' pensions.[63]
So the most we can say about Egypt in this period is that *al-shidda*
- 'crisis' - was, as always, a perpetually recurring state in a
land whose productivity was poised on a fine edge between under-
flooding and overflooding every year.[64]

In Asia it is alleged that the Severan estate confiscations
were disastrous for the 'sound economic structure' of the province[65]
But the Aga Bey inscription referred to earlier shows, if anything,
that those particular tenants of the imperial estates preferred them
to private estates, provided that illicit collections could be controlled. Judging by an inscription found at Pessinus in 1969, it
would appear that cadastration was carried out in 216 in an attempt
to raise taxation (and thus productivity) for Caracalla's eastern
campaigns in at least one town in Asia.[66] The work is on a par with
the Severan *mansiones* which were established for collecting *annona*
supplies, and indicates the general imperial concern for productivity. One cannot tell whether Jones' statistics for fourth-
century Asian cities are typical. They show that one tenth of
city land was classed as *deserta iuga* and as low as one twentieth
at Antioch in Syria. If so, then they compare most favourably with
the 1938 figures for the area corresponding to Antioch's *territorium*,

when only 50% of the land was under cultivation.[67] Besides this,
Antioch, we should remember, was the target for a number of inva-
sions in the third century, one of which was described as a calamity
(Zos. 1.27; cf. 3.32).

It may be that pirate raids too had some effect upon the Syrian
coastal cities (cf. Zos. 1.32f.), but in spite of all this Antioch
itself and Apamea and other inland cities prospered from the extra-
ordinary growth of agriculture on the limestone uplands to the east
and south-west of Antioch, which Tchalenko has described as a veri-
table 'factory' stretching from Cyrrhus in the north to Apamea in
the south, and from the Orontes to Aleppo and Chalcis, a prosperity
that only began in the latter part of the third century and steadily
increased into the sixth, based mainly upon olive culture.[68] Apart
from the very big estates of the Orontes and Afrin valleys, few of
the upland estates were larger than one hundred *iugera*, and were,
Tchalenko thinks, farmed by either veterans, or (more plausibly)
former tenants who had prospered by planting unworked land in a
fashion similar to the metayage contract system outlined in the
Lex Hadriana, and possibly still to be detected in the so-called
'mugarasa' contract today.[69] Nor was this prosperity confined to
olives, since the basaltic uplands of the plain of Chalcis and the
steppes of Euphratensis were growing wheat and showing a similar
increase in population and prosperity.[70]

Without repeating Tchalenko's details, there are two observations to be made of general importance. First, the prosperity of
the period was possible in spite of invasions from Persia, because
the Persian army, and especially the cavalry, were concerned with
the direct route to the cities where wealth was stored, and along
rivers for their water supplies. And, secondly, the period of
high prosperity coincided with Libanius' description of the serious
decline of Cyrrhus among other cities and with John Chrysostom's
preachings concerning the intolerable burden laid upon poor farmers
around Antioch in the late fourth century.[71] This ought to confirm
our suspicions about the purely local conditions or the limited
urban perspective often contained in literary sources.

Further south in Palestine the limestone hills around
Bethlehem and the routes to the Negev went through an olive boom,
not dissimilar to that in Syria although the capital investment

here seems to have come a bit later in the fourth century - and to
be connected with the endowed churches set up on holy sites like
the 'Field of the Shepherds'. By Jerome's time they were exporting
oil to Egypt (PL 25.923). But Gichon's work on the frontier settlements of the Negev, which were established as early as the third
century, shows the transplanting of farming communities to the
desert fringes and thus the opening up of new agricultural land,
possibly prompted by the need for a new protected route via Elath
and the Red Sea, if Persia had closed the trade routes eastwards.[72]
This, be it noted, is in the same period as Jones records 'insolvent
names' (ἄπορα ὀνόματα), who were a public liability for unproductive
land in Palestine.[73]

If we turn to the West, we find that Dalmatia seems to have
avoided many of the ill-effects of the third-century invasions.
Wilkes describes a process not unlike that in Syria, which probably
began in the third century and certainly extended into the fourth.[74]
That is, the appearance of quite small villae rusticae of about
eight rooms, in clusters of three or so buildings which were constructed every three to five kilometres up the inland valleys of
the Narenta (north of Navona) and the Una (on the Pannonian border).
Quite obviously they belonged to small native farmers, although
occasionally there is a larger house of twenty rooms which suggests
a bailiff or the owner of a large estate. Alföldy's study of family
names would indicate that some of these farmers had moved up from
the coastal districts, while the coastal lands in turn were occupied
during the third century by Syrian or eastern settlers, some of
whom themselves moved inland in later generations.[75] Once again
therefore we find an impressive extension of cultivation, which
helps to explain the strength of this region as a recruiting ground
in the later Empire.

In Pannonia the picture is not dissimilar. If we follow
Thomas's categories, the farms of the 'inland region' were local
inhabitants from pre-Roman society whose nucleated settlements
differed from the single, large farm houses of the Italian settlers
- the 'large land owners'.[76] But the main lesson of Thomas's study
is that in spite of some signs of dislocation and destruction,
proved by such evidence as coin hoards dating from c. 260 around
Lake Balaton, the number and prosperity of the inland villas

generally increased in importance in the third and fourth century,
though this development is coupled with a growing tendency to
abandon single farms and to cluster around large property owners for
security. This is strikingly illustrated by the enormous fortified
complexes, such as that at Fenékpuszta on Lake Balaton, which Mócsy
is surely correct in believing to be imperial estates that developed
in the fourth century. The production of distinctive local villa
pottery from the late third century in fortified rustic villas
around Balaton stresses the vigour and autarky of their economy,
while on the west bank of the lake from about the time of Aurelian
until Valentinian a line of fortified farms developed as a second
defence to protect the western approaches to Pannonia Prima. Far
from collapse and desertion under the undoubted pressure of raids,
many rustic villas, like the one near Tác, reached their peak of
prosperity in the later third century.[77] By the fourth century
there was sometimes even an export of surplus grain, as Ambrose
notes (*Ep.* 18.21 = *PL* 16.978), and the *expositio* describes the
province as *terra dives in omnibus, non solum fructibus et
iumentis* (57). One further point is the number of third-century
epigraphic references in Pannonia to exploitation of the *territorium
legionis* and the *prata legionum*, which shows that the frontier
regions here too were probably developed in this period.[78] Evidently the work of Probus and Galerius in drainage and plantation
was more than mere propaganda.

In Gaul the breakdown of the frontiers in the mid-third century
and especially in 276 has left its clear mark on archaeological remains. There are, for instance, many coin hoards which terminate
with pieces of Tetricus; and although there are problems about
accepting the evidence of coin hoards alone, their message appears
to be confirmed by many burnt layers in farm buildings along the
major roads to Trier - especially along that from Cologne - which
can plausibly, if not always specifically, be assigned to this
troubled time.[79] Perhaps there was also a flight from Gaul to
Britain or the East. It has been suggested, for instance, that
this would account for the growth of large estates and luxury farm
houses in places such as Woodchester or Bignor in Britain which
display a great deal of similarity to Belgian villas.[80]

t is therefore difficult to resist the conclusion that there was certainly some abandoned land, as the writer of the Panegyric claimed. But it is worth underlining once again a number of limitations in the assessment we may make of this evidence. A villa destroyed is not the same as land abandoned. Many which had been destroyed were rapidly put back into commission by the end of the third century.[81] Wightman shows furthermore that it was only farms along the major roads in Treveran territory which suffered, while those on the high Eifel or even on the routes other than the Cologne-Trier road show no sign of disturbance and support the conclusions of Tchalenko in Syria, that raiders tend to make quickly for cities.[82] In addition to this, we find that inscriptions dating from the mid-third century begin to record a number of inland *burgi* or towers and *castella*, almost certainly raised in association with *vici* by private enterprise; one such example is that at Bitburg in Treveran territory put up by the *iuniores vici* in 245 (*ILS* 7056). These were not just signal towers and home guard posts but also points for storing corn or, like the Montauban double wall system, they served as refuges for cattle – *non castra sed horrea Belgis* (*Pan. Lat.* 6.16.1; cf. Amm. Marc. 18.2.3-4, Aus. *Mos.* 456-7).[83] Far from a shrinkage in the number of farms, many completely new and more luxurious buildings appeared in the late third century, although they were increasingly nucleated settlements in the pattern of *vicos circa villam* described by Frontinus in Africa.[84]

Agache's aerial surveys in Picardy and the Somme valley, which have in recent years opened up such an astonishingly huge, new area for investigation, reveal that in this region the farms were generally of quite a modest size, in clusters of three to five buildings, with *vici* in some places found to be situated between estates.[85] This size, together with the association of some of the farms with a 'Celtic field' system, would suggest the expansion of local, native agriculture, which was doubtless due to the nearby frontier markets. But there were some enormous estates, too: one of Agache's farmhouses is 330 m long; and some similar estates in Belgium and on the Rhine were of the order of 700 to 1,000 acres in extent.[86] As yet there is nothing to date the development and duration of these farms. Agache himself is inclined to assign their high period to the middle Empire and the destruction of many

of them to the invasions *c.* 275. But he is properly cautious about
such guesses and he relies almost exclusively upon the literary
evidence, which we have seen to be less than conclusive. The pattern of nucleated settlements of these villa complexes corresponds
to that described in Dalmatia in the later third century, and we
should note the evidence, which Agache quotes, from burial grounds
to show a vigorous rural population in parts of this region, at
least, during the later Empire.[87] Whether this was the specific
consequence of importation of foreign labour (*Pan. Lat.* 8(4).21),
or whether – as seems more probable – this is evidence of continuity
of prosperity in spite of disruptions from across the frontiers, the
fact is that centres like Amiens remained remarkably wealthy throughout the fourth century. Elsewhere in the Gallic provinces huge
estates were stimulated by conditions of the later Empire. At
Tholey in the Saarland one large luxury villa stands at the centre
of a widespread network of smaller 250 acre farms, suggesting that
it was a seigneurial estate controlling the rest. The celebrated
south Eifel estate at Welschbillig, which was almost certainly an
imperial property surrounded by a forty-mile perimeter 'Landmauer',
enclosed 55,000 acres made up of between 100 and 200 farms, again
probably controlled from a large central home farm. The enclosure
wall at least dates from the late third or early fourth century.[88]

In Britain we have to begin with the quite specific and personal intervention of Septimus Severus, who was aiming to establish
a deep frontier zone that reached into the Scottish lowlands, with
a series of long-range forward forts of which the solid stone
building at Carpow was perhaps one. There were certainly others
such as those at Risingham and High Rochester. They were set up in
conjunction with farming settlements of pro-Roman civilians, such
as the Votadini, who probably occupied the land which Dio (76.13.4)
tells us had been compulsorily abandoned by hostile tribes, building
new stone farmstead clusters to command the Stirlingshire plain on
former Iron Age sites.[89] Crock Cleuch in Roxburghshire, for
instance, was occupied from the late second to the sixth or seventh
century.

But while these settlements would, no doubt, have contributed
to some extent to the frontier supplies – and one notes here, too,
the number of inscriptions recording military *conductores* and

peccuarii[90] - the real increase in productivity in Britain was taking place elsewhere, in the so-called 'Celtic fields' of upper Wharf-
dale and Cumberland, or on the farms of the east Yorkshire wolds and
the Vale of York, reaching a peak in the third century. These farms
grew mainly grain for the troops. Parallel to this was the specta-
cular drainage and development of the Fens, which Salway now believes to have been principally in order to rear cattle and horses
for the frontier army.[91] It is true there was a 'third-century
gap' in the low level lands which Salway attributes to the breakdown
of drainage in the period of the imperium Galliarum, but which
Cunliffe in the Somerset levels associates with a rise in sea level.
But the fact is that by the late third century and perhaps, not for
the last time, under the influence of Dutch Batavian and Frisian
labour, the prosperity and productivity of the Fenlands was restored
to at least its mid-second-century level of population density.
This was almost certainly the consequence of central imperial
planning.[92] A recent count of country villas in Britain reveals
over fifty new ones built in the third century and over two hundred
in the fourth century without any clear sign of much abandonment of
existing second-century buildings.[93] The one place where there is
evidence of a dwindling population is in the Salisbury Plain /
Cranbourne Chase region. But the reason was not because land was
being deserted. Here estates which had once probably been imperial
grain producers for the legions of the south-west were turned over
to sheep and cattle runs of considerable size in the third to fourth
century, much to the obvious prosperity of the few farms which remained to service the ranches. It was these estates which supplied
the British wool manufacturers who first appear early in the third
century.[94] On this evidence, Britain in the late third century was
indeed terra tanto frugum ubere, tanto laete numero pastionum (Pan.
Lat. 8(5).11.1)[95] and, says Ammianus (18.2.3), quite often able to
supply grain to Gallic farmers in times of hardship - annona a
Britanniis sueta transferri[96] - another way incidentally in which
damage by frontier raiders was endured in Gaul. For 'they could
live off part of the corn and sow part of it and have the necessi-
ties of life until harvest time' (Zos. 3.5).

    Africa, which has been left until the last of the provinces,
is the least difficult to prove as a major growth area in the third

century, and the evidence is too well known to need full repetition.
It starts with the vigorous Severan frontier policy which has a remarkable affinity with that already noted in Britain and in the
Negev; that is, a system of deep forward antennae based on forts
such as Bu Ngem, Gheria el-Garbia, Cydames and Si Aioun in Tripolitania, or Castellum Dimmidi and a series of *hiberna* stretching
westwards into Mauretania, which operated in conjunction with a
strategic barrier of fortified farms (the 'gsur' or *burgi*).[97]
The complicated hydraulic and road systems of these forward areas
was the means of bringing wide stretches of the land under cultivation which, as we know from later legislation, was considered
highly desirable.[98]

The purpose of these frontiers may have been primarily to
control transhumance nomads, but in carrying out such a programme
huge new territories were opened up for exploitation. Not only
did frontier zones develop, such as the high Djebel of Tripolitania
or the southern Chotts of Algeria, but the main nomadic routes were
now secured and controlled for sedentary farmers. So, for instance,
the plains of Sitifis and southern Constantine became a vast grain-
growing region which developed, according to the inscriptions of
the area, between 190 and 250. In the southern part of eastern
Algeria, south of the town of Tebessa (ancient Theveste), and on
the southern Djebel of Tripolitania we find - as in Syria - new
prosperity emanating from major olive-growing districts. To judge
by the milestones collected by Leschi in the Algerian olive planta-
tions, the district was opened up between 268 and 324.[99] It may be
no more than coincidence that the first of these dates is just ten
years after the last dated Spanish potsherd from Monte Testaccio.
Crude African oil, as we know, had begun to enter the Italian market
in the second century; but a more refined quality of African oil
now probably replaced Spanish cooking oil completely and coincides
with a remarkable take-over of the Italian and southern Gallic
coastal markets by an African red slip ware, which from about 250
for the next three hundred years became the principle fine table
ware of the whole Mediterranean seaboard.[100]

The particular reasons for this 'golden age' of Africa are not
of direct relevance here, since our concern is with the simple fact
of expansion of territory and exports. If the secret of the success

was the Mancian and Hadrianic laws, which are often supposed to
have produced a vigorous class of *cultores* whose petty transactions
some believe can be detected in the fifth-century Tablettes
Albertini, then the whole progress of such a development is shrouded
in mystery. It is true that Tchalenko inclines to this sort of
theme as an explanation for the Syrian oil boom also. But in
neither Syria nor Africa can one treat such an hypothesis - and
that is all it is - with more than gingerly respect. What we do
know is that it was the imperial, and particularly the Severan,
frontier policy and their concern for full *horrea* in Rome which
created the demand and the proper conditions for this development.
This is nicely illustrated by an inscription from the Hodna in
Algeria recording the direct intervention of the emperor's *mensores*
in making assignations of *agri et pascua et fontes* to new settlers,
and is one of a series of references to *coloni* and *conductores* in
the region south of Bou Saada, where nomads and cultivators still
compete.[101]

   There remains the problem of the well-known legislation of
Honorius in 422 (CTh.11.28.13), which is now generally believed to
have been an instruction to magistrates in the provinces of Africa
and Byzacena forbidding taxation by *epibole* of large deserted tracts
of imperial estates. The size of the figures are usually interpreted as a sign of cumulative and disastrous decline in agrarian
prosperity. But the conclusion of both Warmington and (more recently) Lepelley is that the proportion of land represented by these
figures - that is, about 5/9 of the surface area - is almost exactly
the same as that which is regarded as too marginal to be cultivated
in present-day Tunisia. As an index of the rise of deserted land
in Africa therefore the figures are no help either way, but when
set against the undoubted ubiquity of African exports *paene...
omnibus gentibus* (*Expos.tot.mun.* 61) in the same period one cannot
credit the argument that African agriculture was going through a
crisis.[102] Neither Goodchild nor Oates detects any diminishing of
the Tripolitanian olive prosperity in the course of the third or
early fourth century.[103] Even the 'catastrophe', whose effects
they comment upon in their excavations, cannot be dated conclusively
to the fourth century, and in any case appears to have been local
to the eastern Djebel and not evident in the rest of Africa.

Italy is by far the most difficult area to judge in terms of deserted land and productivity. Before the imposition of direct taxation under Diocletian and as long as the law of compulsory investment for senators was in force, there is no reason why more than the most marginal land should have been abandoned. The 1968 Report on the *ager Veientanus* speaks of 'no hint of a break' in prosperity up to about 250, but of 'a dramatic change' in occupation patterns by the end of the third century with 72% of former sites abandoned. The authors of the Report however are properly cautious about whether this means more *agri deserti* or simply larger estates, and, although they incline to the former view, Percival prefers the latter.[104] In his earlier study of the *ager Capenas* G.D.B. Jones showed that during the period in which red polished ware (i.e. African red slip ware) was in use much of the northern part of the *territorium* and the Ciminian forest were opened up for the first time, and it is tempting to associate this development with Trajan's and Marcus Aurelius' legislation on land investment. But since the author does not divide red polished ware, which lasted for about five centuries, into chronological types his pottery dates are a somewhat blunt instrument for our purposes.[105] One point however about Etruria which is not noted in the study of the *ager Veientanus* is that by the later fourth century it had indeed become a region of large estates, as can be detected from the fact that in this, and in some other northern Italian districts alone of all Italy, mounted shepherds were not forbidden by law.[106]

Clearly Aurelian's measure of tax relief for deserted lands had no relevance to Italy, which was tax-free up to Diocletian, but its reaffirmation by Constantine might have had, and it might therefore be an indication of dereliction if we could be sure it applied to Italy.[107] The principal argument for large-scale desertion of land in Italy derives from the provision a century later, in 395, now recorded in the Theodosian Code (11.28.2), by which some 528,042 *iugera* of Campanian land were formally declared *deserta*; this was about one tenth of the territory, according to Jones's estimates.[108] The remission was followed up by a statement some twenty years later (CTh.11.28.12) which claimed that Campania had in the past been subject to an unusually heavy tax assessment. Was this then because Campanian agriculture had been declining? And was it

symptomatic of the whole of Italy? There were numerous occasions
before the concession of 395 on which food shortages or harvest
crises were said by Symmachus to have occurred in Rome; most notably
that of 384, when he claimed a general failure of crops throughout
the Mediterranean (*Ep.* 2.6, *Rel.* 3.15-16).[109] It does not follow,
of course, that the inadequacies of the *annona* supply had anything
to do with the state of Italian agriculture, and we must not forget
Ambrose's well-known scepticism about even such a crisis as that of
384 (*Ep.* 18.17.21 = *PL* 16.977; *de off.minist.* 3.7.48-9), which he
firmly believed to have been a year of *fecunditas* in northern Italy
and in the northern provinces.[110] Both Ambrose and Symmachus had
axes to grind. The problem is, as before, to distinguish between
economics and politics, and thereby to avoid exaggerating the nature
of the crisis. The petition of the Campanian *curiales* in 395, which
Symmachus himself probably supported (*Ep.* 4.46), was granted at a
time of extreme political sensitivity, when the African *annona* supply
was being manipulated with some success by Gildo, and when Honorius,
following the death of Theodosius in January of that year, needed
all the friends he could find – especially in view of the bitterness
which must have existed among the supporters of Nichomachus Flavianus
after his defeat at the River Frigidus in September 394.[111] These
years therefore produced very special circumstances, from which it
is rash to generalize. Nevertheless, it is difficult to discount
entirely Symmachus' pessimistic portrait of a downturn in the agrarian economy of Italy in the fourth century, which is consistent
with the repeated legislative concessions to landowners and tenants
of imperial estates (e.g. CTh.11.16.2(323); 11.16.9(359); 11.16.12
(380); 11.28.4(408)), and I cannot help but be impressed by Hannestad's general accumulation of arguments that the fourth century
was not a period of rural prosperity.[112] But the cause of his de-
pression could have been no more than the removal of the artificial
value given to land by its tax-free status before Diocletian. Once
Italy became subject to taxes like the rest of the empire it would
have been surprising in fact if some marginal land had not gone out
of production.

IV

The chief object of this paper has been to set the general and

mainly literary evidence against the detailed and mainly archaeological evidence from the provinces. On the whole the two por-
traits do not match. But there is a theoretical issue at stake
here too. Unless one can sustain the proposition of a manpower
crisis or of a downturn in the forces of production, implying new
and less efficient agricultural methods or combinations of labour
– neither of which is possible, in my opinion[113] –agricultural productivity must have remained relatively static. The literary evidence of contemporaries, by concentrating on vivid but relatively
isolated phenomena such as wars and plagues, found it impossible
to see this simple fact. Perhaps one analogy will illustrate the
argument most effectively. In the Black Death of 1349 and the
Grey Death of 1361 it is estimated that the population of Britain
was reduced by two fifths. Yet the numbers had been restored by
the end of that century, and by the end of the fifteenth century
they had doubled, in spite of thirty or more recorded outbreaks of
plague. At the same time, that is during the fifteenth century,
the Wars of the Roses and uncontrolled bandits were facts of every-
day life. Yet the many battles of those wars, we have been reminded, involved no more than twelve to thirteen weeks of actual
fighting in thirty-two years and the great campaign from Milford
Haven to Bosworth lasted a mere fourteen days. The Battle of St
Albans left a grand total of one hundred and twenty dead. Most
of all, the fifteenth century is now regarded in retrospect as one
of the most prosperous ages of the English peasant.[114] But this
same age was described at the time by Edward IV as an example of
God's vengeance through 'intolerable persecution, punicion and
tribulation, whereof the likes hath not been seen or heard in any
other Christian realm...'

What one hopes has emerged from this survey is that, while
certainly some land was going out of use permanently, there was a
great deal of marginal land fluctuating in use between good and
bad years. This was accompanied by movements of population – to
the Fenlands or to the Syrian limestone plateaux; from inland to
the frontier zones of Africa; from imperial to private estates in
Asia. At the same time new patterns of farming and farm dwellings
evolved in Syria, in the Dalmatian valleys, and in the Fens, providing support for Percival's belief that the demesne system was

on the increase. But, as Percival has also reminded us, seigneurial farming is not inconsistent with growth.[115]

NOTES

Chapter 1. Introduction

1 Heitland (1921), Weber (1909); on Greece and Rome separately, Guiraud (1893), Weber (1891). The bibliography at the end of this volume provides a fair, though of course not complete, guide to modern work.

2 Because of the differences in both the focus and the procedure, this book is in important respects not comparable to the Greek volume which I edited a few years ago, *Problèmes de la terre en Grèce ancienne* (Paris and The Hague, 1973).

3 How landowners marketed their crops is an obviously missing piece in our account, and I doubt if the evidence exists for a satisfactory discussion.

4 Finley (1973), 118-19.

5 If it were my intention to present a full research programme for the future, I should have said something about archaeological discoveries, which, in bulk, constitute the fundamentally new evidence available today.

Chapter 2. Some configurations of landholding in the Roman empire

1 The modern work that I have found most useful is Jones's 'Census records of the later Roman Empire' (Jones (1974) 228-56), which provided the numerical résumé of the Hermopolis register on which the analysis here is based. I am indebted for bibliographical help to Mr M.J. Farrell and for statistical advice to Dr A.D. Barbour. For an attempt to establish how far Egyptian patterns of land-division into large and small units follow a statistically 'normal' pattern, see Hansen-Schiöler (1965).

2 For further description, cf. Weber (1891). For the position in Egypt, see for example Westermann (1920) and (1922); Hohlwein (1938) at 35-53.

3 See e.g. Sicinius Flaccus 157L. A.H.M. Jones, *Studies in Roman law and government* (Oxford, 1960), 143-9. Cf. *Atti del convegno internazionale sul tema: I diritti locali nelle province romane con particolare riguardo alle condizioni giuridiche del suolo, 1971* (1974) (Problemi attuali di scienza e di cultura, no. 194).

4 It is very difficult to identify types of land-use from the list of estates. Though *saltus* is associated with *montes* in *oblig.* 48, the term does not necessarily seem to refer to any one particular type of terrain or exploitation when used in the Veleian register (*CIL* XI 1147; de Pachtere (1920), 60, etc.

consistently associates the *saltus* with pasture and forest land). The jurists use the term variously to denote a large estate (Ulpian D.11.4.1.1; Proculus D.41.2.27), or pasture land (Ulpian D.33.7.8.1; 19.2.19.1, etc.). In the parlance of land-measurement, *saltus* could mean a very large unit of designated size (800 *iugera* according to Varro, *r.r.* 1.10.2, 5,000 *iugera* according to Siculus Flaccus 158.20L), though it merely denotes a large estate (of unspecified size) in the passage from Agennius Urbicus cited in n.58.

5 Veleia: *CIL* XI 1147; Ligures Baebiani: *CIL* IX 1455. Theoretically references to peripheral holdings can provide misleading information about their scale. A small estate which happens to border five other estates may be mentioned as a neighbour five times, whereas an estate the same size that is completely hedged in by two much larger estates can be mentioned as neighbour at most twice. Nevertheless references to neighbours (of which there are almost 700 at Veleia, though only 58 at Ligures Baebiani) seem to provide a usable index of the scale of landownership, taken en masse. The seven largest Veleian landowners received 76 mentions as neighbour, an average of 10.9 (accepting Bormann's identification of Cornelia Severa as daughter and heir of L.Cornelius Severus, cf. Duncan-Jones (1964), 141, n.104). The seven smallest landowners receive seven mentions as neighbour, an average of 1.0 (*CIL* XI, pp.229-31). The seven largest estates are worth on average 17.1 times as much as the seven smallest. Thus the ratio of land-value between the two groups is 17.1, and the ratio of mentions as neighbour is 10.9. This points to a significant tendency for larger landowners to be mentioned as neighbour more frequently than smaller ones. Furthermore, the estates of known size which are also 'neighbours' are on average much larger than those which are not: the two differ by a factor of 4.22 at Veleia, and by 2.92 at Ligures Baebiani. The Veleian and Baebian landowners are tabulated in order of size in Duncan-Jones (1974), 211-15; for neighbours at Veleia see p.196 and n.4, together with lists in *CIL* XI, pp.229-31, and *CIL* IX, p.13.

6 See chapter 3.

7 See n.4.

8 *Liber Pontificalis* cap. 34 (*M.G.H.*, *Gest. Pont. Rom.* I 47-72). The estimate of area assumes that the rental was a gross 6% (cf. Duncan-Jones (1974), 133) and the land-value on average 5 *solidi* per *iugerum* (it cost 5½ in a sixth-century sale at Faventia in northern Italy, Jones (1964), 822).

9 Jones (1964), 415-16. The figures for Africa show (if demonstration was needed) that Pliny's statement (*NH* 18.35) that Nero put to death six men who owned 'half of Africa' is mere hyperbole.

10 Although the *Res Gestae* implies that city lands were used for the veteran settlements as a whole, Augustus/Octavian had evidently attempted to evict many private landowners in his earliest land-settlements (Dio 48.6.8; Appian 5.12-13).

11 From the evidence published by Piganiol (1962), 104ff., which

includes many editorial restorations of fragmentary sections,
not all of which can be accepted, it would appear that of a
total of 50,630 *iugera* whose status can be determined in the
three cadasters, 15,803 or 31.2% was 'returned to the Tri-
castini', a neighbouring tribe; but virtually all of this
land appears to have been uncultivated. Out of 9,961 *iugera*
of land in this category whose condition can be determined,
9,566 *iugera* or 96% are described as uncultivated.

12 *CIL* XI 1147, *ob.* 43; IX 1455.3.23.

13 Piganiol (1962), 57-60. For the explicit leasing of municipal
land to private tenants in perpetuity see *AE* 1967, 531 (Apoll-
onia) and juristic evidence in Bove (1960), 65ff. (Gaius 3.
145; D.6.3.1 pr.-1; 39.4.11.1). For subleases for 5 years or
other short periods, see Hyginus 116-17L, Siculus Flaccus
162L.

14 See list in Duncan-Jones (1974), 313 n.3. For *ager vectigalis*
as municipal land, see Crook (1967), 158.

15 Jones (1964), 146-7; 732.

16 An exception is Sulla's endowing the temple of Diana Tifatina
with land, whose boundaries Augustus and Vespasian confirmed
(A.de Franciscis, *Rend.Acc.Arch.Nap.* 41 (1966), 241-6). For
the Greek world, Guiraud (1893), 362-81; A.H.M. Jones, *The
Greek City* (Oxford, 1940), 309-10; Rostovtzeff (1957), 655-7;
Jones (1974), 28-9. Theories of the omnipresence of temple-
land in Hellenistic Asia, already contested by Jones, were
laid to rest by Broughton (1951). For Egypt, cf. Evans (1961)

17 Kent (1948).

18 R. Dareste, B. Haussoulier, Th. Reinach, *Recueil des inscrip-
tions juridiques grecques* I (1891), no. 12. For dating, see
F. Sartori in B. Neutsch (ed.) *Arch. Forsch. in Lukanien* II
(Heidelberg, 1967; *Mitt. Deutsch Arch. Inst. Rom. Abt.* 11
Ergänzungsheft), 39; for estimates of the Heraclean *schoenus*
varying from 33.32 to 39.6 metres see Sartori 41. Cf. F.
Ghinatti in A. Uguzzoni, F. Ghinatti, *Le tavole greche di
Eraclea* (Rome 1968), 98-9; 182.

19 Larsen (1938), 365; Johnson (1936), 122. Appian indicates
that Antium, Lanuvium, Nemi and Tibur were richest in temple
treasure after Rome in the second century A.D. (5.25). For
temple treasure in Africa, see Duncan-Jones (1974), 110, nos.
381-2.

20 Jones (1964), 415-16; 732-3.

21 Jones (1964), 894-910; 933.

22 Cf. e.g. Salmon (1969); Frederiksen (1973).

23 Siculus Flaccus 156L; cf. Brunt (1971), 295, n.8.

24 Brunt (1971), 332-42.

25 Brunt (1971), 337, n.3; cf. Duncan-Jones (1974), 48-52, 345,
347-8, 366. The value added by the state and type of cultivation is an important variable that cannot be taken into
account. Columella's calculations (*de r.r.* 3.3) purport to

refer to the provinces as well as to Italy, but the passage
as a whole is full of improbabilities (Duncan-Jones (1974),
40 n.5 and 39-50).
Brunt assumes the further difficulty that the release of so
much cash into the land-market would have increased land-
prices substantially. This is certainly likely in a free
market situation (it is illustrated at a later date in Pliny,
Ep. 6.19). But would Augustus have adopted the course of
paying the free market price whatever it might be, at a time
when such a course was so likely to be self-defeating? Hyginus
actually states that Augustus paid compensation 'secundum
reditus' (197.17L), which implies that the price was assessed
by applying a fixed multiple of revenue, and was not necessarily the same as the owner's asking price. This procedure
could circumvent the inflationary effects created by the release of such large funds; and it is reasonable to think that
it resulted in the payment of conservative compensation prices.

26 Cf. G. Forni, *Il reclutamento delle legioni da Augusto a
Diocleziano* (Milan, 1953), 39ff.

27 At the time of writing, *P.Yale* Inv. 296 is still apparently
unpublished, and these details are calculated from the brief
summary given by Oates (1970), 386.

28 Cf. land prices in Johnson (1936), 150-3. The 400-*iugera* veteran holdings conjectured from archaeological evidence in
Pannonia (cf. A. Mócsy, *Die Bevölkerung von Pannonien bis zu
den Markomannerkriegen* (Budapest, 1959), 91) suggest a different order of magnitude and are almost impossible to credit.

29 References for sowing quantity of 5 *modii* (43.65 litres) per
iugerum (0.2517 hectares) and fallowing in alternate years in
Italy in Duncan-Jones (1974), 49, nn.2 and 5; Jones (1964),
636. While a sowing quantity of 1 *artaba* per *aroura* is well
attested in Egypt (see Jones), which of the 25 or more values
of the *artaba* is represented in any one instance is usually
uncertain (cf. A. Segré, *Maia* III (1950), 66-74).

30 Cf. e.g. Crook (1967), 118-32. Le Gall's view (*Revue d'histoire écon. et soc.* LII (1974), 37-50, at 40) that most property was acquired by purchase, not by inheritance, which
appears to be based only on the fact that the writers on agriculture give advice about purchase, is quite unconvincing.
Apart from anything else, the agronomists could scarcely be
expected to give advice about what property to inherit, no
matter how frequent inheritance might be. Pliny the Younger,
one of the few rich men about whom we are informed, inherited
land near Lake Como from his father, his mother and at least
one unnamed source, together with land at Tifernum from his
uncle; inheritances and bequests reached him from four more
named sources, as well as others not mentioned by name
(Duncan-Jones (1974), 19, 21, 25-7). Only once does Pliny
mention adding to his property by purchase, and even then does
not make clear whether the transaction was carried out (*Ep.* 3.
19).

31 Thus Pliny evidently received the landed property of his uncle
as well as that of his parents. Various instances of fragmen-

tation among heirs occur in the Veleia register: four properties for example were split between the third and fourth
largest landowners in the list (*CIL* XI 1147, 3.23, 2.67; 3.30,
3.70, 3.28, 3.69; 3.23, 3.67; 3.32, 3.75, cf. 6.60). Two of
the smallest landowners received their inheritance in equal
shares, though one declares his half of the 'saltus Tuppelius
Volumnianus' as HS51,000, while the other half is declared as
HS50,000 (*oblig.* 7 and 29).

32 Duncan-Jones (1974), 324.

33 For vast estates as a conventional form of economic megalo-
mania, see Petronius, *Sat.* 48; 53; 77; Seneca, *de ben.* 7.10.5;
Columella, *de r.r.* 1.3.12.

34 Bormann lists the estate-valuations and the component valuations on which loans were secured in *CIL* XI pp.223-5.

35 The estates are listed in Duncan-Jones (1974), 211. The average number of *pagi* represented in the five largest estates is
9.8. A similar pattern of dispersal of holdings within large
estates can be seen at Hermopolis, from analysis of the *pagi*
mentioned there (Jones (1974), 252 and 249).

36 For further evidence about the size of estates in Italy, see
Duncan-Jones (1974), 323-6; for estate-sizes in the Later
Empire, see Jones (1974), 781-8.

37 If 18,000 *modii* represented a true tithe, the total wheat crop
would be 180,000 *modii*. A gross yield of six-fold, a sowing
quantity of five *modii* per *iugerum* and fallowing in alternate
years (n.29) would imply a total wheat acreage of 12,000 *iugera*.
Assuming as before that other crops would increase acreage by
at least one sixth, total area becomes 14,000 *iugera*, an average for 252 farmers of 55.6 *iugera*. Cicero indicates typical
gross yield of wheat at Leontini, much the best wheat-growing
area in Sicily (2.3.47; 2.3.109), as eight-fold, with ten-fold
in better years (2.3.112).

38 A detailed analysis and commentary is given in Jones (1974),
244-52. The total of landowners holding estates listed here
(which corresponds to the total tacitly given by Jones's
analysis) differs from the total referred to in Jones's text
because of differences of classification referred to on pp.
245-6.

39 Analysis in Jones (1974), 252-3.

40 Estates listed in descending order of size in Duncan-Jones
(1974), 211-15. The size of the loans assigned to the nine
estates whose valuations are missing implies that they fell
within the same range as the 57 estates whose valuations
survive.

41 The Gini coefficient is a product of the Lorenz curve. The
Lorenz curve uses percentages to plot property against number
of owners, from a distribution arranged in ascending order of
property-size. If the position is one of perfect equality
where all properties are the same size, the 'curve' will be a
straight line. Otherwise, any deviation from equality creates
a curve below the straight line. The Gini coefficient measures

the area of the gap between this curve and the straight line, expressing it as a decimal fraction of the area of the triangle defined by the line of perfect equality (the area of the triangle being 1). The greater the inequality, the higher the Gini coefficient.

The Gini coefficient is a crude measure which can take no account of the shape of the Lorenz curve; and it has been persuasively argued that, in common with more sophisticated conventional units of measurement, the coefficient does not provide a complete index of inequality. However it is not practical to incorporate the suggested alternative, involving inferences about how far total wealth would have to be raised to reach a situation of perfect equality, when the data do not represent a typical social cross-section. (For the Gini coefficient, see e.g. R. Floud (ed.), *Essays in quantative economic history* (Oxford, 1974), 17. For criticisms of this and other measures, see A.B. Atkinson (ed.), *Wealth, income and inequality; selected readings* (Harmondsworth, 1973), 46–68.) In the diagrams reproduced here, the data about differentiation is shown in the form of histograms, which are generally more informative as a method of visual presentation than Lorenz curves.

42 For Ligures Baebiani the coefficient is now .348, while that for Veleia is .359.

43 7 out of 57 peripheral holdings at Ligures Baebiani belong to imperial estates.

44 Déléage (1945), 221–3. The *millena* is attested as a land-measure for tax-purposes in Val. III Nov.5.4 (A.D. 440); Maj. *Nov.* 7.16 (A.D. 458); Justinian, *App.* 7.26 (A.D. 554); (Jones (1964), 62; 254; 453; 820). W. Goffart (*Caput and colonate* (Toronto, 1974) (*Phoenix* Supplementary Volume 12), 113–14) contests the reading 'M(illena)', but his claim that the *modius* (which he prefers) was 'a very standard Italian land measure' is invalid. Goffart's suggestion that the Volcei document itself could be an *obligatio praediorum* akin to the alimentary inscriptions is most unlikely; the alimenta seem to have vanished in the inflation of the third century (cf. Duncan-Jones (1974), 319). The register, with its senatorial organizer (for whom see *PLRE* Apronianus 9), has much more the appearance of a tax-document, especially since it belongs to a period when intensive census activity was in progress, and falls within two years of the attempt in 305–6 to take a census in Rome itself (Jones (1964), 62–3).

45 *CIL* VIII 18587 with de Pachtere (1908), who gives a commentary and incorporates further readings by Gsell.

46 The fourth veteran has an entitlement of 350 'K'. This might refer to an ex-auxiliary whose retirement bonus was smaller than that of legionaries, or it might be only part of the lands held by the veteran concerned.

47 There is no reason to assume that the 15 *iugera* at Philadelphia (cited above) indicates a standard allotment of exactly this size, least of all if it represents the expenditure of a cash bonus by each individual. However, the overall implications

for interpreting the Lamasba register will not vary greatly
if a figure of 10 *iugera* or one of 20 is substituted.

48 O. Kern, *Inschriften von Magnesia am Maeander* (1900), 122.
Jones (1974), 234-7 (cf. 229-31) provides a useful analysis
and commentary (the figure given on p.238, n.48 as *iuga* 4½ ¼
$\frac{1}{20}$ should read *iuga* 6½ ¼ $\frac{1}{20}$).

49 Among 81 farms of known tax-value, 4 owners have three farms,
6 have two farms and 57 have one. The alphabetical list contains at least 37 farms beginning with the letter beta. If
we extrapolate from the ratio of beta to the rest of the
alphabet in the place-name index in the *Corpus Inscriptionum
Graecarum*, the projected total number of farms in the original
list is about 1,066. It may be noticed that in the Veleian
list only 4.9% of the valuation units are the same as estate-
valuations (11 out of 226); all the remainder belong to estates
containing 2 or more such components.

50 Jones (1974), 250.

51 If uncultivated land in Italy typically cost not more than
HS500 (cf. Duncan-Jones (1974), 48-51), cultivated land might
have been worth not more than double on average.

52 Assuming that 75% of the area was arable and 25% vines, etc.,
the *iugum* would equal roughly 81 *iugera* from the figures
suggested by Jones (1974), 230. These are derived from an
inscription at Thera which gives totals both in *iugera* and in
iuga, though they depend on emendation of one of the totals.

53 Jones (1964), 554-7, using evidence about the fortunes of
senators in East and West.

54 The registers are those from Ligures Baebiani and Volcei on
the one hand, and those from Magnesia and Hermopolis on the
other.

55 He owned 12 villas in different parts of Italy, and lands in
Samnium, Apulia, Sicily and Mauretania; see Jones (1964), 554;
781-2.

56 Cf. e.g. examples cited by R. MacMullen, *Roman social relations*
(New Haven, 1974), 159-60, nn.33-4.

57 Cf. Vicus Annaeus, Vicus Haterianus, Vicus Phosphori (P.
Salama, *Les voies romaines de l'Afrique du Nord* (Paris, 1951),
139-40).

58 Agennius Urbicus (C. Thulin (ed.) *Corpus Agrimensorum Romanorum*
1 (1913) 45). For the *fundus Petrensis* built up 'in modum
urbis', see Ammianus Marcellinus 29.5.13. For the self-
sufficiency of large estates cf. D.33.7.12.5 (an estate may
have its own bakers, barbers, masons and weavers), and in
general Duncan-Jones (1974), 37-8.

Chapter 3. Imperial estates

1 The basic study is that of Hirschfeld (1913), cf. 528-44; see
also Pelham (1890); Beaudouin (1897, 1898); Rostowzew (1910)
and Rostovtzeff (1957); Kornemann (1924); Broughton (1934);
MacMullen (1962).

2 See Baldacci (1969) with earlier (extensive) bibliography.

3 See for example Stevens (1966), 109. For the type of inscription, cf. *ILS* 5567. Such repairs were, one suspects, often
only superficial.

4 Phillips (1970), 7, 10. The unguent flask from Colchester
with the inscription *[vec]t[i]gal patrim[oni]*, *JRS* (1956),
149 might support the identification (for the type see F.
Haverfield, 'Roman Britain in 1913', *British Academy Supplementary Papers II* (Oxford, 1914)) but it has recently been
argued that such flasks contained balsam from Judaea:
Baldacci (1969) with Pliny *NH* 12.54.111-12 cf. 123. For this
area, cf. Whittaker above, p.159.

5 Anderson (1899 and 1937); Ramsay (1890 and 1895-7); J.Keil
and A.von Premerstein, 'Bericht über eine Reise in Lydien'
etc., *DAW* LIII 2 (1908-9); LIV 2 (1911); LVII 1 (1914-15);
P.Herrmann, 'Neue Inschriften zur historischen Landeskunde
von Lydien', *DAW* LXXVII 1 (1959).

6 E.g. *CIL* III 431; 6071; 6075; 6077; 6082; 7121; 7123; 7126-7;
7130; 7132; 13677.

7 See Appendix, pp.59-63.

8 Geremek (1969), 48-50.

9 *Pap.Chic.*; *BGU* 31; 104; 105 (= *W.Chrest.* 346); 160; 172; 204;
206; 210-11; 262; 280; 284; 438; 441; *P.Cairo Goodspeed* 18;
24. My calculations differ somewhat from those of
Parássoglou (1972), 101 table 4.

10 These inscriptions have been frequently republished and discussed; the bibliography is enormous. See for example Frank
(1938), 83-102; van Nostrand (1925); Kotula (1952-3); Kolendo
(1963 and 1965). Saltus Burunitanus, *CIL* VIII 10570; Philomusianus, 14603; villa magna Variana, 25902; saltus Neronianus, 25943.

11 As P.A.Brunt, 'The 'fiscus' and its development', *JRS* LVI
(1966), 88-9, in an important article.

12 G.Charles-Picard, *La Civilization de l'Afrique romaine* (Paris,
1959), 60; cf. p.42 above.

13 Pflaum (1960-1), no.328.

14 E.g. *ILS* 327; *CIL* VI 9021, her procurator; Fronto, *Ad M.Caes.*
2.16-17 (37-8 Nab.); *Ad amicos* 1.14 (183 Nab.), her will.

15 For further examples see Hirschfeld (1913), 547.

16 *SB* 9150.4; *P.Lond.* II 445 = p.166. 5-8; *P.Mich.* IX 560.8; *PSI*
33.11-12 (?); 1028.13; *P.Ryl.* II 126 = *CPJ* 420b.6-8; *P.Mil.*
6.2; *P.Weill inv.* 104 = *BASP* 1975, 85.

17 *P.Lond.* II 445 = p.166. 5-8 (A.D. 14-15); *SB* 9150.4 (A.D. 5).

18 *P.Bouriant* 42; *Pap.Chic.* 6; 10; 31; 70; 81; *BGU* 160; 441;
810. ii 7; 1894.111-12; *P.Mich.* IV 223-5; VI 372. ii 23-5;
374. ii 10; IX 540.6; *P.Mich.Michael* 14.6; *P.Hamb.* 3.10-12;
P.Phil. 19.5-6; *P.Ryl.* II 134.7-9; 207.14; *P.Ross.Georg.* II
12. i 2, 14-15; iii 15, 21; *P.Col.* 1 verso 1a. 45; *P.Louvre*
= Rostowzew (1910), 121.

19 *P.Mil.* 6.2 (A.D. 26), cf. *P.Wisc.* 34.4 (144); *P.Mich.* 617.2
    (145-6), perhaps referring to the same land. *SB* 10536.15-16
    (25-6) records the joint property of Julia Sebaste and the
    children of Germanicus at Tebtunis; cf. *BASP* 1975, 87, Phila-
    delphia.

20 *PSI* 1028.13 (A.D. 15); *IGRR* IV 1204; 1213 ἄρκη Λειβιανή (= *ILS*
    8853, ἀρχή), cf. Pflaum (1960-1), no. 218 ter, unwilling to
    connect the land with Livia; A.H.M.Jones, *The cities of the
    eastern Roman provinces*[2] (Oxford, 1971), 84.

21 Josephus, *Ant.Jud.* 18.31. For C. Herennius Capito as her pro-
    curator here, see Pflaum (1960-1), no. 9.

22 Wife of Drusus: *P.Oslo* III 123.6; *P.Oxy.* 244.1-3; *P.Ryl.* II
    140.7; 141.7-8; 171.4; *P.Ross.Georg.* II 12. iii 6, 8 + *P.Rain.*
    178. Daughter of Claudius: *P.Ryl.* II 138.4-5; *P.Bouriant* 42.141;
    P.Fay. 40.7-8. As 'Αντωνιανή (probably the wife of Drusus):
    P.Lond. III 900 = p.89 = Tomsin (1954), 96, introd. 3-7; *P.Phil.*
    19.7-8; *BGU* 199 verso. 9; 212; 277. i 6-7; 280; 653.11; 1893.
    93-4, 484-5, 625-6, 649-50; 1894.100-01, 155-62; *P.Mil.Vogl.* (+*BI*
    II 75; *P.Fay.* 60.6; *Pap.Chic.* 7; *P.Col.* 1 verso 1a. 71; verso
    4. 83-4, 105, 109, 125-6, 134; *P.Berl.Leihg.* 1 verso. ii 16,
    iii 5; *P.Mich.* IV 224; 225; *P.Strassb.* 551.[1]; *P.Aberdeen* 24.5;
    P.Giess. Univ.-Bibl. 52.11.

23 *P.Ryl.* II 87.4, 7; IV 684, 3; *W.Chrest.* 367.8; *P.Flor.* 40.8;
    P.Rain. 2, cf. Rostowzew (1910), 122; *SB* 6019.

24 *W.Chrest.* 176.5; *P.Ryl.* II 171.1-2; *P.Oxy.* 2197.216

25 *P.Bouriant* 42; *BGU* 438 (+*WB*); 1894.94; *P.Berl.Leihg.* 1 verso.
    iv 8-9; *P.Berol.inv.* 11534.11; *P.Mich.* IV 224; 225; VI 372.
    iii 1-8; *P.Phil.*·19.15-16; *P.Strassb.* 267.6-7; *P.Ryl.* II 171.
    13-14; 207.5, 17; *P.Mil.* 65.4; *P.Lond.* II 195 = p.127 = *P.Ryl.*
    II pp.254-5. a. 15; *P.S.A. Athen.* 50 verso. 5. For Italy see
    Phlegon of Tralles, *de long.vit.* IV, Sabinum.

26 *P.Bouriant* 42; *P.Oslo* II 21.5; *Pap.Chic.* 52; *P.Mich.* IV 223;
    224; *P.Strassb.* 210.10-11; *P.Mil.Vogl.* II 75; *P.Ryl.* II 99.3-4;
    171.1-3; *SB* 9205.2; 10512. ii 2, 7, iii 4, 8; *P.Berol.inv.* 7740
    recto. 4 = Świderek, 'ΙΟΥΔΑΙΚΟΣ ΛΟΓΟΣ', *JJP* XVI-XVII (1971), 61.

27 Egypt. *P.Berol.inv.* 7440 recto. 6-7. Sardinia: *CIL* X 7640;
    7980; 7984; 8046[9]; *ILS* 2595; Sotgiu (1957). Italy: *ILS* 1742;
    7386; 7396; 7409; *CIL* VI 15027; XI 1414; XV 7835.

28 *CIL* X 7489, cf. VI 4358 and 9066 (Tiberius and Livia). But
    this is at the very beginning of the system.

29 *IGRR* IV 887-93; *HA, Marc.* 4.7; 7.4. Some may have come from
    her father M.Ummidius Quadratus, cos. 167, cf. praedia Quadra-
    tiana at Ladik, *MAMA* I 24.8-9 (Severus Alexander). Broughton
    (1934), 223-7 discusses this estate.

30 See Hirschfeld (1913).

31 Herakleides division of Arsinoite nome: *BGU* 181.3-7; 889 = *CPJ*
    449.21-2; *P.Bouriant* 42; *P.Mich.* IV 223; 224; 357; *P.Mich.inv.*
    2964.17, 22; *Pap.Chic.* 23; 42; 61; 65; 81; *P.Tebt.* II 343.76-
    80; *SB* 4414.13; 9224.10, 15; *P.Oslo* 26a. 9; *P.Mich.* VI 372.
    ii 15-19; *P.Aberdeen* 50.8; *P.Ryl.* II 207.26; 383; *P.Hamb.* 3.4;

34.10-11; *P.Berol.inv.* 11534.16; *P.Berl.Leihg.* 1 verso. iii 16, iv 5; *P.Ryl.* II 171.14; *BGU* 1894.179-86, 204-5; 1895.33; *P.Col.* 1 verso 1a. 68, 75. Polemon division: *P.Mich.* V 274.8; *SB* 7742.3; *P.Aberdeen* 29.9.

32 Herakleides division: *Pap.Chic.* 32; 36; 39; 41; 48; 49; 50; 78; 87; *BGU* 105 = *W.Chrest.* 346; *BGU* 284; *P.Mich.* IV 224; *P. Mich.inv.* 2964.23; *P.Petaus* 77-8; *P.Bouriant* 42; *P.Hamb.* 3.10. Themistos division: *SB* 10512. ii 8, 12, iii 3; *BGU* 1893.260, 547-8, 651, 658-9, 309-10; *P.Berl.Leihg.* 1 verso. iv 12; *P. Ross.Georg.* V 53. ii 8a; *P.S.A.Athen.* 19.10.

33 Tiberius: *P.Ryl.* II 134.7-9; cf. *P.Lond.* II 195 = p.127. 1-14 with *P.Ryl.* II p.254. Gaius: *P.Ryl.* II 148; *P.S.A.Athen.* 32. 4-7; *P.Mil.* 6.1-3 (as son of Germanicus). Claudius: *P.Ryl.* II 148; *BGU* 650 = *W.Chrest.* 365 (previously of Petronius); *P.Mich.* II 121 recto i. xii 1, iii. x 1; V 244.3, 13; 274-5.8; *P.Oxy.* 2837. Nero: *P.Lond.* II 280 = p.193. 3-7; *BGU* 181 3-7 (from Maecenas). *SB* 4226 may refer to one of the later Julio-Claudian emperors, see Parássoglou (1972), ch.3, n.23.

34 They were recorded in a *liber beneficiorum*, see Nipsus (ed. Lachmann) p.295, *quaeris si in libro beneficiorum regionis illius beneficium alicui Augustus dederit.*

35 E.g. Rostovtzeff (1957), 295; Tomsin (1957).

36 Parássoglou (1972) to be published in *American Studies in Papyrology*; cf. Rostowzew (1910), 126-7 for *ousiai* as private land.

37 Arsinoite nome, Herakleides division: *P.Bouriant* 42; *BGU* 104; 172; 202; 1894.196-203, 206-7; *Pap.Chic.* 5; 16; 18; 26; 53; 62; 65; 67 (= *SB* 4417); 71; *P.Mich.* IV 223; 224; 225; *P.Mich.* VI 382.59; *P.Aberdeen* 50.7; *P.Ryl.* II 207.7, 15; *P.Hamb.* 3.9; *P.Berl.Leihg.* 1 verso. ii 20, iv 11; *P.Lond.* III 900 = p.89. 15-17 + Tomsin (1954), 91-9; *P.Col.* 1 verso 1a. 76; *SB* 10512. ii 6. Polemon division: *SB* 10512. iii 13-14; *P.Giess.Univ.- Bibl.* 52.16-17. Arsinoite, unspecified: *P.Fay.* 338; *P.Flor.* 337.1; *P.Aberdeen* 152.7. Hermopolite nome: *PSI* 448.2, 22, 25; *P.Ryl.* II 99.4. Herakleopolite nome: *P.Hib.* 279.3. Oxyrhynchite nome: *P.Oxy.* 2873.7; 3051.7; *P.Lips.* 115.5-6; *BASP* 1975, 91. For Seneca's unconcern for these estates see *Ep.* 77.3. For Pallas and Narcissus see nn. 24-5.

38 Suet. *Tib.* 49.2 but cf. Tac. *Ann.* 4.6.7 *rari per Italiam Caesaris agri.* Pliny, *NH* 18.7.35; Tac. *Ann.* 14.22,57-60; cf. Dio 62 (61).26.1.

39 Cf. Carcopino (1906).

40 *IGRR* III 335 (= *OGIS* 538, making Nero part of the date), with a fuller publication with new copies in G.E.Bean, 'Notes and inscriptions from Pisidia Part I', *AS* IX (1959), 85 no. 30; cf. *CIL* III 6872 (= Bean, 84) *finis Caesaris n.* from Kılıç north of the lake. On Nero's procurators see Tac. *Ann.* 13.1 and 33, P.Celer, an eques and Helius, a libertus.

41 *HA, Sev.* 12.3 reading *magnam partem agri* (von Domaszewski, *PhM* LIV (1899), 312); contrast *HA, Avid. Cass.* 7; *ILS* 1370; cf. 1421, proc.Aug. *ad bona cogenda in Africa*; 1422-3 and *CIL* XIV 5344, proc.ad bona damnatorum.

42 See above, p.53, eventually for the most part under the *ousiakos logos*. But some ousiac land came under the *dioikesis* cf. *P.Mich.* IV 224.4258-65 (172-3), part of the Severan land under the *idios logos* and part under the *dioikesis*; cf. *P.Bouriant* 42 p.164 (167) where the land of Antonia daughter of Claudius at the Drumos of Hiera Nesos is, exceptionally, under the *kuriakos logos*. *P.Phil.* 19 (first to second century), recording livestock on ousiac land, lists some under the *strategos* and some under the control of an imperial freedman (line 12: ὑπὸ φρ[ο]ντίδα ἀ[πε]λ(ευθέρου) τοῦ Σεβαστοῦ, suggested reading of Dr J.Rea).

43 Chersonese: Dio 54.29.5; Broughton (1934), 219-20 suggests somewhat unconvincingly that this came to Agrippa through Atticus' daughter; Rostovtzeff, *Anatolian studies presented to Ramsay* (Manchester, 1923), 365, land earlier of Pergamene kings. See *ILS* 1419 for a procurator. In Campania, at Boscotrecase: *CIL* IV 6499; 6996-7; X 924. See Rostovtzeff (1957),552 n. 31. For his estates in Sicily see Horace, *Ep.* 1.12.1-2; possibly also in Egypt, *BGU* 1047. ii 14.

44 See P.R.C.Weaver, *Familia Caesaris* (Cambridge, 1972), 213, with references and discussion.

45 Cf. A.Arvanitopoullos, 'Θεσσαλικαὶ ἐπιγραφαί', Ἀρχ.Ἐφ. (1910), 335, for livestock in Thessaly. See further Anderson (1899); Ramsay (1926).

46 Robert (1937), 340-3. On imperial ranching in the area in the third century see *IGRR* III 2; Rostovtzeff (1957), 704 n.40.

47 Cf. *IGRR* III 17 (earlier) with Flam-Zuckermann (1972), somewhat speculatively.

48 Anderson (1937), 19, cf. H.G.Pflaum, 'Note de lecture', *ZPE* VII (1971), 277-8.

49 Notes 27, 31 and 37.

50 A reply to Nero's similar treatment of his own land.

51 Whittaker, pp.140-1, argues that this passage and others like it do not prove that imperial land was lying idle before it was sold.

52 *IG* II - III² 1100 with J.H.Oliver, *The ruling power* (Philadelphia, 1953), 960-3, recording the sale of the confiscated land of Hipparchus, father of Herodes Atticus (Philostratus, *Vita soph.* 2.547). The wording, τὰ 'Ιππάρχου χωρία τὰ ὑπὸ τοῦ φίσκου πραθέντα, is closely paralleled in *P.Bouriant* 42, 116, 148 (167) ἐκ τοῦ κυριακο(ῦ) λόγου πεπραμένω(ν), of ousiac land once of Antonia daughter of Claudius which, similarly, has been sold but which is still accounted for by the authorities. For the sale of other imperial land in Egypt see: *SB* 10527.7-11 (152-3); *BGU* 210 (158-9); *P.Giess.Univ.-Bibl.* 52. 15-16 (222 or 223).

53 Some examples (in chronological order): *SB* 7742; *BGU* 650; *P.Oxy.* 2873; *Stud.Pal.* XX 1; *P.Oxy.* 986; *BGU* 619 (+*BL*), 22; *P.Wisc.* 34 cf. *P.Mich.* 617; *P.Fay.* 82; 60; *BGU* 1893, cf. p.48; *P.Oslo* 91; *P.Lond.* II 339 = p.200. See Kuhnke (1971).

54 Note 9 above.

55 *BGU* 650.1-3, 10; 1669.1-2; *SB* 9150.3; *P.Oslo* III 123.3-4; *P. Ryl.* II 138.3-4; *W.Chrest.* 176.7.

56 *P.Mil.* 6.1; *P.Mich.* V 312.6, 50; *P.Oxy.* 2837.1.

57 Keil and Premerstein, *DAW* LVII 1 (1914-5), no.55 = F.F.Abbott and A.C.Johnson, *Municipal administration in the Roman empire* (Princeton, 1926), 478-9, no.142.

58 *AE* 1916.128, a dedication to Juno. *CIL* XIII 4228, a dedication to Mercury. Neither of these examples is explicitly imperial.

59 Other examples in *ILS* 5567; *ILAf.* 9; *ILS* 5965, coloni Kasturrenses; Février (1966), 218-21, coloni Perdicenses from south of Sitifis; *AE* 1896.34, col(oni) vici Aug(usti) n(ostri); Pflaum (1960-1), no.328.

60 *Inscr.It.* X 1.592 a and b. For imperial estates in the neighbourhood see *Inscr.It.* X 1.593n.

61 *Inscr.It.* X 2.229, possibly 222 (both taken as servile) and X 1.599, with doubtful reading.

62 In practice their condition may have differed little from that of the neighbouring slaves, cf. Martial 4.66.11.

63 φόρος προβάτων on imperial *ousiai*: *P.Phil.* 19 (first to second century), Philadelphia; *SB* 8972 (156/7 - 161), cf. *P.Hamb.* 34 (159-60), Euhemeria; *BGU* 1894 (157), Theadelphia. The administration of these flocks is not straightforward; collective responsibility seems to have been introduced in the reign of Antoninus Pius, C.Préaux, *CE* XVI (1941), 143-4.

64 *CIL* VIII 25902. i 31; cf. 10570. iv 29; 23022.3.

65 *CIL* VIII 10570. iii 16, iv 7. For *forma* see Fronto, *Ad M.Caes.* 5.37 (p.87 Nab.), with Weaver, *Familia Caesaris* (1972), 269.

66 *CIL* VIII 25902. i 23-4. Cf. the later definition of conductores as those *qui reditus domus nostrae debitos quodannis iuxta consuetudinem arcariis tradunt*, CTh. 10.1.11 (367).

67 Put up by *conductoris* (read: *-es*) *praediorum regionis Thuggensis* See further *CIL* VIII 26467-70; *ILTun.* 1389; 1391; 1513; *ILAf.* 515; 569; *AE* 1951. 75.

68 Cf. Thomsin (1964), 90.

69 *IGRR* IV 889; 894; 897; *MAMA* I 292; W.M.Ramsay, 'The cities and bishoprics of Phrygia II', *JHS* VIII (1887), 498. But how many of these are imperial? See Broughton (1934), 227.

70 Ramsay (1895-7), I 272, nos.192 (= *IGRR* IV 927); 194.

71 For an *actor* married to a *vilica* (in Noricum) see *CIL* III 5616.

72 But this man may have been rather a tax-collector. *ILAlg.* I 99, with a vilicus, Enaris, is undated.

73 On the use of slaves in African agriculture see Gsell (1932).

74 Kuhnke (1971), 64-71, especially 64-5.

75 Świderek (1970).

76 Robert, *Hellenica* X 83 n.3.

77 Above note 57; *CIL* III 14191 = *OGIS* 519 = *IGRR* IV 598 (Aragua);
   see now Ballance (1969), 146.

78 Anderson (1899), 124, no.134; (1937), 19.

79 C.H.E.Haspels, *The highlands of Phrygia* (Princeton, 1971),
   appendix no. 31, giving details of earlier publications.

80 *IGRR* IV 634, Lydia; Keil and Premerstein, 'Bericht über eine
   dritte Reise in Lydien', *DAW* LVII 1 (1914-15), no.11 cf. p.6,
   Lydia. Elsewhere: *IGBulg.* 2319, near Thessaloniki; *ILS* 5542,
   Italy; Rostovtzeff (1957), 690 n.100, Waldfischbach, Belgica;
   in Africa: *ILAlg.* I 324; *CIL* VIII 6976; 24697; cf. 25902. iii
   16, *custodes*. On the duties of the *saltuarius* see Pomponius
   in D.33.7.15.2, *custodia agri* just as the wife is *villae custos*.

81 *IGRR* IV 897, Alastus (private ?); Robert, *Hellenica* XIII 99-
   100 with an improved reading of Ramsay (1890), 178 from
   Karaağaç, the tomb of an *orophylax* murdered ὑπὸ λῃστῶν, cf. the
   similar fate of a soldier from the saltus Philomusianus recorded
   in *CIL* VIII 14603. The procurator might also control his own
   soldiers, *CIL* VIII 10570. ii 11; Josephus, *Ant.* 18.158.

82 *P.Amh.* 77.20 (139). There seems no reason to connect the
   paraphylakitai of *IGRR* IV 896; Ramsay (1895-7), 308, no.116,
   with an imperial estate.

83 *CIL* VIII 12590-13214; 24678-707.

84 See Pflaum (1960-1), 547, on the African divisions. For the
   Bagradas valley Kolendo (1968) has established a hierarchy in
   which the procurator tractus has several *regiones* under him.

85 Rostowzew (1910), 327; T.R.S.Broughton, *The romanisation of
   Africa Proconsularis* (London, 1929), 114-15.

86 See Pflaum (1960-1), 381-5; Kolendo (1968).

87 Above note 57.

88 W.M.Calder, *JRS* II (1912), 81; cf. from Egypt, *P.Oxy.* 62 = *W.
   Chrest.* 278 1-2 (242) (ἑκατόνταρ)χ(ος) ἐπὶ κτήσ(εων) [θεο(υ)(?)
   Τ]ίτου.

89 Ballance (1969).

90 Rostovtzeff (1957), 670, generally accepted but cf. the caution
   of *W.Grund.* 299.

91 *P.Strassb.* 267. 6-7; *P.Mil.* 65. 4; *BGU* 1646. 8; 1894. 93; *SB*
   10512. i 6; *P.Berl.Leihg.* 1 recto. iii 6, 18, iv 3, 11, vi 4,
   7, 13; verso. i 18, ii 4; 4 recto. iii 22, iv 2, 17, vi 20,
   vii 4, 11, 20; *P.Bouriant* 42.78 and *passim*; *P.Strassb.* 551;
   P.S.A.Athen. 30 verso; *P.Giess.Univ.-Bibl.* 52.11. The third
   century appearance of οἱ ἀπὸ τοῦ οἴκου θεῶν Οὐεσπασιανοῦ καὶ
   Τίτου, *P.Oxy.* 3047 (245), cultivating various categories of
   non-ousiac land is puzzling.

92 *P.Oxy.* 1434.16 (107-8). The terminology is not new but
   appears in the edict of Tiberius Julius Alexander, line 30;
   see G.Chalon, *L'Édit de Tiberius Julius Alexander* (Olten and
   Lausanne, 1964).

93 *CIL* VIII 25943. ii 2; 26416. i 3-4, 7; 10570. iii 4-5, 25.

94 See above, p.50.

95 H.G.Pflaum, *Les Procurateurs équestres sous le haut empire* (Paris, 1950), 58-67.

96 *P.Giess*. 4.8 (118); *P.Hamb*. 59.6 (138). After Hadrian the term οὐσιακὸς καὶ δημόσιος γεωργός becomes regular, e.g. *P. Phil*. 15.2 (153-4); but it may just be chance that these terms do not occur earlier.

97 E.g. *BGU* 1047. ii 14-15. Individual estates earlier had their own *logoi*, cf. *P.Mich*. 524 (98).

98 *P.Oxy*. 58 = *W.Chrest*. 378 (288).

99 αἱ δεσποτικαὶ ἀποφοραὶ καὶ ψῆφοι; see note 57.

100 See Chalon (note 92 above), lines 10-15; cf. *SB* 9224.9-10 (50-1).

101 See Tomsin (1964), 85-6 with references.

102 Parássoglou (1972), chapter 4, 164-71.

103 Poethke (1969 a and b).

104 *P.Strassb*. 267.5-6 (126-8). For references see Tomsin (1964), 95-7; *P.Petaus* 75-8, introduction; *SB* 10761. *Epiteretai* seem to have held office for a limited period only, cf. D.49.14.3.6, Hadrian freeing conductores after a lustrum.

105 Cf. the complaints in Keil and Premerstein, *DAW* LVII 1 (1914-15), nos. 28 and 55; Herrmann, *DAW* LXXVII 1 (1959), no.9; *Syll.*³ 888, Scaptopara; Aragua, n.77 above.

106 *P.Vars*. 11.2 also mentions *ateleia* but the reading is doubtful and the reference not necessarily imperial.

107 S.L.Wallace, *Taxation in Egypt* (Princeton, 1938), 121-4.

108 Eusebius, *Hist.Eccl*. 10.6, recording orders to the ἐπίτροπος τῶν κτημάτων to provide as many funds as required by the bishop of Carthage.

Chapter 4. Classical Roman law and the sale of land

1 This is therefore the point at which to remind the reader of one general rule concerning conveyance of land. Land in Italy and in communities possessing *ius Italicum* was *res mancipi*. Title to it (*dominium*) was conveyable only by the formal cere-mony of *mancipatio*: if such *mancipatio* had not taken place the transfer of title had to await the completion of *usucapio* by uninterrupted possession for two years. Not all land, be it noted, was *res mancipi*, and not all *res mancipi* were land.

2 E.J.Jonkers, *Economische en Sociale Toestanden in het Romein-sche Rijk blijkende uit het Corpus Juris* (Wageningen, 1933), 21-5.

3 D.26.7, passim, but especially 26.7.3.2; 26.7.5 pr.; 26.7.7.2-3; 26.7.49.

4 Daube (1957a).

5 Buckland (1932 or 1963), 486-93; Zulueta (1945), 42-51; and for the late Republic, Watson (1965), 70-91.

6 In the well-known document from Dacia recording sale of part of a house (*Fontes Iuris Romani Antejustiniani* III, *Negotia*, ed. V.Arangio-Ruiz (Florence, 1943), no.90) the *stipulatio* is taken in spite of the fact that there has been a *mancipatio*; but of course the *mancipatio* of non-Italian land is the real irregularity.

7 See, for example, *Pauli Sent.* 2.17.2.

8 D.19.1.36. For *damnum infectum* see Watson (1968), 125-54.

9 Cicero, *de officiis* 3.54-67.

10 D.21.2.75 (cf. 21.2.48); 18.1.59; *FIRA* III, no.90 (applying to house property) and no.92 (in a formulary applying to land, though for *fiducia*, not sale).

11 See *Tabula Herculanensis* no.60, in *PP* IX 55.

12 See Buckland (1932 or 1963), 492-3 on D.21.1.1 pr. and 21.1.49.

13 D.19.2.25.1. This and other relevant texts are discussed by J.A.C.Thomas, 'The sitting tenant', *Tijdschrift voor Rechtsgeschiedenis*, XLI (1973), 35-44.

14 Apart from texts in the law of *locatio conductio*, CJ.4.65.9, a rescript of Severus Alexander, on precisely the present topic, bears the same implication.

15 Cicero, *pro Caecina* 54 and *Topica* 23.

16 This is to ignore certain possible complications about ownership of the materials embodied in the building - a topic much beloved of the modern inventors of 'problems' in Roman law. See Buckland (1932 or 1963), 212-15.

17 D.18.1.57 pr., heavily interpolated after the second sentence; so that in the case of partial destruction 'the classical law is not certain' (Buckland (1932 or 1963), 482). A similar problem arises if you buy land with timber on it for the sake of the timber, and the timber has ceased to exist, D.18.1.58.

18 See Chap.7.

19 Crook (1967), 261-2.

20 L.Homo, *Rome impériale et l'urbanisme dans l'antiquité* (Paris, 1951), 602-3.

21 D.43.8.2.17 and 43.8.7.

22 See H.F.Jolowicz, *Digest XLVII.2 'De Furtis'* (Cambridge, 1940), xvi-xvii. As Jolowicz points out, there were other remedies; but that is not the matter that concerns us here.

23 *Lex Iulia et Plautia*: Gaius, *Institutes* 2.45.

24 Gai. *Inst.* 2.51.

25 Gai. *Inst.* 2.52-6. Incidentally, in that case *usucapio* even of land was effective in the shorter period of one year.

26 Cicero, *de legibus* 1.55; CTh.2.26.5

27 In Daube (1959), 26-38.

28 *PP* VIII 455.

29 In D.21.2.11 pr. lands are bought *in Germania trans Renum*; but the problem that arises is not one of error.

30 For some comment see Watson (1965), 91-2.

31 See Kaser (1959) II, 284 n.25; but add H.F.Jolowicz, *Juridical Review* XLIX (1937), 50-72.

32 V.Arangio-Ruiz, *La Compravendita in Diritto Romano*, I. Second edition (Naples, 1956), 144.

33 Carrelli, *SDHI* III (1937), 446-50, was not necessarily right to reject CJ.2.36.1 and 2.36.3.1 as precursors because they concerned improper influence by imperial officials.

34 C.Longo, *Bullettino dell' Istituto di Diritto Romano* XXXI (1921), 40-50; Buckland (1932 or 1963), 496-8; Zulueta (1945), 55-7; Watson (1965), 98.

35 The reader is reminded that in Roman law a joint heir, before partition, owns, jointly with the other heirs, his appropriate fraction of everything: if he is heir to half, he owns a half share of every field of land, half of every chair and spoon, and half the cat.

36 D.10.2.22.1-2 says the same, though it also says that 'even if there has been a bidding the court can adjudicate a particular item to a particular person'.

37 The text of 3.37.3.1 (only this half is of concern) seems slightly amiss syntactically. It is necessary to understand *agri* or *fundi* with *singuli* and to infer some such words as *aut posse* or *ut possit* between *ex sociis* and *sua pecunia*. The sense is in any case over-compressed.

38 The estate of Matidia in Fronto, *ad Ant. imp.* 2.1 (M.P.J.Van den Hout, *M. Cornelii Frontonis Epistulae* I (Leiden, 1954), 98) was in danger of being put to public auction; but that would have been a 'compulsory' auction resulting from the refusal of heirs to enter.

39 See the remarks of Miss Rawson on pp.85-9 above.

Chapter 5. The Ciceronian aristocracy and its properties

1 The only one mentioned by D'Arms (1970), see esp. 61ff.

2 A.W.Lintott, 'Cicero and Milo', *JRS* LXIV (1974), 62, on the legal position. Note *A.* 5.8.2-3 on the sale of Milo's property; *de ND* 3.86, Rutilius Rufus' loss of his estate at Formiae.

3 G.E.Mingay, *English landed society in the eighteenth century* (London, 1963).

4 For the reasons for fragmented holdings, see Duncan-Jones in chapter 2.

5 Badian (1973), 122. Cf. D'Arms (1968), 27.

6 Schmidt (1899).

7 But see D'Arms (1970), 173: the villa of Antony at Baiae had belonged to his father and grandfather; and the villa of the Pisones was probably to remain in the family for a number of

generations. Cf. Schneider (1974), 67.

8 Frank (1966).

9 It was bought by Lepidus, *A.* 13.47a. Q. Cicero buying in Rome and selling in Tusculum, *A.* 1.14.7.

10 Varro had property at Tusculum (*F.* 9.1.2, also Varro, *RR* 3.13. 1, 3.3.8 - bought from M.Piso); in Campania (*F.* 9.1.2); at Casinum (*RR* 3.4.2, 3.5.8, cf. Cicero, *Phil.* 2.103); Reate (*RR* 2.2.9) and probably the south, where his flocks wintered (*RR* 2.2.9).

11 And he has rented his old house in the Carinae to the Lamiae, who are *mundi habitatores*. Cicero's friend L.Aelius Lamia may be meant; he was a leading *eques* and ultimately entered the Senate.

12 See Crook (1967), 143. *F.* 7.23.4 may refer to a rented house, but this was an arrangement between relatives.

13 Lepidus was paying 6,000 sesterces, Sulla 3,000, which does not look like terrible indigence. Caelius, on the smart Palatine and later, paid 10,000 for his flat, according to Cicero - 30,000, according to the prosecution.

14 Mingay (*op. cit.* note 3), 157.

15 Cf. Mr Bingley, to whom 'Netherfield Hall was let at last'. He was of a good family, but his father had made money in trade and died before buying an estate as he intended.

16 D'Arms (1970), 171ff. lists known owners.

17 Id., 69-70.

18 E.g. Plut. *Antony* 21.2; *Caesar* 51.2; Cicero, *Phil.* 2.104, *A.* 14.6.1, 10.2.

19 Crook (1967), 132.

20 Appian, *BC* 1.104; Pliny, *Ep.* 1.6 and (a friend fishing and hunting) 2.8.

21 Writing to Brutus about the town's investments in Gaul, or putting his son and nephew into the aedileship to tidy up its finances (*F.* 13.11).

22 Caesar, *BC* 1.34 and 56.

23 I cannot find any discussion of the possibility that senators might not be allowed to own land abroad in Mommsen's *Staats-recht*, which may be why most scholars seem unaware of it. E. Badian, *Publicans and Sinners* (Oxford, 1972), 88 however takes the ban for granted.

24 2.3.93, also perhaps 152; a senator's wife, 97.

25 It is sometimes thought that M.Crassus' silver mines were in Spain, where he certainly had connections (Plut. *Crassus* 2.5; F.Adcock, *Marcus Crassus, millionaire* (Cambridge, 1966), 1; T.F. Carney, *A biography of Gaius Marius* (*PACA* Supplement I, 1961) 23, argues that Marius also owned mines in Spain, but this is very uncertain. C.Aquillius Gallus, the lawyer, a rich man, owned a property in the island of Cercina, off the coast of Africa, where Ser. Sulphicius in youth studied with

him (Pomponius 43); Gallus was subsequently praetor, in 66,
but may have entered the Senate late - Pliny, *NH* 17.2 calls
him an *eques Romanus*. Schneider (1974) takes the following
possibly to be senators: T.Pompeius, with land in Gallia
Transalpina, Varro, *RR* 3.12.2; P.Quinctius, ditto, Cicero,
pro Quinct. 12,19 (but see 1 on his poverty and lack of
gratia); C.Caelius, Africa, *pro Cael*. 73 (but strictly only
his father, an *eques*); Cn.Calidius, *Verr*. 2.4.42 (again, only
a senator's father); C.Anicius, Cicero, *F*. 21.4 (no evidence
his business is landowning). J.Hatzfeld, *Les Trafiquants
italiens dans l'Orient hellénique* (Paris, 1919), 64 believes,
on *F*. 13.42, that L.Lucceius had land in Epirus, but what his
procurators are doing there is unclear; and *A*. 6.1.19 and 6.
5.2 are too mysterious to let us assert with Broughton (1934)
that Cicero owned land in the Chersonese. (List in I.Shatzman,
Senatorial wealth and Roman politics (Brussels, 1975) Table
VII: all uncertain or erroneous, except *Schol. Bub*. 90.)

26 *F*. 13.2: Strabo 10.445. G.Crifò, *Ricerche sull'exilium nel
periodo repubblicano* I (Milan, 1961).

27 Cicero's friend L.Aelius Lamia may have kept lands in Africa
after he became, belatedly, a senator, *F*. 12.29; see Wiseman
(1971) Appendix II C. Professor K.Hopkins points out to me
that, other things being equal, estates in Italy were likely
to be more profitable than those in the provinces, as they
carried no tax; but other things would not be equal for great
men, who could surely acquire estates cheap or for nothing by
devious means. *Q*. 1.1.8 lists the things a governor might be
tempted to acquire in Asia; land is not mentioned. For the
considerable information we have on Pompey's properties in
Italy, see below, note 32. For the considerable information
we have on the interests of the Claudii in the East, see my
'The Eastern clientelae of Clodius and the Claudii', *Historia*
XXII (1973) 219 and 'More on the clientelae of the Claudii',
forthcoming. Referring primarily to the Lex Claudia, which
forbade senators to own ships of any size, Cicero *Verr*. 2.5.45
says *antiquae sunt istae leges et mortuae*; he may well also be
referring to a ban on owning property abroad, which might in
fact be a provision of the Lex Claudia itself.

28 Seneca, *Ep. Mor*. 87.7. The Republican ban, if there was one,
would seem to have lapsed shortly after the Ciceronian period,
when Agrippa acquired estates in Sicily (as Professor Finley
points out to me); he later left Augustus estates in the
Chersonese, Dio 54.29.5.

29 An Argive decree in honour of Cn.Octavius, 170 B.C. (Moretti,
Iscrizioni Storiche Ellenistiche no.42) gives him the right to
own house and land; this raises no presumption he could take
advantage of it, for compare the way in which Greek cities,
especially Athens, pressed citizenship on Romans, who did not
always realize they could not take it without losing their
own (Cicero, *pro Balbo* 30).

30 E.g. Plut. *Crassus* 6.7; Cicero, *pro Tullio* 14. Aemilius
Paullus retired to Velia as a health resort with medical tra-
ditions (see *PP* (1970), articles by Nutton, Pugliese Carratelli
and others) rather than because he already owned property

there. He did have a *fundus* somewhere, Val. Max. 4.4.9; Poly-
bius 18.35, more plausibly, mentions properties in the plural.

31 Juventius Thalna (*A*. 16.6.1) is counted as a senator by Wiseman
(1971), 194. A senatorial family, certainly.

32 Pompey owned a house in town as well, and a suburban villa,
property at Alba, Tusculum, Cumae, the ager Falernus, Baiae,
Alsium, Formiae and presumably Picenum (Miltner *RE* XXI 2.2210);
not necessarily all at once. But he never increased his properties by buying up neighbouring land (Pliny, *NH* 18.35) and
avoided extravagant building (id., ib. 9.170).

33 Schneider (1974) lists known estates of senators and *nobiles*;
Wiseman (1971), App. III those of senators in Italy, but without drawing any conclusions; Harris (1971), 295 suggests that
Roman owners were expanding into Etruria and Umbria in the
fifties and forties. See also Jaczynowska (1962). For villas,
as opposed to smaller farm-houses, close to roads, see Kahane
etc. (1968).

34 Trimalchio also took pride in self-sufficiency, Petronius,
Sat. 38.1.

35 *F*. 16.21.7 - because they will all make use of it and it will
revert to the family on Tiro's death? This is probably the
Puteolan property that Suetonius tells us Tiro lived on till
extreme old age (Jerome, *Chron*. 194.1). D'Arms (1970), 200
unconvincingly makes him inherit Cicero's grand Puteolanum,
which was surely confiscated.

36 Furius Bibaculus *ap*. Suet. *de gramm*. 11.

37 *Catalepton* 8; cf. D'Arms (1970), 57, but note Aulus Gellius
6.20.1 (for Nola).

38 Retired persons of all kinds bought farms, e.g. the gladiator
in Horace, *Epist*. 1.1.5. Pompey gave his protégé Balbus land
for *horti*, but this was exceptional munificence.

39 S.Treggiari, *Roman freedmen during the late Republic* (Oxford,
1969), 109.

40 Not all Roscius' wealth will have been in these *fundi* - there
was a house at Rome; and Cicero may have exaggerated his
client's standing. Cf. Schneider (1974), 63 for conclusions
fairly similar to mine. (*Fundi* worth HS20,000 or less are
common units for the less well-off under the Empire, see
Duncan-Jones (1974), 231 n.669.)

41 Frank (1933), 393. But in the time of Pliny, *NH* 14.49-50,
farms near Rome were often cheap; Duncan-Jones (1974), App. 8
observes that this remark goes against the other evidence,
even of Pliny himself.

42 F.M.L.Thompson, *English landed society in the nineteenth century* (London, 1963), 123.

43 Varro, *RR* 3.2.14-15; market-gardening, Cato, *de agric*. 1.7,
7.1; Pliny, *NH* 18.29; Columella 3.2.1. Varro, *RR* 3.13.8 shows
us that *pastio villatica* was only treated piecemeal by Greek
and Punic authors. Note also his Menippean Satire *Gerontodid-*

askalos, perhaps mentioning an estate which formerly had a
granary and wine-presses, but now flocks of peacocks, not to
mention doors inlaid with African citrus wood (Bücheler 181ff).

44 *F*. 16.18.2, to Tiro; it is a pity we have not more letters to
members of Cicero's household. The text is disputed: some
emend *abutor* to *abundo*. Horace, *Sat*. 2.4.15 reports a complaint
that field-grown vegetables taste better than those from an
artificially irrigated garden.

45 See Wiseman (1965).

46 Brunt (1971), 345 discusses the various parts of it in detail.

47 To the other evidence for *coloni* in this period, perhaps add
Priapea 2 - a small farmer, but a *vilicus* about, so the farmer
may be a tenant. For the use of hired labourers, Varro, *Sat*.
Menipp. 564 is not always noted: *utrum mercedem accipit is
qui meas venit segetes ut sariat, an ego ab illo*? Note this
is not harvest time, often said to be the only period when
day-labourers would be needed (haymaking and vintage, Varro,
RR 1.17.2).

48 In place of *silva viridicata* has been conjectured *silva vitium
ridicata*, 'a plantation of vines supported on sticks', but
Cicero is now talking of the ornaments of the estate, and perhaps of the welcome shade he has already mentioned. Dio 46.4.2
makes Calenus in his invective against Cicero talk of his father
profiting from his vines and olives, as well as the fulling
works; not much stress can be laid on this. *Verr*. 2.3.119
suggests that Cicero thought of the normal farm as mixed, and
with valuable timber.

49 *A*. 7.3.9, 13.45.3, *de fin*. 2.84. (Note Hortensius' villa at
Laurentum as well as his Campanian properties, Varro, *RR* 3.13.
2.) In A.D. 174 the rent for the office at Puteoli for the
statio Tyrensium was the huge sum of HS100,000 (*IG* XIV 830:
Duncan-Jones (1974), 210, 236 - possibly even HS400,000).
Juvenal 3.223 shows that in his time rents in Rome were dis-
proportionately greater than the cost of buying in country
towns, and indeed Suet. *DJ* 38 shows that rents in Rome were
already much higher than elsewhere - Caesar remitted those up
to HS2,000 in the capital, only up to HS500 in the rest of
Italy.

50 D'Arms (1970), 171ff. lists prominent Romans with houses in
Naples - note esp. *A*. 1.6.1, *F*. 9.15.5.

51 Columella 3.3.2 says many think it more profitable than vineyards. See also *de leg. agr*. 2.18.48.

52 Showing Atticus as well rented *ager publicus*.

53 *A*. 12.32.2, 15.17.1, 15.20.4, 16.1.5. Or could the money from
these *dotalium praediorum*, in Cicero's hands after the divorce
from Terentia, have earlier been part of *Tullia's* dowry rather
than her mother's?

54 Atticus, M.Crassus, L.Lucceius, M.Caelius, P.Clodius. See
chapter 7.

55 First, we must accept Constans' emendation of *Bovillanum* (*Q*.

3.1.3) to *Fufidianum*, or chaos, and yet another property,
result. Next we must identify the Manilianum and the Arcanum
as a single estate which could be called either after its previous owner or its locality. In fact Cicero visited both on
the same day; 3.7.7 shows that like the Manilianum of 3.1.1
the Arcanum has a *piscina* and is being altered by the unsatisfactory Diphilus; 3.3.1 only mentions two estates, the Arcanum
and Laterium. (N.B. *F*. 1.9.24 - Quintus wants to *adiungere* a
farm to his *patrimonium*.)

56 He himself had at least three villas on the shores of Lake Como.

57 *F*. 16.18.2, with Tyrell and Purser's commentary.

58 Shackleton Bailey ad loc. suggests that Pilia had been asked
   also to look after the Puteolanum, which is perhaps unlikely.

59 There were or could be state architects (e.g. *de leg. agr.* 2.
   32) and these might be responsible for official valuations
   such as those made of Cicero's damaged properties in 56. Who
   valued the land used to pay debts under Caesar's legislation
   - *agrimensores*? Or *praediatores* (see note 65)?

60 Münzer, *RE* IIA 1713 and D'Arms (1970), 19-20. All information
   on him probably comes ultimately from a speech of L.Crassus
   (Val. Max. 9.1.1, Pliny, *NH* 9.168ff., Cicero, *de or.* 1.178,
   de off. 3.67, *de fin.* 2.70 and *ap.* Augustine, *de beata vita*
   26, which calls him *ditissimus, amoenissimus, deliciosissimus,*
   the possessor of health, friends and influence.

61 But acc. Festus, from his two large gold rings. Macrobius,
   Sat. 3.15.2.

62 Thus Porphyrio and Pseudo-Acro respectively; Festus shows
   Coctio means haggler, and for the meaning of Cerdo cf. Petronius, *Sat.* 60.8; the name is not uncommon epigraphically. To
   combine quality building with statuary was sensible till recently; cf., from the productive end, the family of the
   Cossutii (Wilson, op. cit. in note 25, 97 n.1, and myself, 'The
   activities of the Cossutii', forthcoming. I also hope to say
   a little more elsewhere about Damasippus as an art-dealer).

63 *RE* X 1034; the commentators on Cicero, even Shackleton Bailey,
   think of the senator Licinius Damasippus, while Treggiari (op.
   cit. note 39), 105 note 7 believes he might be a freedman.
   He could conceivably be the Junius of *A*. 12.14.2, where he is
   dunning Cicero for money as surety for Cornificius; the *praediator* Appuleius is mixed up in the affair, probably as another
   creditor. (For *praediatores* see Gaius, *Inst.* 2.61: *qui merca-
   tur a populo praediator appellatur*. If this is correct, he is
   then a specialized sort of dealer only, concerned with confiscated property.)

64 Wiseman (1971), 81 compares, as 'operating an estate agent's
   business', the (Vettius) Scato of Cicero, *de domo* 116. But
   Cicero says it is ridiculous that so poor a man should be
   supposed to have bought so rich a house, so he is clearly a
   private individual.
   It is not clear how much M.Crassus sold of the vast amounts
   of property which he acquired by dubious methods, especially
   in Rome and its suburbs (for example, by making up to a

Vestal Virgin); Plutarch says that he had over five hundred
slaves trained as architects and builders (*Crassus* 2.5). They
must have been employed in rebuilding and improving this property, for instance that damaged in the fires that allowed
Crassus to buy it up cheap - if that story is not too good to
be true. Crassus himself used a single house and was contemp-
tuous of φιλοικοδόμους; he even sold his father's palazzo on
the Palatine to Cicero (*F.* 5.6.2), but this might prove
stinginess rather than a policy of selling valuable houses
and estates.

Chapter 6. Private farm tenancy in Italy before Diocletian

1 Note the phrasing in a rescript of 231 (CJ.4.65.8): *si tamen
expressum non est in locatione aut mos regionis postulat.*

2 See most recently D.Hennig, 'Die Arbeitsverpflichtungen der
Pächter in Landpachtverträgen aus dem Faijum', *ZPE* IX (1972),
111-31.

3 See generally Mayer-Maly (1956), ch. 1; p.76 above for a
neat example with respect to sale of land.

4 Brockmeyer (1971), 740.

5 This point was clearly made long ago by Gummerus (1906), 64-5.

6 As an example of a methodologically correct analysis, see
Mayer-Maly (1956), 140-7, on the Severan administrative steps
designed to 'protect' agriculture. On the latter, see also
pp.142-3 above.

7 Heitland (1921), 307-8. Cf. Gummerus (1906), 83, on the mis-
understandings that have arisen because of Columella's use of
colonus in both senses.

8 See J.Kolendo, *Le Traité d'agronomie des Saserna* (*Archiwum
filologiczne* XXIX, 1973).

9 See Heitland (1921), 215-16.

10 Cic. *ad Att.* 9.9.4, taken with Sen. *Ben.* 4.12.3, as elucidated
by Shackleton Bailey in his commentary on the letter (which
still leaves much obscure); *CIL* XI 1147, sect. 39: *ex reditu
aestimatus est.*

11 See most recently Duncan-Jones (1974), ch. 2.

12 One common subject in land leases elsewhere, the incidence of
taxation, was missing because Italian land was not at this
· time subject to tax.

13 See the references in Kaser (1971), 464-6; more fully, Mayer-
Maly (1956), passim; and the protest by Kaser (1957), 155-6.

14 The rhetoric of Seneca, *Ben.* 7.5.2-3 - *nec conductum meum,
quamquam sis dominus, intrabis,* etc. - is exaggerated to the
point of falsity.

15 The fundamental work on the subject is Steinwenter (1942).

16 I take the quotation from Neratius which follows in this
passage to refer to customary practice, derived from the
agricultural writers, not to a general legal obligation; see

Mayer-Maly (1956), 122.

17 See briefly, p. 73 above.

18 See on all this Kaser (1957), 155-86; cf. A. Berger, 'A labour contract of A.D. 164: *CIL* III, p.948, no. X', *CP* XLIII (1948), 231-42, at 239-42.

19 See Heitland (1921), 366-7, with further source-references.

20 R.A.C.Parker, 'Coke of Norfolk and the agrarian revolution', *Econ.Hist.Rev.*, 2nd ser., VIII (1955), 158.

21 D.19.2.55 is a selection from Paul's *Sententiae*, but even if that work is to be dated *c*. A.D. 300, it does not follow automatically, the possibility of interpolation apart, that the rule under consideration is very late, and certainly not that it is Diocletianic.

22 D.33.7.20.3 refers to a *cautio* offered by a tenant for payment of an unpaid balance, which is a different matter.

23 I myself have no doubt of the authenticity of *tacite* in D.20. 2.7 pr., mentioned in my text; of CJ.8.14.3 and briefly Kreller (1944), 323 n.64.

24 This statement means that I accept the authenticity of D.20. 2.4 pr., and that I hold generalized statements about pledged *illata* always to imply a prior agreement on the subject; note the words *voluntas* and *scientia* in CJ.4.65.5. On the rural-urban distinction in the context of the *interdictum Salvianum*, which I shall not discuss, see Kreller (1944), esp. 322-3. Urban tenants of course produced no *fructus* which the landlord could seize.

25 Kaser (1957), 177-86.

26 Heitland (1921), 365. Cf. the even more sweeping conclusion of Brockmeyer (1971), 740: the inclusion of *reliqua colonorum* in inheritances 'zeigt dass das Kolonatssystem anscheinend bereits zur Beginn seiner Entwicklung keine besonders rentable Wirtschaftsform war'.

27 Professor P.A.Brunt, who kindly read and commented on my manuscript, reminds me that, since rents were not paid in advance, a landlord would commonly have *reliqua colonorum* on his death, that is, rents due without any implication of default.

28 Duncan-Jones (1974), 21.

29 *PP* VIII (1953), 455. I have not indicated dotted letters and supplements as the text I have reproduced is certain.

30 The label 'draconic' comes from Weber (1891), 232; cf. Schulz (1951), 544-5.

31 It may be relevant that there is no discernible lexical trend in the use of the word *colonus* before the shift to the sense of 'tied tenant' in fourth-century legal texts.

32 On public land, see Kaser (1942), 36-7; Weber (1891), 136-9.

33 Fustel de Coulanges (1885), 15-24.

34 That this was the effect, direct or indirect, of *addictio*
   seems to me certain, despite the notorious paucity and obscur-
   ity of sources on the subject. F.v.Woess, 'Personalexekution
   und cessio bonorum im römischen Reichsrecht', *ZRG* XLIII
   (1922), 485-529, remains fundamental.

35 D.Daube, *Studies in Biblical law* (1947), 45.

36 See H.Bellen, *Studien zur Sklavenflucht im römischen Kaiser-
   reich* (1971), pt. III.

37 See Duncan-Jones (1974), ch. 2.

38 See e.g. G.Duby, *Rural economy and country life in the medieval west*, transl. Cynthia Postan (1968), 273-8, 312-27.

39 Weber (1891), 244-7.

40 Heitland (1921), 252-4.

41 Gummerus (1906), 85.

Chapter 7. Urban property investment

1 Frank (1933), I 394-6.

2 Rostovtzeff (1957), 31; 17.

3 The precise meaning of this sentence remains obscure.

4 *ad A.* 12.33; Plut. *Crassus* 2.4; see above p.187 n.64.

5 Cf. Juv. 3.212ff. Other examples of intentional demolition,
  varied in context and motive, include Str. 5.3.7; Hor. *Ep*.1.1.
  100; D.19.2.30; 39.2.45. I make no attempt to provide here a
  comprehensive analysis of the subject of speculation.

6 Salvioli (1906), 31ff.; 61ff. See e.g. 54: 'La spéculation
  édilitaire, qu'Atticus a également pratiqué...'.

7 R.Feger, 'Atticus', *RE* Supp. VIII 516-17.

8 Frank (1933), I 394; A.H.Byrne, *T.Pomponius Atticus* (Bryn
  Mawr, 1920), 13.

9 Frank (1933), I 393-5. For the influence of Tenney Frank on
  later scholars, see e.g. Smutny (1951), 54, on the 600,000:
  'this amount, as Frank points out, approximately equals
  Cicero's own income'.

10 Observed by Smutny (1951), 53.

11 *ad A.* 13.46.2; 14.9.1, 10.3, 11.2; cf. 12.25.1: *voluptuarias
   possessiones.*

12 *ad A.* 12.32.2, 7.1, 24.1; 16.1.5.

13 E.g. 100,000 sesterces might represent a return of 10% on an
   investment of 1,000,000 sesterces. But the capital outlay
   might be somewhat greater, for 10% is an unusually high yield.
   See Duncan-Jones (1974), 33ff.

14 J.Carcopino, *Cicero: the secrets of his correspondence*
   (London, 1951), I 54: the bulk of Cicero's productive land was
   near Arpinum, this land was roughly of equal value to the
   Tusculan, and the latter was worth about 1,000,000 sesterces.

15 This statement is controversial and will have to be defended in detail in another place.

16 Salvioli (1906), 36-7.

17 These properties were at Puteoli.

18 Provided, of course, that the owners were citizens of Ostia and the profits did not go to outsiders. Meiggs (1960), 235 ff.; Packer (1971); Boethius (1960), 128ff.

19 Etienne (1960).

20 E.Boeswillwald, R.Cagnat, A.Ballu, *Timgad, une cité africaine sous l'empire romain* (Paris, 1905), 325-6; *CIL* VIII 2395, 2399; 17904-5; *ILS* 5579; *BAC* 1932-3, pp. 185-6 (Plotius Faustus). We are in no position to calculate the returns coming to house-owners in Africa. If Faustus had invested 400,000 sesterces, the equestrian census, in rural land, he might have received 24,000 sesterces per annum at 6%. His shops might have been worth 12,000 sesterces per annum (i.e. less than 1,000 sesterces per room, which seems a low estimate). The ratio 2:1 between income from rural and urban sectors might be a significant result for an agricultural town. For some rents in late Republican Rome see Yavetz (1958), 504; cf. D.19.2.7-8,30 pr.

21 Basic reference-works include J.Overbeck, *Pompeji in seinem Gebäuden, Alterthümern und Kunstwerken*[3] (Lepizig, 1875); Maiuri (1942), 97ff.; della Corte (1954). This is not the place to undertake a critique of Maiuri's influential theory, the essence of which is that the Pompeian aristocracy was forced to invest in commerce and industry as a result of its losses in the earthquake of A.D. 62. I find little concrete evidence to support this argument.

22 Hypsaeus: Maiuri (1942), 165-6; Overbeck (op.cit. note 21), 345, fig.192; della Corte (1954), 46. Of course many owners of bakeries, dye-works, fulleries, and so on, would have been merely *rentiers*.

23 Lex Tar. 32ff.; lex Urs. 75; lex Malac. 62. Texts in *FIRA* I, pp.168; 184; 214.

24 See note 40 below.

25 Clearly not every wrecker who did not immediately rebuild can properly be termed a land hoarder. Delay in rebuilding was inevitable if builders and architects proved unavailable, or materials were not to hand, or cash was short and credit tight. Housing was no doubt an extremely volatile industry. Probably only monopolists like Crassus with his slave-builders and limitless resources were unaffected by its instability. It may be that in Spanish colonies, where, as the charters show, permission to demolish had to be obtained, a petitioner had to satisfy the council that he could rebuild without delay.

26 Phillips (1973), 88-91, goes too far in arguing that the prescriptions of the charters were designed to protect the inhabitants of cheap, sub-standard housing against redevelopment and the inevitable higher rents. This interpretation is linked with the strange thesis that the charters ruled out demolition altogether, but were circumvented by the (unregu-

lated) practice of demolishing after sale. The weak points
are the construction placed on the words *non deterius resti-
turus erit* and *se reaedificaturum*, and the manipulation of
Str. 5.3.7 (p.87). His rejection of a humanitarian purpose
behind the S.C. Hosidianum is at least paradoxical (p.94,
quoted n.39 below).

27 *FIRA* I nr. 45, p.288.

28 Note *auctore divo Claudio* in the S.C. Volusianum, *FIRA* I nr.
45, p.289 1.26, the language of the prolegomenon of the
Claudian decree, and the archaic dative *pace* (1.10).

29 This might be inferred from the reference to Italy in the
opening clause, the mention of *villae* as well as *domus*, and
the location of the houses whose demolition is discussed in
the Neronian decree. But I do not agree with Phillips (1973),
95 that the charters and decrees 'in the main concerned different types of property', i.e. *domus* and *villae* (*rusticae*)
respectively. (This is the supposition that underpins the
thesis that the two sets of legislation had different object-
ives.) Note 'tectis urbis nostrae', emphatically placed and
more specific than 'totius Italiae aeternitati', which can
easily degenerate into a mere slogan. 'Exemplo suo' in the
following clause I take as a reference to specific building
or public works undertaken by Claudius in the first years of
his reign. Claudius goes on to profess concern for the pre-
servation (*custodia*) of public and private buildings.

30 On the penalty see V.Arangio-Ruiz, *SDHI* II (1936), 518, with
reference to D.39.2.48.

31 I translate *mutare* as 'sell', not 'change'; cf. Plaut. *Capt.*
27-9; Virg. *Ecl.* 4.38; Hor. *Sat.* 1.4.29; 2.7.109; Sall. *Jug.*
44.5; etc. Contrast, e.g. Hor. *Ep.* 1.1.100; Nepos, *Atticus*
13.2 ('nihil commutavit'). Remodelling is not here excluded,
but rather the disposing of part of a house for pecuniary advantage; cf. in the Neronian decree, *neve quis negotiandi
causa eorum quid emeret venderetve*, where *eorum quid* may be the
equivalent of *aliquas partes earum*, and refer to parts of
houses. (A prohibition against buying and selling houses for
profit makes no sense to me.) Against, Daube (1957b). See
D.18.1.52, preserving the wording of the Neronian decree, with
the roughly contemporaneous 39.2.48: *si quis ad demoliendum
negotiandi causa* vendidisse domum partemve domus *fuerit con-
victus.*

32 de Pachtere (1912).

33 E.g. *CAH* X 695 (Charlesworth); V.A. Scramuzza, *The Emperor
Claudius* (Cambridge, 1940), 173. Against de Pachtere I have
seen only Phillips (1973), 92-3, with whom I am in general
agreement, having reached similar conclusions by independent
investigation. But see note 29 above.

34 See note 29 above.

35 Augustus set the pattern. See Suet. *Div.Aug.* 29; *CAH* X 570ff.
On the municipal level, cf. Dio's plan to beautify Prusa, not
appreciated by the poorer classes. See *Or.* 40.8-9; 45.12; 46.
9; 47.11 and 15.

36 Claudius' projects in and around Rome included work on the
   Tiber bank to prevent flooding, the harbour at Ostia, a new
   distribution centre and granaries, the draining of the Fucine
   lake, the repair of Aqua Virgo, and the construction of Aqua
   Claudia and Aqua Anio Novus. See Blake (1959), 25ff.

37 Martial, de spect. 1.2.7-8: Hic, ubi miramur velocia munera
   thermas/abstulerat miseris tecta superbus.

38 FIRA I p.290, 11. 36ff.: eaque aedificia longa vetustate dila-
   berentur neque refecta usui essent futura, quia neque habitaret
   in iis quisquam nec vellet in deserta ac ruentia commigrare.

39 Cf. Phillips (1973), 94: 'It affected better class property
   rather than slums and was concerned with appearances, not with
   the social necessity of providing housing for the poor.'

40 The attractiveness of marble to wreckers is brought out as
   early as the reign of Vespasian: Negotiandi causa aedificia
   demoliri et marmora detrahere edicto divi Vespasiani et senatus consulto vetitum est. See CJ.8.10.2. In D.30.41.1, reference is made to a S.C. of A.D. 122, an amendment to the
   earlier decrees: 'ea quae aedibus iuncta sunt legari non poss-
   ent'. §2 shows that marble and columns are at stake. In §3
   the transference of materials from one house to another is
   permitted, where the same man owns both houses and intends to
   retain them (possessoribus) ... id est non distracturis. See
   §§5, 7-9, 12 for other amendments. In D.18.1.34 pr. Paulus
   indicates that a house might be bought for its appurtenances
   among which are listed marble statues and paintings.

41 See CJ.8.10.2: sed nec dominis ita transferre licet, ut inte-
   gris aedificiis depositis publicus deformetur adspectus (A.D.
   222); 8.10.6 pr.: si quis post hanc legem civitate spoliata
   ornatum, hoc est marmora vel columnas, ad rura transtulerit,
   privetur ea possessiones, quam ita ornaverit. See also R.
   MacMullen, 'Roman imperial building in the provinces', HSPh
   LXIV (1959), 207-36. Derelict housing becomes a matter of
   concern to the imperial authorities for the same reasons. See
   IGRR IV 1156a = SIG³ 837 (A.D. 127); D.17.2.52.10 (Marcus);
   CJ.8.10.4 (Philip); 11.29.4 (Diocl./Max.); 8.10.8 (A.D. 377);
   D.1.18.7; 39.2.7.2; 15.21.

42 I am grateful to Mr J.J.Nicolls for acute comments on the
   Claudian decree.

Chapter 8. Agri deserti

1 See for example the general theory of devastation recorded
  by Ed. Meyer, 'Die Bevölkerung des Altertums' in Hwb. d.
  Staatswiss. (3rd ed. 1909), III.912; followed by V.G.
  Simkhovitch, 'Rome's fall reconsidered', Pol. Science Quart.
  XXXI (1916), 227. For a recent statement see Salmon (1974),
  159, 177.

2 Jones (1964), 1039.

3 Martin (1971), 14.

4 References collected by Boak (1955), 47.

5 The date of Boniface's crossing to Africa and his appointment
  are discussed by P.Romanelli, *Storia delle province dell'
  Africa* (Rome, 1959), 636-8.

6 As Jones (1964), 813, agrees. Finley (1958), 162, notes that
  legislation on *coloni* does not prove manpower shortages but
  only a failure to check peasant mobility.

7 E.g. Syn. *Ep.* 122,125,132; cf. Goodchild (1952/3), 147, demonstrating that Synesius' gloomy account must be balanced by the
  known prosperity of Libya during the later period of the Empire.
  Synesius himself (*Ep.* 148) extols the pleasures and richness of
  his estate up-country.

8 R.Rémondon, *La Crise de l'empire romain* (Paris, 1964), 279.

9 πρῶτον μὲν γὰρ πᾶσαν τὴν κατ' ᾽Ιταλίαν καὶ ἐν τοῖς λοιποῖς
  ἔθνεσιν ἀγεωργητόν τε καὶ παντάπασιν οὖσαν ἀργὸν ἐπέτρεψεν,
  ὁπόσην τις βούλεται καὶ δύναται, εἰ καὶ βασιλέως κτῆμα εἴη,
  καταλαμβάνειν, ἐπιμεληθέντι τε καὶ γεωργήσαντι δεσπότῃ εἶναι.
  ἔδωκέ τε γεωργοῦσιν ἀτέλειαν πάντων ἐς δέκα ἔτη καὶ διὰ παντὸς
  δεσποτείας ἀμεριμνίαν. Presumably the γεωργοῦσιν of the last
  sentence are the recipients of the deserted land.

10 φημὶ τοίνυν χρῆναί σε πρῶτον μὲν ἁπάντων τὰ κτήματα τὰ ἐν τῷ
   δημοσίῳ ὄντα ... πωλῆσαι, πλὴν ὀλίγων τῶν καὶ πάνυ χρησίμων σοι
   καὶ ἀναγκαίων ... (the money thus realized to be loaned out at
   a low rate of interest). οὕτω γὰρ ἥ τε γῆ ἐνεργὸς ἔσται,
   δεσπόταις αὐτουργοῖς δοθεῖσα ... (and this will result in a
   regular source of income for public and military expenditure).

11 Gabba (1962), esp. 49-56; P.Brunt, 'The fiscus and its development', *JRS* LVI (1966), 88 discusses the emperor's occasional
   need for ready cash and obviously one cannot discount such a
   motive in Dio's proposal, but there is nothing in Dio's words
   to suggest the concern for small proprietors which Gabba detects. Crawford, on pp.41-2, notes cases where imperial land
   was returned to private ownership.

12 Cf. Haywood (1938), 94-95.

13 By for instance J.F.Gilliam, 'The plague under Marcus Aurelius', *AJPh* LXXXII (1961), 225-51; cf. Salmon (1974), 135-9.

14 E.g. Augustus settled 50,000 Getae in Moesia - Strabo 7.3.10;
   Nero settled more than 100,000 also in Moesia - *ILS* 986.

15 I.A.Richmond, *JRS* XLV (1945), 15; A. Mócsy, *Pannonia and Upper
   Moesia* (London and Boston, 1974), 272.

16 Frank (1933-40), I 85.

17 In Phillips (1970), 13.

18 CJ alone contains eighteen pronouncements on the *fiscus* and
   eleven directions to fiscal officials; cf. T.Pekáry, *Historia*
   VIII (1959), 479 for references. The *apokrimata* dossier is
   P.Columbia 123, published by W.L.Westermann and A.Schiller,
   Apokrimata (New York, 1954), corrected by Schiller and Youtie,
   CE XXX (1955), 332-4.

19 E.g. *P.Cattaoui* II.6-8 (from the Fayum) required a return of all Egyptians to their own *oikiai* in 207 and had the same objective as *P.Hamburg* 11, dated 202/3, putting high taxation rates on uninundated land.

20 *SB* 7361, dated 211/12, referring to earlier edicts of the same content.

21 E.g. a new garden tax recorded in *P.Oxy.* 2129; cf. Johnson (1936), 528.

22 *CIL* VIII 26416. The same aim lies behind the *longae possessionis praescriptio* legislation found in Egypt in 199/200, *P. Strasb.* = *FIRA* I 54-5.

23 *fenus publicum trientarium exercuit, ita ut pauperibus plerisque sine usuris pecunias dederit ad agros emendos, reddendas de fructibus*; cf. 26.2-3.

24 Gabba (1962), 58-9, quotes and rejects objections from the CTh noted here, but strictly on a *priori* grounds.

25 *et decrescit ac deficit in arvis agricola, in mari nauta, miles in castris, innocentia in foro, iustitia in iudicio,* etc... *minuatur necesse est quicquid fine iam proximo in occidua et extrema devergit... haec sententia mundo data est, haec Dei lex est, ut omnia orta occidant et aucta senescant.*

26 Alföldy (1974), 91; although most of Alföldy's subsequent observations concern the political crisis, he assumes social and economic distress must follow.

27 Alföldy (1974), 96-7, summarizes his own earlier discussion of Cyprian in *Historia* XXII (1973), 479-501.

28 The remarks here derive from W.H.C.Frend, 'The Roman empire in eastern and western historiography', *PCPhS* XIV (1968), 19-30; cf. also, J.Danielou, 'The conception of history in the Christian tradition', *J. Religion* XXX (1950), 171-9; W. den Boer, 'Some remarks on the beginnings of Christian historiography', *Stud. Patristica IV* = *Texte und Untersuch. z. Gesch. der Altchrist. Lit.* LXXVIII (1961), 361.

29 Boak (1955), esp. 26; Salmon (1974), 145.

30 *habemus enim, ut dixi, et hominum numerum qui delati sunt et agrorum modum, sed utrimque ne<qua>quam hominum segnitia terraeque perfidia. unde enim nobis Remus aut Nervius aut ipse ille de proximo Tricassinus ager aut arator, quorum reditus cum labore contendunt?*

31 *Pan Lat.* 8(4).21, actually discusses other restoration work but still makes no reference to Autun's land problems; *Pan. Lat.* 9(5), delivered by Eumenes in 298, requests a new school.

32 Jones (1964), 817, 819.

33 S.Gagnière and J.Granier, *Provençe historique* XIII (1963), 234; R.MacMullen, *Enemies of the Roman order* (Cambridge, Mass., 1967), 194-201, collects references for which see comments below (note 48).

34 Wightman (1970), 55, makes this point and presents a balanced judgement on the worth of such evidence.

35 *cum vastatum Illyricum ac Moesiam deperditam videret, provinciam Transdanuvia<m>Daciam...sublato exercitu et provincialibus reliquit...abductosque ex ea populos in Moesia conlocavit.*

36 Victor, *Caes*. 37.3-4 mentions other work done by Probus; cf. *Epit.de Caes*. 37.4, *HA, Prob*. 18.8, 21.2, Eutrop. 9.17.2; Eusebius, *Chron*. 224a (Helm). Mócsy (op. cit. note 15), 298, comments on the importance of this work, and some parallel private agrarian development which took place at the same time.

37 *cum divus Aurelianus parens noster civitatum ordines pro desertis possessionibus iusserit conveniri et pro his fundis, qui invenire dominos non potuerunt quos praeceperamus, eorundem possessionem triennii immunitate percepta de sollemnibus satisfacere, servato hoc tenore praecepimus ut, si constiterit ad suscipiendas easdem possessiones ordines minus idoneos esse, eorundem agrorum onera possessionibus et territoriis dividantur.*

38 L.Homo, *Essai sur le règne de l'empereur Aurélien* (Paris, 1904), 150-1, 179-80; Groag, *RE* V.1411 'Domitius 36' (1903).

39 Rostowzew (1910), 391-2.

40 Poethke (1969b), 70.

41 Lewis (1937), 69; A.E.R.Boak, 'Irrigation and population in the Fayum', *Geog. Rev*. XVI (1926), 362-4. Geremek (1969), 6 note 4; T.C.Skeat and E.P.Wegener, 'A trial before the Prefect of Egypt, etc.', *JEA* XXI (1935), 224-47, make a case for widespread economic decline *c*. 250; and S.I.Oost, 'The Alexandrian seditions under Philip and Gallienus', *CPh* LVI (1961), 1-20, demonstrates the disturbed political state of Egypt in the mid-third century.

42 For refs., see note 36.

43 Reynard (1959), 51, makes the point.

44 *HA, Claud*. 9.4-6, *Prob*. 15.1f., 18.1-2, Zos. 1.68, 1.71, *Pan. Lat*. 5(8).18, etc.

45 Tac. *Ann*. 13.34; *HA, Claud*. 9.4 (although the reading is not certain).

46 E.g. Salway (1965), 196-7.

47 In Phillips (1970), 75.

48 MacMullen (op. cit. note 33), 197.

49 All except the Scaptopare inscription (*CIL* III 12336) can conveniently be found in vol.IV of Frank (1933-40), 96-102, 656-61.

50 A.Calderini, 'οἱ ἐπὶ ξένης', *JEA* XL (1954), 19-22; Poethke (1969b), 70.

51 *HA, Firm*. 12.1-2; cf. Eutrop. 9.17.1, *Epit. de Caes*. 37.2, *HA, Prob*. 18.5-8.

52 Jones (1964), 68. Salmon (1974), 146, still quotes Diocletian's measures as evidence of a deteriorating economy without qualification.

53 *adeo maior esse coeperat numerus accipientium quam dantium, ut enormitate indictionum consumptis viribus colonarum, des-*

ererentur agri et culturae verterentur in sylvam.

54 pass. Tip. 1; W.H.C.Frend, The Donatist church[2] (Oxford, 1971)
   109-10; T.D.Barnes, JRS LXIII (1972), 29-46, now makes a good
   case for the date of Lactantius' writing being between 313 and
   315.

55 Larsen (1938), 466-80, for a general discussion of Greece in
   this period. Day (1951) demonstrates that conditions in
   Euboea were not as bad as Dio argued in spite of certain similarities between his advice and the Thisbe inscription; contra
   Gabba (1962), 57-8, who believes Dio to have had serious intentions, for all his rhetorical inaccuracies.

56 M.H.Callender, Roman amphorae (London, 1965), 50ff. CIL XV 2.
   3840 is the last dated amphora. R.Thouvenot, Essai sur la province de Bétique (Paris, 1940), 51ff., 272f.

57 Or. mar. 442-3; cf. 271-2, which Boak (1955), 44, accepts as
   the truth.

58 CTh.13.5.4 and 8 records Constantine's legislation. Hannestad
   (1962), 11, warns against wholesale acceptance of the evidence
   of the expositio totius mundi, but this is certainly not the
   view of J.Rougé, Text, translation and commentary (Paris,
   1966), esp. 85. Thouvenot (note 56) adds corroborative evidence of prosperity.

59 Rostovtzeff (1922), 13-14; Lewis (1937), 70ff.; Boak, Geog.
   Rev. XVI (1926), 353-63.

60 Wesseley, CPR 58 (256/5) = Rostovtzeff (1957), 429, 742 note 32.

61 Geremek (1969), 48-52, collects evidence and previous discussion
   on ancient canals. The University of Michigan excavation report
   of Socnopaiou Nesos is published by A.E.R.Boak, Soknopaiou Nesos
   (Ann Arbor, 1935), esp. 21 and 38. For the pottery dates, see
   J.W.Hayes, Late Roman pottery (London, 1972), 2.

62 P.Bouriant 42, BGU 835; I am indebted to Dr D.J.Crawford for
   this example. Cf. Geremek (1969), 89, for other examples of
   Karanis' cleruchies.

63 Rémondon (op. cit. note 8), 279, with references; R.S.Robinson,
   Sources for the history of Greek athletics (rev. ed. Ann Arbor,
   1955), 208-9, who also quoted an application in 267 for a pen-
   sion payment of 2 talents, 3,090 drachmae by a single athlete,
   P. Hermop. 54.

64 There is a useful modern study of 'Evolution of irrigation
   culture in Egypt' by G.Hamdan in L.Dudley Stamp, A history of
   land use in arid regions (UNESCO, 1961), 119-39; Hamdan, 124-6,
   stresses the perpetual fluctuations of Egyptian agriculture and
   poses the possibility of the great 1½ million acre desert region of the northern Berari, already known to early Arab chro-
   niclers, being the result of earlier neglect of drainage which
   prevented the washing through of saline deposits; but there is
   no date suggested for the start of the decline.

65 Broughton (1938), 903.

66 ἀγαθῇ τύχῃ. (Caracalla's name and titles follow) ἀγροὺς πάσης
   χώρας τῆς λα[μ]πρᾶ[ς] Πεσσινουντίων πο|λοως (sic) μετρηθῆνε

ἐκέλευσε σὺν τῇ εἱερᾷ| γραμῇ ἐφεστῶτος Κησίου Φηλικισσίμου Π Π
(= ? πριμιπιλαρίου). The full text and discussion given by
J.Devreker, *Latomus* XXX (1971), 352ff.

67 Jones (1964), 815-16, J.H.W.G.Liebeschutz, *Antioch: city and
imperial administration in the later Roman empire* (Oxford,
1972), 41; the figures for deserted land in Jones' example only
represent those actually included in the tax lists, and there
may have been more which no one bothered about.

68 Tchalenko (1953), esp. I.422.

69 Tchalenko (1953), I.414-15.

70 R.Mouterde and A.Poidebard, *Le limes de Chalcis* (Paris, 1945),
esp. 234-5; Tchalenko (1953), I.425.

71 Liban. *Ep.* 1071, τὰ μὲν ἄλλα πέπτωκέ τε καὶ κεῖται, κτλ. *PG*
58.591f. = *in Matt. homil.* 3-4. τοῖς [sc. γεωργοῖς] γὰρ ἐν
λιμῷ τηκομένοις ... καὶ τελέσματα διηνεκῆ καὶ ἀφόρητα ἐπι-
τιθέασι, κτλ. Cf. Lemerle (1958), 42.

72 Avi-Yonah (1958), 41; Gichon (1967), 181, 186, 191-2.

73 Jones (1964), 814 and note 103.

74 J.J.Wilkes, *Dalmatia* (London, 1969), 416ff.

75 G.Alföldy, *Bevölkerung u. Gesellschaft der röm. Provinz Dal-
matien* (Budapest, 1965), 207.

76 Thomas (1964), 380.

77 Thomas (1964), 389ff.; Mócsy (op. cit. note 15), 299-308,
gives an up-to-date summary of the evidence.

78 E.g. *CIL* III 14356[3a], *cond(uctor) prat(i) Fur(iani)*, who was a
soldier of leg. XIV in 205 at Carnuntum. A.Mocsy, 'Das Territorium Legionis und die Canabae in Pannonien', *AArchHung* III
(1953), 179-200; P.Oliva, *Pannonia and the onset of the crisis
in the Roman empire* (Prague, 1962), 312-18.

79 Wightman (1970), esp. 55-7; the invasion of 276 recorded in
HA, Prob. 13.6, 15.3 has been much exaggerated, as Wightman
notes; just as was the destruction in 355, which Ammianus
does not even think worth recording.

80 Applebaum (1966), 104.

81 Reynard (1959), 47.

82 Wightman (1970), 162.

83 Wightman (1970), 173-80.

84 *Grom. vet.* 53; Applebaum (1964), 775.

85 The most recent comprehensive study is Agache (1970), esp.
179-205; but cf. also Agache (1964), 117; (1966), 57-60;
Wightman (1970), 160, notes a strip field system that probably
served peasants in the Mayen area but not attached to any
central villa system.

86 Agache (1970), 192-203; (1966), 60.

87 Agache (1970), 204-5, 213-14; cf. A. van Doorselaer, *Les
Necropoles d'epoque romaine en Gaul septentrionale* (Bruges,

1967), map 7.

88 Wightman (1970), 154, 170.

89 Steer in Richmond (1958).

90 Salway (1965), 188-9.

91 Salway in Phillips (1970), 13-14; S.Frere, *Britannia* (London, 1967), 273.

92 Hallam in Phillips (1970), 71-5; Cunliffe (1966), 72; Salway in Phillips (1970), 17.

93 J.Liversidge, *Britain in the Roman empire* (London, 1968), 289; Rivet (1964), 127.

94 E.g. *CIL* XIII 3162; J.Teall, 'The age of Constantine: change and continuity in administration and economy', *DOP* XXI (1967), 19; Rivet (1964), 117-18; Frere (op. cit. note 91), 274, 280.

95 *(Britannia) terra tanto frugum ubere, tanto laeta numero pastionum, tot metallorum fluens rivis, tot vectigalibus quaestuosa, tot accincta portibus, tanto immensa circuitu.*

96 *(Julianus) id inter potissima mature duxit implendum, ut civitates...receptas...communiret, horrea quin etiam extrueret pro incensis, ubi condi possit annona a Britanniis sueta transferri.*

97 The main studies of the frontiers are found in R.Goodchild and J.M.Ward-Perkins, *JRS* XXXIX (1949), 81-95, XL (1950), 30-8, P. Salama, *Libyca* (Arch.epig.) I (1953), 231-61, III (1955), 329-67, G.Ch.-Picard, *Castellum Dimmidi* (Paris, 1945).

98 J.Baradez, *Fossatum Africae* (Paris, 1949), passim; CTh.7.15.1; cf. J.Guey, 'Note sur le limes romain de Numidie et le Sahara au IVe siècle', *MEFR* 56 (1939), 220-3, 244.

99 Leschi (1957), 294-5, who concludes, 'It is in the second half of the third century and during the course of the fourth century that this part of Numidia [i.e. in S.E. Algeria] was the most inhabited and also the most civilised.' Frend (op. cit. note 54), 45-7, gives a good general survey of the evidence; Février (1966), collects many of the Setif inscriptions.

100 For African oil, the studies of F.Zevi and A.Tchernia, 'Amphores de Byzacène au Bas-Empire', *AntAfr* III (1969), 173-214, make it clear that African produce, including oil, was reaching all parts of the Mediterranean from *c.* 270/280 until the seventh century A.D. For African red slip ware, see Hayes (op. cit. note 61), 423.

101 *ex auctoritate impp* (names and titles of Severus and Caracalla follow) *...agri et pascua et fontes adsignata...ma?...curantibus Epagatho et Manlio Caeciliano corniculario praef.* etc. *AE* 1946, 38, Leschi (1957), 75.

102 B.H.Warmington, *The North African provinces from Diocletian to the Vandal conquest* (Cambridge, 1954), 64; Lepelley (1967), 135-44, although curiously L. still accepts a 'diminution of cultivated surfaces' as a 'certainty' (p.141). Salmon (1974), 158, while prepared to accept Augustine's word that Africa was richer than Italy at the end of the fourth century (*de ord.* 1.3.6), yet believes in a sudden deterioration by 422 for no

accountable reason.

103 Goodchild (1951), 64; Oates (1953), 112–13.

104 Kahane/Threipland/Ward-Perkins (1968), 152–3; Percival (1969), 458.

105 G.D.B.Jones (1963), 132ff.; the Roman legislation is quoted by Pliny, *Ep.* 6.19, *HA, Marc.* 9.8 and was probably still in force after Diocletian, according to Hannestad (1962), 9, who quotes CTh.9.30.2(364), Symm. *Ep.* 6.81(82), 7.126; but Jones (1964), 525, does not insist on the point.

106 CTh.9.30.1, 2.5; Hannestad (1962), 11.

107 As has been argued in an article I have not seen by de Robertis (1948), 100,102, quoted by Hannestad (1962), 8; see above, pp.147–8 for the suggestion that Aurelian (and possibly Constantine?) was legislating for Egypt.

108 Jones (1964), 816.

109 Evidence collected by H.P.Kohns, *Versorgungskrisen und Hungers-revolten in spätantiken Rom* (Antiquitas Reihe 1.6, Bonn, 1961). Salmon (1974), 154, finds it significant when Symmachus (1.5) reports that Italy could not feed herself in 375; but when had this ever been the case since the annexation of Sardinia and Sicily?

110 O.Seeck, *Mon.Germ.Hist.* VI.cxix-x, J.R.Palanque, *REA* XXXIII (1931), 346–56. I am grateful to Dr John Matthews for advice on this and other points. M. is sceptical about Palanque's two separate famines in 383 and 384, but leaves the choice of year open.

111 For Gildo, see Kohns (op. cit. note 109), 57. J.Matthews, *Western aristocracies and imperial court, A.D. 364-435* (Oxford, 1975), 249, notes Ambrose's plea for loyalty to the new emperor on the grounds of other tax concessions (*de ob. Theod.* 5): and (in correspondence) agrees that this is a plausible context for CTh.11.28.2.

112 Hannestad (1962), esp. ch.2.

113 See the two articles by Finley (1958) and (1965). Alföldy (1974), 101–2, still accepts the theory of manpower shortage without reference to Finley's refutation; Ulpian's comment in D.50.6.3 concerning shortage of men available for urban *munera* is of course a social, not a demographic, statement. There is nothing in the recent work of Salmon (1974) which is either new or a challenge to Finley's criticism of Boak; Salmon appears to favour the general notion of population decline while admitting there is no evidence for it which will stand up to examination.

114 J.R.Lander, *Conflict and stability in fifteenth-century England* (London, 1969), 22, 35; the quotation from Edward IV also comes from this book.

115 Percival (1969), 457.

BIBLIOGRAPHY

Note. The purpose of this bibliography is to provide a list of the works cited in the text and notes which are concerned either wholly or in the main with land and property. The only exceptions to this rule are the few general works which it would be too cumbersome to keep on repeating in the notes. All other studies are fully documented in the notes wherever they are relevant. Journal titles have been abbreviated according to the initials used by *Année philologique* or in a fashion which is self-explanatory. Other abbreviations refer to ancient authors or to standard collections of inscriptions, legal texts, etc. which it is hoped will be familiar to most readers.

Agache,R. (1964). 'Aerial reconnaissance in Picardy', *Antiquity* XXXVIII 113-19

Agache,R. (1966). 'Recherches aériennes de l'habitat rural gallo-romain en Picardie', *Mélanges...A.Piganiol* I. Paris. 49-62

Agache,R. (1970). *Détection aérienne...dans le bassin de la Somme et ses abords*. Bull.Soc.préhist du Nord, 7 no. spéc. Amiens (the 2nd edition in 1971 has a map added)

Alföldy,G. (1974). 'The crisis of the third century as seen by contemporaries', *GRBS* XV 89-111

Anderson,J.G.C. (1899). 'Exploration in Galatia cis Halym II', *JHS* XIX 52-134

Anderson,J.G.C. (1937). 'An imperial estate in Galatia', *JRS* XXVII 18-21

Applebaum,E.S. (1964). 'The late Gallo-Roman rural pattern', *Latomus* XXIII 774-87

Applebaum,E.S. (1966). 'Peasant economy and types of agriculture', in Thomas,C. (1966), 99-107

Avi-Yonah,M. (1958). 'The economics of Byzantine Palestine', *IEJ* VIII 39-51

Badian,E. (1973). 'Marius' villas: the testimony of the slave and the knave', *JRS* LXIII 121-32

Baldacci,P. (1969). '*Patrimonium* e *ager publicus* al tempo dei Flavi. Ricerche sul monopolio del balsamo giudaico e sull'uso del termine *fiscus* in Seneca e Plinio il vecchio', *PP* CXXIV 349-67

Ballance,M.H. (1969). 'Regio Ipsina et Moeteana', *AS* XIX 143-6

Beaudouin,E. (1897-8). 'Les grands domaines dans l'Empire romain, d'après des travaux récents', *Nouvelle revue historique de ̄roit français et étranger* XXI 543-99, 673-720; XXII 27-115,

194-219, 310-50, 545-84, 694-746

Blake,M.E. (1959). *Roman construction in Italy from Tiberius through the Flavians*. Washington

Boak,A.E.T. (1955). *Manpower shortage and the fall of the Roman empire in the West*. Ann Arbor, Michigan

Boethius,A. (1960). *The Golden House of Nero: aspects of Roman architecture*. Ann Arbor

Boren,H.C. (1961). 'The sources of Cicero's income: some suggestions', *CJ* LVII 17-23

Bove,L. (1960). *Ricerche sugli agri vectigales*. Naples

Brockmeyer,N. (1971). 'Der Kolonat bei römischen Juristen der republikanischen und augusteischen Zeit', *Historia* XX 732-42

Broughton,T.R.S. (1934). 'Roman landholding in Asia Minor', *TAPhA* LXV 207-39

Broughton,T.R.S. (1938). *Roman Asia*, in vol.IV of Frank.T. (1933-40)

Broughton,T.R.S. (1951). 'New evidence on temple-estates in Asia Minor', *Studies...in honor of A.C.Johnson*. Princeton. 236-50

Brunt,P.A. (1971). *Italian manpower 225 B.C.-A.D. 14*. Oxford

Buckland,W.W. (1932 or 1963). *A text-book of Roman law from Augustus to Justinian*. 2nd or 3rd ed. Cambridge

Carcopino,J. (1906). 'L'inscription d'Aïn-el-Djemala', *MEFR* XXVI 365-481

della Corte,M. (1954). *Case ed abitanti de Pompei*. 2nd ed. Rome

Crook,J.A. (1967). *Law and life of Rome*. London

Cunliffe,B. (1966). 'The Somerset levels in the Roman period', in Thomas,C. (1966), 68-73

D'Arms,J.H. (1968). 'The Campanian villas of C.Marius and the Sullan confiscations', *CQ* XVIII 185-8

D'Arms,J.H. (1970). *Romans on the Bay of Naples*. Cambridge, Mass.

Daube,D. (1957a). 'Finium demonstratio', *JRS* XLVII 39-52

Daube,D. (1957b). 'Three notes on Digest 18.1, conclusion of sale', *Law Quarterly Review* LXXIII 379-98

Daube,D. (1959). 'Certainty of price', *Studies in the Roman law of sale*, ed. D.Daube. Oxford. 9-45

Day,J. (1951). 'The value of Dio Chrysostom's Euboean discourse for economic historians', *Studies...in honor of A.C.Johnson*. Princeton. 209-235

Déléage,A. (1945). *La capitation du Bas-Empire*. Nancy

Duncan-Jones,R. (1964). 'The purpose and organisation of the alimenta', *PBSR* XXXII 123-46

Duncan-Jones,R. (1974). *The economy of the Roman empire: quantitative studies*. Cambridge

Etienne,R. (1960). *Le quartier nord-est de Volubilis*. Paris

Evans,J.A.S. (1961). 'A social and economic history of an Egyptian temple in the Greco-Roman period', *YClS* XVII 149-283

Février,P.A. (1966). 'Inscriptions inédites relatives aux domains de la région de Sétif', *Mélanges...A.Piganiol* I. Paris. 217-28

Finley,M.I. (1958). Review of Boak (1955). *JRS* XLVIII 156-64

Finley,M.I. (1965). 'Technical innovation and economic progress in the ancient world', *Econ.Hist.Rev.* XVIII 29-45

Finley,M.I. (1973). *The ancient economy*. London

Flam-Zuckermann,L. (1972). 'Un exemple de la genèse des domaines impériaux d'après deux inscriptions de Bithynie', *Historia* XXI 114-19

Frank,C.L. (1966). *The villas of Frascati*. London

Frank,T. (1933-40). *An economic survey of ancient Rome*, 5 vol. Baltimore

Frederiksen,M. (1973). 'The contribution of archaeology to the agrarian problem in the Gracchan period', *DArch* IV-V (1970-1) 330-67

Fustel de Coulanges,N.D. (1885). *Recherches sur quelques problèmes d'histoire*. Paris

Gabba,E. (1962). 'Progetti di riforme economiche e fiscali in uno storico dell'età dei Severi', *Studi Fanfani* I 41-68

Geremek,H. (1969). *Karanis. Communauté rurale de l'Egypte romaine au IIe-IIIe siècle de n.è.* Warsaw

Gichon,M. (1967). 'The origin of the Limes Palaestinae, etc.', in *Studien z.d.Militargrenzen Roms* (Vorträge des 6. Internat. Limeskongresses in Suddeutschland). Köln. 174-93

Goodchild,R.G. (1951). 'Roman sites on the Tarhuna plateau of Tripolitania', *PBSR* XIX 43-77

Goodchild,R.G. (1952/3). 'The decline of Libyan agriculture', *Geographical Magazine* XXV 147-56

Gsell,G. (1932). 'Esclaves ruraux dans l'Afrique romaine', *Mélanges Gustave Glotz* I. Paris. 397-415.

Günther,R. (1965). 'Die Entstehung des Kolonats im I Jahrhundert vor unser Zeit in Italien', *Klio* XLIII 249-60

Guiraud,P. (1893). *La propriété foncière en Grèce jusqu'à la conquête romaine*. Paris

Gummerus,H. (1906). *Der römische Gutsbetrieb* (*Klio*, Beiheft 5)

Hannestad,K. (1962). *L'évolution des ressources agricoles de l'Italie*. Copenhagen

Hansen,H., Schiöler,Th. (1965). 'Distribution of land based on Greek-Egyptian papyri', *Janus* LII 181-92

Harris,W.V. (1971). *Rome in Etruria and Umbria*. Oxford

Haywood,R.M. (1938). *Roman Africa*, in vol.IV of Frank,T. (1933-40)

Heitland,W.E. (1921). *Agricola*. Cambridge

Hirschfeld,O. (1913). 'Der Grundbesitz der römischen Kaiser in den ersten drei Jahrhunderten', *Kleine Schriften*. Berlin. 516-75

Hohlwein,N. (1938). 'Le blé d'Egypte', *EPap* IV 33-120

Homo,L. (1951). *Rome impériale et l'urbanisme dans l'antiquité*. Paris

Jaczynowska,M. (1962). 'The economic differentiation of the Roman nobility at the end of the Republic', *Historia* XI 486-99

Johnson,A.C. (1936). *Roman Egypt*, in vol.II of Frank,T. (1933-40)

Jones,A.H.M. (1964). *The later Roman empire 284-602*, 3 vol. Oxford

Jones,A.H.M. (1974). *The Roman economy*. Oxford

Jones,G.D.B. (1963). 'Capena and the ager capenas. Part II', *PBSR* XXXI 100-58

Kahane,A., Threipland,L.M., Ward-Perkins,J. (1968). 'The ager Veientanus', *PBSR* XXXVI 1-218

Kaser,M. (1942). 'Die Typen der römischen Bodenrechte in den späteren Republik', *ZRG* LXII 1-81

Kaser,M. (1957). 'Periculum locatoris', *ZRG* LXXIV 155-200

Kaser,M. (1959). *Das römische Privatrecht*. 1st ed. Munich

Kaser,M. (1971). *Das römische Privatrecht* I. 2nd ed. Munich

Kent,J.H. (1948). 'The temple estates of Delos, Rheneia and Mykonos', *Hesperia* XVII 243-338

Kolendo,J. (1963). 'Sur la législation relative aux grands domaines de l'Afrique romaine', *REA* LXV 80-103

Kolendo,J. (1965). 'Sur le colonat en Afrique préromaine', *Neue Beiträge zur Geschichte der alten Welt* II 45-56

Kolendo,J. (1968). 'La hiérarchie des procurateurs dans l'inscription d'Aïn-el-Djemala (*CIL* VIII.25943)', *REL* XLVI 319-29

Kornemann,E. (1924). 'Domänen', *RE* Suppl.IV 227-68

Kotula,T. (1952-3). 'Stosunki spoeczno-gospodarcze w afrykánskich *saltus* w I-II w.n.e.', *Eos* XLVII 139-74

Kreller,H. (1944). 'Pfandrechtliche Interdikte und Formula Serviana', *ZRG* LXIV 306-45

Kuhnke,H.C. (1971). Οὐσιακἡ γῆ. *Domänenland in den Papyri der Prinzipatszeit*. Diss. Köln

Larsen,J.A.O. (1938). *Roman Greece*, in vol.IV of Frank,T. (1933-40)

Lemerle,P. (1958). 'Esquisse pour une histoire agraire de Byzance', *RH* CCXIX 32-74, 254-84

Lepelley,C. (1967). 'Déclin ou stabilité de l'agriculture africaine au Bas-Empire?', *AntAfr* I 135-44

Leschi,L. (1957). *Etudes d'épigraphie, d'archéologie et d'histoire africaines*. Paris

Lewis,N. (1937). 'Μερισμὸς ἀνακεχωρηκότων. An aspect of the Roman oppression in Egypt', *JEA* XXIII 63-75

Liversidge,J. (1968). *Britain in the Roman empire*. London

MacMullen,R. (1962). 'Three notes on imperial estates', *CQ* n.s. XII 277-82

Maiuri,A. (1942). *L'ultima fase edilizia di Pompei*. Rome

Martin,R. (1956). *L'urbanisme dans la Grèce antique*. Paris

Martin,R. (1971). *Recherches sur les agronomes latins*. Paris

Mayer-Maly,T. (1956). *Locatio conductio*. Vienna

Meiggs,R. (1960). *Roman Ostia*. Oxford

Oates,D. (1953). 'The Tripolitanian gebel', *PBSR* XXI 81-117

Oates,J.F. (1970). 'Landholding in Philadelphia in the Fayum (A.D. 216)', *Proc. XII Internat.Congr. of Papyrology 1968 (Am.Stud. in Papyrology*, vol.VII) 385-7

de Pachtere,F.G. (1908). 'Le règlement d'irrigation à Lamasba', *MEFR* XXVIII 373-400

de Pachtere,F.G. (1912). 'Les Campi Macri et le sénatus-consulte Hosidien', *Mélanges Cagnat*. Paris. 169-86

de Pachtere,F.G. (1920). *La table hypothécaire de Veleia* (Bibl. de l'Ec. des Hautes Et. 228). Paris

Packer,J.E. (1971). *The insulae of imperial Ostia*. Rome.

Parássoglou,G.M. (1972). *Imperial estates in Egypt*. Yale, unpublished PhD thesis

Pelham,H. (1890). *The imperial domains and the colonate*. London. (Reprinted in his *Essays*, ed. F.Haverfield, Oxford 1911, 275-99)

Percival,J. (1969). 'Seigneurial aspects of late Roman estate management', *EHR* LXXXIV 449-73

Pflaum,H.G. (1960-1). *Les carrières procuratoriennes*. Paris

Phillips,C.W. (1970). *The fenland in Roman times*. London

Phillips,E.J. (1973). 'The Roman law on the demolition of buildings', *Latomus* XXXII 86-95

Piganiol,A. (1962). *Les documents cadastraux de la colonie romaine d'Orange (Gallia*, suppl.16). Paris

Poethke,G. (1969a). 'Epimerismos von Bodenflächen verschiedener οὐσίαι der drei Bezirke des Arsinoites', *APF* XIX 77-84

Poethke,G. (1969b). *Epimerismos* (Papyrologica Bruxellensia 8). Brussels

Ramsay,W.M. (1890). *The historical geography of Asia Minor*. London

Ramsay,W.M. (1895-7). *The cities and bishoprics of Phrygia*. Oxford

Ramsay,W.M. (1926). 'Studies in the Roman province Galatia', *JRS* XVI 201-15

Reynard,M. (1959). *Techniques et agriculture en pays trévere et rémois* (Collection Latomus 38). Brussels.

Richmond,I.A. (1958). *Roman and native in north Britain*. London

Rivet,A.L.F. (1964). *Town and country in Roman Britain.* 2nd ed.
London

Robert,L. (1937). *Etudes anatoliennes.* Paris

Robert,L. (1962). *Villes d'Asie mineure: études de géographie
ancienne.* 2nd ed. Paris

de Robertis,F.M. (1948). 'La produzione agricola in Italia dalla
crisi del III secolo all'età dei Carolingi', *Ann.Fac. Economia
e Commercio. Univ. Bari* n.s. VIII 67-271

Rostovtzeff,M. (1922). *A large estate in Egypt in the third century
B.C.* (Wisconsin Univ. Stud. in Soc. Sciences and Hist. 6).
Madison, Wisconsin

Rostovtzeff,M. (1957). *Social and economic history of the Roman
empire.* 2nd ed. Oxford

Rostowzew,M. (1910). *Studien zur Geschichte des römischen Kolonats*
(*Arch. f. Pap.*, Beiheft 1). Leipzig, Berlin

Salmon,E.T. (1969). *Roman colonization under the Republic.* London

Salmon,P. (1974). *Population et dépopulation dans l'empire romaine*
(Collection Latomus 137). Brussels

Salvioli,G. (1906). *Le capitalisme dans le monde antique.* Paris

Salway,P. (1965). *The frontier people of Roman Britain.* Cambridge

Schmidt,O.E. (1899). 'Ciceros Villen', *Neue Jahrb. f. d. klass.
Altertum* II 328-55, 466-97

Schneider,H. (1974). *Wirtschaft und Politik: Untersuchungen zur
Geschichte der späten römischen Republik.* Erlangen

Schulz,F. (1951). *Classical Roman law.* Oxford

Smutny,R.J. (1951). 'The sources of Cicero's income', *Class. Wkly.*
XLV 49-56

Sotgiu,G. (1957). 'La Sardegna e il patrimonio imperiale nell'
alto impero', *Epigraphica* XIX 25-48

Steinwenter,A. (1942). *Fundus cum instrumento* (*SAWW* 221, no.1)

Stevens,C.E. (1966). 'The social and economic aspects of rural
settlement', in Thomas,C. (1966), 108-28

Świderek,A. (1970). 'Les Καίσαρος οἰκονόμοι de l'Egypte romaine',
CE XLV 157-60

Tchalenko,V. (1953). *Villages antiques de la Syrie du Nord* I. Paris

Thomas,B. (1964). *Römische Villen in Pannonien.* Budapest

Thomas,C. (1966). *Rural settlements in Roman Britain* (CBA Research
Reports 7). London

Tomsin,A. (1954). 'Un document de comptabilité fiscale, P.Lond. III,
900, p.89', *BAB* XL 91-9

Tomsin,A. (1957). 'Notes sur les *ousiai* à l'époque romaine', *Studi
in onore di A. Calderini e R. Paribeni* II. Milano. 211-24

Tomsin,A. (1964). 'Le recrutement de la main d'oeuvre dans les
domaines privés de l'Egypte romaine', *Studien...Friedrich*

Oertel. Bonn. 81-100

Tomsin,A., Denooz,J. (1974). 'Application à un groupe de textes papyrologiques grecs relatifs aux ousiai d'un analyse automatique sur ordinateur', *Akten des XIII Internat. Papyrologen-Kongresses* (*Münchener Beiträge* LXVI)

Toynbee,A.J. (1965). *Hannibal's legacy*. Oxford

Van Nostrand,J.J. (1925). *The imperial domains of Africa Proconsularis* (University of California Publications in History XIV)

Watson,A. (1965). *The law of obligations in the later Roman republic*. Oxford

Watson,A. (1968). *The law of property in the later Roman republic*. Oxford

Weber,M. (1891). *Die römische Agrargeschichte*. Stuttgart

Weber,M. (1909). 'Agrarverhältnisse im Altertum', reprinted in his *Gesammelte Aufsätze zur Sozial- und Wirtschaftsgeschichte*, Tübingen 1924, 1-288

Westermann,W.L. (1920). 'The "uninundated lands" in Ptolemaic and Roman Egypt', *CPh* XV 120-37

Westermann,W.L. (1922). 'The "dry land" in Ptolemaic and Roman Egypt', *CPh* XVII 21-36

White,K.D. (1967). 'Latifundia', *BICS* XIV 62-79

Wightman,E.M. (1970). *Roman Trier and the Treveri*. London

Wiseman,T.P. (1965). 'The potteries of Vibienus and Rufrenus', *Mnemosyne* 4th ser., XV 275-81

Wiseman,T.P. (1971). *New men in the Roman senate, 139 B.C. - 14 A.D.* Oxford

Yavetz,Z. (1958). 'The living conditions of the urban plebs in republican Rome', *Latomus* XVII 500-17

de Zulueta,F. (1945). *The Roman law of sale*. Oxford

INDEX

M4